THE 12 Amazing SECRETS OF MILLIONAIRE INVENTORS

Smart, Simple Steps for Turning
Your Brilliant Product Idea
into a
Money-Making Machine

HARVEY REESE

Published by John Wiley & Sons, Inc., Hoboken, New Jersey.
Published simultaneously in Canada.

Wiley Bicentennial Logo: Richard J. Pacifico

For general information on our other products and services or for technical support, please contact our Customer Care Department within the United States at (800) 762-2974, outside the United States at (317) 572-3993 or fax (317) 572-4002.

Wiley also publishes its books in a variety of electronic formats. Some content that appears in print may not be available in electronic books. For more information about Wiley products, visit our web site at www.wiley.com.

Library of Congress Cataloging-in-Publication Data:

Reese, Harvey.
    The 12 amazing secrets of millionaire inventors : smart, simple steps for turning your brilliant product idea into a money-making machine / Harvey Reese.
       p.   cm.
    ISBN 978-0-470-13549-5 (pbk.)
       1. Inventions–Marketing.   I. Title.   II. Title: Twelve amazing secrets of millionaire inventors.
          inventors.
    T339.R44   2007
    658.8–dc22

                                                                                2007007080
Printed in the United States of America.

10 9 8 7 6 5 4 3 2 1

I of course dedicate this book to my family: Thelma, Andrea, Tory, Gerson, Jacob, and Emma. However, I would like to also dedicate this book to the thousands of inventors who have honored me by sending me their product ideas and inventions for my opinions, suggestions, and recommendations.

To all of you, I offer my admiration for your creativity, inventiveness, talents, and ingenuity. Some of you, I know, have gone on to achieve substantial rewards, while others of you are still working to make that happen. However, it's the striving that I admire, not the end result. Not many are able to think creatively as you folks have done, and not many are brave enough to put their new ideas under their arms and go out to meet the world. You are the men and women who have done it, and to you I tip my hat.

CONTENTS

> *It is time to stand and cheer for the doer, the achiever—*
> *the one who recognizes the challenge and does*
> *something about it.*
> —Vince Lombardi, coach, Green Bay Packers

> You have brains in your head.
> You have feet in your shoes.
> You can steer yourself
> any direction you choose.
> You're on your own.
> And you know what you know.
> And YOU are the guy who'll
> decide where to go.
> –Dr. Seuss, *Oh, the Places You'll Go!*

Do you know those dumb reindeer antlers that folks put on their pet dogs and cats every Christmas? I created that product years ago (Santa's Reindog) and have been collecting royalties on it every since. I get royalties on other products as well; creating and licensing products is my business. I mention the antlers in particular, however, because it's one of those silly little products that any of you could have easily thought up yourself (and maybe did). It doesn't take a genius to dream up these ideas, which is the whole beauty of this business. I don't claim to be any smarter or more creative than you are, but having been doing this work for so long, I believe I do have two advantages at the moment. However, the whole point of this book, by telling you what I know, is to make those advantages disappear.

My first advantage is that I'm not in love with any of the products I create, and I've created and licensed or marketed more than 100 of them. Before I do anything, I do the research to determine if my idea is truly original and if it really has the potential that I believe it does. If I find I'm wrong—if the idea's not particularly original or has limited commercial value—I simply put it aside and move on.

If I can create one idea, I know can create another one. I have no emotional attachment to my product ideas, and I don't view any of them as "my baby." And most of all, I don't just hear what I want to hear. If someone in the business in whom I have confidence tells me the idea stinks, I don't take that to mean that *I* stink—any more than if he tells me the idea's great, that it makes me great. It's just an idea and it's just business; nothing more, nothing less.

My second advantage, at the moment, is that if the product's originality and value meet certain standards, I know the sure steps to take to make it pay off for me, either through licensing or marketing. I've been an entrepreneur all of my adult life—manufacturing, importing, retailing, and licensing—and along the way I've managed to assemble a great bag of tricks. I know what works and I know what doesn't, and whatever I know, I'm happy to have you know. Why learn by suffering from your own mistakes when I've already made them for you?

I have a website (www.money4ideas.com) where inventors send me their ideas for evaluation with the hope that I'll like the idea enough to offer to try to get it licensed or find them a backer or investor. I'm in contact with thousands of inventors in this manner, so I have a good idea of the kind of advice, guidance, and information inventors like you are seeking. This book, I hope, will give you the kind of on-target answers and information to help you achieve great success and recognition. Why not? I don't feel that I'm creating competitors; I'm creating associates. The need for new products in our fast-moving society is so great, and there are so few talented folks like you around who have the creativity to dream them up, that I need all the help I can get!

If you're hoping to license your product, any idea that offers the promise of high sales and that requires no more start-up costs than seem justified by anticipated profits is something that any manufacturer would probably be willing to pay for. Of course, you have to prepare the idea in the right way, present it in the right way, and show it to the right person—but I'm going to show you how to do all of that. And if you're thinking of marketing your idea yourself, I'm going to show you what it takes to be an entrepreneur and how to launch your business so that you can have an enterprise to be proud of. I've been where you are and I've done what you're preparing to do.

I assume we're meeting on these pages because you're at a crossroads; you have a great product idea and don't want to blow it. Should you license it, should you sell it, should you look for investors to make it yourself? Not only do you want to determine the right path for your own goals, talents, and circumstances, but you want to know how to launch your venture in the surest, most effective manner. I can help you do that; I'm sure of it.

This book is not just a pep talk. Telling you to do your best is OK, but best what? First you want to know what your best goals should be, and then you want to know the best way to achieve them. This book is designed to do both: to help you recognize the goals that work for you and to offer precise, step-by-step information to help you achieve the riches that your talents entitle you to.

"Just follow the yellow brick road," the Oz Munchkins advised Dorothy, but did you know there was such a road for inventors as well? Yes, there is, and it starts on the very next page. Just follow me.

ONE

The 12 Amazing Mistakes, Bloopers, Errors, Wretched Miscalculations, Boners, Goof-Ups, and Simply Stupid Moves Made by Many New Inventors (Not Meaning You, Of Course)

> *Sometimes I wake up at night and ask, "Where have I gone wrong?" Then a voice says to me, "This is going to take more than one night."*
> —Charlie Brown

When I made the decision to write this book, my first move was to reach out to successful inventor/ entrepreneurs I knew to ask what tips and advice they might offer to help my readers achieve similar successes. All of these men and women, either through licensing or self-marketing, have personally achieved what every inventor hopes for himself: to see his dream turn into reality and to earn profits from his creativity. Who these inventors/entrepreneurs are and the success secrets they've agreed to share is the subject of Chapter 11, but I thought it would be useful to start this book on an entirely different tack.

Since in Chapter 11 I review the 12 brilliant success moves you should make, isn't it equally useful to know the 12 dumb, disastrous moves to avoid? Brilliant moves at one end; blunders, boners, and bloopers to avoid at the other; and with lots of information and guidance in between seems like the perfect formula to give you the kind of hands-on guidance you have a right to expect by opening this book's covers.

I've been an inventor/entrepreneur all my adult life and have been around others for just as long. Many of these folks are quite successful, and in thinking about how they got that way, I've been struck by two observations. First, as exemplified by the inventors/entrepreneurs you'll later meet, successful folks come in all shapes and sizes, and there are no predictors, at least none that I could ever determine, based on age, gender, race, intelligence, or anything else. I've met successful inventors/entrepreneurs who are young and old, male and female, black and white, highly educated and with scarcely any education at all. So what connects them? Why have they succeeded when so many other equally bright folks have not? Yes, certainly, it's a given that they share characteristics like enthusiasm, drive, ambition, skill, and energy—but it became apparent to me that they share something else as well.

What became apparent is that virtually all of these successful inventors and entrepreneurs suffered through business failures, reversals, bankruptcies, and even jail terms earlier in their careers, giving them the hard-won lessons that brought them to their current professional heights. I've certainly had my own share of failures, and Thomas Alva Edison failed so many times that he could be our poster boy. You could almost call failure a rite of passage. Think of the successful inventors/ entrepreneurs you know and I believe you'll come to the same conclusion. One thing that makes America so great is that we're willing to give anyone a second or third chance if he or she has the determination and zeal to try again. Guys like Walt Disney, Henry Ford, Milton Hershey, among others, all experienced setbacks or financial failure, some more than once, before achieving their later successes.

I figured that lessons learned are lessons learned—and so if these folks would just tell us where they went wrong, we could skip the bankruptcy part and go right on the success phase. That sounded like a plan, and so I traveled the country interviewing successful inventors/entrepreneurs whom I had come to know personally, all with backgrounds of failure and financial reversal. These folks were all were happy to tell me about their earlier goof-ups, missteps, and bonehead decisions that they later learned to avoid. To their own most frequently mentioned mistakes, I added some that I gleaned myself from years of dealing with inventors all across the world; then I narrowed the field down to the 12 most important ones. Whatever I learned, I'm happy to share. After all, others' failures can be our successes, if we learn from them.

12 Most Important Dumb Mistakes

Mistake No. 1: Not Understanding the Concept of a Fully Developed and Marketable Idea

As I mentioned in the preface, I have a website, money4ideas.com, visited by thousands of inventors every year, many of whom send in their ideas for my evaluation. It never ceases to amaze me how many of these folks simply have no concept of what it takes to gain the attention of the manufacturers, licensors, or investors who have the power to make their dreams come true. Most of these folks are obviously perfectly intelligent, but they either have not done their homework, or their life experiences have not prepared them to understand what it takes to create something of value to put on the table that might pique the interest of the person it's being presented to.

Ideas alone, I'm sorry to say, have little commercial value; we all get them, they float in and out of our minds continually. Investors and licensors are interested in *inventions or fully formed products*, and an idea doesn't become one until it's been fully developed, reduced to practice, and can be demonstrated to do what the inventor claims for it. It's precisely what you yourself would expect to see if someone wanted you to invest in his or her own new idea. "Show me how it works," you'd say. Companies are no different, no matter how big they are. As the inventor, you are expected to put something into the investor's hands or the licensee's hands and be able to say "Look at this exciting new product I've invented! Look how easy it works! Look at the great things it does!" Anything less is simply an idea for a product, and no one invests in those. The "what" is fine for starters, but it's the "how" that might pique an inventor's or licensee's interest.

Someone might send me a little pencil drawing of a teddy bear, accompanied by a note that says: "I've got this great idea for a new teddy bear with an American flag in his paw. You squeeze the button on its other paw and the bear jumps in the air, does a back flip, lands on his feet, waves the flag, starts to tap dance and sings 'You're a Grand Old Flag.'" "Wow," I might say, "how does it work?" "Like I say," the inventor impatiently answers, "you squeeze the button on his paw." Yes, that's an exaggeration, but sadly, not by much.

Another "inventor" (this time a true story) sent me an idea to make a popular product in smaller, single-portion package so a woman can carry it in her purse. That was a reasonable suggestion and I thought perhaps the actual invention was some sort of clever packaging—but no, there was nothing else; just the few sentences needed to tell me what she had in mind. This woman expected Procter & Gamble to proceed with her idea and pay her a royalty for each smaller package that left the factory. Yeah, sure, dream on, lady, I told her (but politely).

Many folks have an idea or the notion that a certain type of product could be useful, and will submit it to me on the assumption that I can find a company willing to invest its own resources, expertise, and money in trying to turn the idea it into a reality. Any company presented with that proposal would rightly wonder why, since they're taking the risks and doing all the work, they're being asked to pay someone else a royalty. After all, that's supposed to be the inventor's job—having actually invented the product is the singular accomplishment that might entitle a person to ask for rewards. That's how this business works. Otherwise, I'm afraid the best that one can hope for is a polite "thank you for your suggestion" note from the company, signed by some third-level clerk.

Mistake No. 2: Not Thoroughly Researching the Product Idea for Value and Originality

There are certain logical, sequential steps for anyone to take who wants to earn money from his or her million-dollar idea. First you do Step A, then you do Step B, then you do Step C, and on and on.

The first couple of steps, carefully researching the idea for its value and originality, can be taken without spending any money, without quitting your job, and without making any career-changing commitments. Yes, if you follow my advice, you might at some point hire a professional to do the patent search for you, but hopefully the cost (a few hundred dollars) won't be enough for you to feel it.

Depending on how you fare with these preliminary steps, you can either plunge ahead with enthusiasm or just walk away, no harm done. However, since these are the only virtually free-ride steps, and since those that follow *do* require money to be spent and *do* require decisions with consequences, it stands to reason that you'd want to do the preliminary steps as thoroughly and honestly as you know how. Doesn't that make perfect sense? Would you be surprised to know that most inventors don't do it, won't do it, or think they've done it when they haven't?

Time after time I've seen inventors blithely plunging ahead without doing any investigation whatsoever, thinking they know everything they need to know, continuing to throw money at the idea, until one day reality finally stares them in the face. Not doing the research is like not going to the doctor for fear that she'll find something terribly wrong with you. You're healthy as long as you don't go. In their mind's eye, the inventors' idea remains brilliant until proven otherwise—and proving otherwise is not high on their agenda.

In succeeding chapters we'll explore this issue in great detail: how to successfully research your idea and how to make sure that it really is the moneymaker you expect it to be. For now, I think I can safely say that of all the mistakes so many inventors make, this one would have to be among the most prevalent—and the one with the most potentially devastating effect.

Mistake No. 3: Overestimating the Idea's Potential Market Value

If you ask any attorney to name the single most important factor in screwing up a product licensing negotiation or an investor negotiation, he will tell you without hesitation that it's the inventor's inflated view

DUMB MISTAKE NO. 3:
Overestimating the Product Idea's Market Value

of the value of her idea and the impossible demands made because of it. That's not hard to understand. A person dreams up an original idea, perhaps spends the money to get it patented, perhaps spends the money to make an impressive prototype, and perhaps spends the money to create a winning presentation. Why wouldn't she think that the world is eager to beat a path to her door? At some point, however (unless she actually did discover a cure for cancer), she will come face to face with steely-eyed professionals who know the true value of the idea—and unless she's willing to face the true facts and return to mother earth, getting someone to invest in her idea is not likely to happen.

Here's a typical scenario. An inventor will send me his idea and say, "There are at least a hundred million gardeners in America who can use this new garden weeder. If we just sell to 5% of them, at $10 apiece, that means sales every year of $50,000,000!" That sounds perfectly reasonable and prudent to the poor guy (after all, he could have projected selling to 10%) because he simply has no concept of what it takes to sell $50,000,000 or $100,000,000 of anything, yet alone something as mundane as a new gardening tool. Some simple research can give him reliable predictors as to how many such tools can logically be sold, and unless he's prepared to take a more realistic view, the idea will remain simply a pipe dream.

An inventor without a realistic understanding of the market and the value of things will always ask for too much from the investor or licensor he's hoping to win over—*so much* too much that negotiations probably will seem futile to the one who's being asked to open up his purse strings. Or worse yet, the inventor with stars in his eyes is liable to empty out his own bank account in anticipation of the big payday just around the corner. Whatever the scenario, the licensee will walk away, the investor will walk away, and without question, the inventor's own money will walk away as well.

Mistake No. 4: Rushing Off to See a Patent Attorney

They say that talk is cheap—but believe me, it's not cheap when you talk to an attorney. Applying for a utility patent for a simple product idea can easily cost $10,000 or more in legal fees, and often what you have to show for it is meaningless. I don't mean that the patent attorney isn't delivering what he's asked to deliver, but patents often simply have no commercial value. Inventors will commonly take this step: They think up an idea, make a sketch, and rush off to get it patented. What they don't realize is that many products don't require patents in order to be successful, that products will get knocked off by other companies, patented or not, and that trying to protect the patent through the court system can easily cost $500,000 or more in attorney fees and court costs. How many ideas are worth that?

If this strikes close to home, if you've just dreamed up a new idea yourself and if you have it in mind to apply for a patent for it, please wait, at least until you read the chapter on patents, trademarks, and copyrights before committing yourself to the process. Sometimes patents are crucial to the success of a new product, but more often they're not. Later I will show you how to tell which is which, and I'll review other ways to protect an idea that are a lot cheaper and may serve the same purpose. Please read on.

Mistake No. 5: Rushing Off to See an Invention Marketing Company

Anyone who stays up to watch late-night TV has seen the ads on the local cable channels. "*Attention, inventors. If you have a new invention or just an idea for one, call this toll-free number for our free inventors' kit. . . .*" These invention promotion companies make it all sound so easy—the answer to any inventor's prayers. They understand that what gives the inventor pleasure is the actual process of inventing; everything that's supposed to follow—finding the prospects, pitching the idea, asking for money—is distasteful, unpleasant, and demeaning. "Now, now," says the invention marketing company's smiling salesman, "you let us worry about those nasty matters. You just stay in your warm, comfortable workshop and wait for the checks to start rolling in." As the comedian George Carlin properly observed, any salesman who keeps smiling is probably selling you something you don't need.

The lure is irresistible to many, and what the heck, the "inventors' kit" is free, so why not get one? In a few days a big envelope arrives with lavishly prepared material about all that the company can do for the inventor. Next come the calls from a company representative inviting the inventor to submit her invention for a "free professional evaluation." Why not? What the heck, it's free. Then, in a few weeks, the company issues its report, enthusiastically telling the inventor how brilliant the idea is, what a genius the inventor is, and how excited the company is to be working with her. Of course the company has never seen an idea that was less than brilliant or an inventor who was less than a genius. And now that they have the inventor puffing her chest out with pride, dreaming of riches beyond belief, they're ready to move in for the kill.

There's a whole menu of products the invention company sells to the inventor: a "research report" on the product's market potential, which is obviously and laughably one boilerplate paragraph following another, a patent search, a patent application (often for a next-to-worthless design patent), presentation material for investors and licensees, and a program to present the idea to supposedly "eagerly waiting prospects." The company can easily lift $10,000 to $20,000 from the inventor's wallet before she realizes what hit her. Later these inventors often come to me, sadder and wiser, and I'm too much of a gentleman to tell them what chumps they've been.

Mistake No. 6: Fear of Showing the Idea to Others

I wrote an article for *Inventor's Digest* called "The Heimlich Maneuver," in which I told the story of the kindly inventor who, many years ago, toiling selflessly away in his basement laboratory, finally discovers the cure for some dreaded disease. The archvillain, Otto Heimlich, learns of the discovery and sends his thugs to steal the formula, leaving the kindly inventor beaten and unconscious. The story goes on about how the inventor's niece swears revenge and goes about avenging her kindly uncle's beating and the theft of his magic formula.

It's a familiar tale and I won't bother you with the details—except to add that some evil specter managed to implant this story into the brains of all inventors, young and old, many of whom will even now swear that Otto Heimlich remains alive, secretly maneuvering to steal their own ideas and inventions. The only way to keep their ideas safe, some sadly and illogically conclude, is by not showing them to anyone.

Forget logic; I've encountered this inventor fear more often that you might think. It's an urban myth that if a company sees a chance to steal the inventor's idea, they'll do it in a New York minute. That attitude is precisely why so many companies don't want to deal directly with inventors and make them sign lengthy legal disclosure agreements before allowing them to step foot in the door. I'm an agent for inventors, and companies are happy to work with me but (nothing personal) often prefer not to meet with the inventors like yourself. First of all, as discussed, inventors often have an inflated view of their idea's worth, and second, many inventors are so fearful that their idea will be stolen that they're ready to call the cops if anyone in the company even looks at them funny.

As you of course realize, unless you're willing to put your idea out front, patented or not, nothing will ever come of it. There are many ways to do that safely, and there are many reasons why companies won't steal your idea, even if it's as brilliant as you believe it to be. All of these matters are clearly reviewed in a later chapter—and if you have any such fears, I believe they will all swiftly be allayed through logic and your own good sense.

Mistake No. 7: Not Properly Preparing the Idea

There are lots of product ideas that are apparent on their face, and so a beautiful drawing or picture may be all that's needed. However, if what you've invented is supposed to do something or accomplish some specific result, and if how it's accomplished is not obvious, then it's your responsibility as the inventor to create a working prototype to prove that the product will do precisely what you claim for it. Those are the rules; there are no passes. The inventor is expected to invent the product, or at least cause the product to be invented. However it happens, the investor or licensee expects to be handed a fully developed, fully working prototype to see, examine, use, and determine for himself if it has the commercial potential for him to make the required investment to bring the idea forward.

It's not uncommon for someone to dream up an idea that's beyond her skills to create. That's OK, that's what experts are for. It is *still* the inventor's idea, even if she has to hire an electrical engineer or a scientist or some other professional to work out the details.

She can pay the professional outright for his services, she can give him a share of the hoped-for profits, or she can make him a partner. However she acquires the expert's services, the end result should be a working prototype that proves to whoever is interested that the inventor is able to deliver the goods. No investor and no licensee and no manufacturer will agree to pay thousands of dollars to an inventor if there's doubt as to whether his invention really would work. Nobody would do that.

Also, even the most experienced executive will pause longer over a beautifully prepared presentation than he will over something that appears to be cobbled together. If the inventor doesn't show respect for his idea by presenting it beautifully, then his task of getting the licensee or investor to view it in that manner is even harder. These observations seem so obvious—that an inventor needs a fully working prototype and professional presentation material— that I'm always perplexed why so few inventors venture forth armed in this manner. I will commonly receive from an inventor a few scribbled sentences and nothing else. Trying to understand the idea, I'll ask, "Do you have any drawings, or pictures or plans or sketches or anything?" "Gosh," comes the reply, "I can't draw a straight line." Is that any way to get someone excited about a new product idea?

Some ideas might actually be so brilliant that a sketch on a napkin is enough to get companies clamoring to be partners. I've never seen any, but I'll concede that it's possible they exist. At the other end, some ideas are so stupid on their face that even if they're presented with full orchestra accompaniment, no one will view them seriously. (Those I have seen, in abundance.) However, most ideas, probably yours and definitely mine, lie somewhere in between—and like any other commodity, they need to be sold. Salespeople are usually armed with samples of their products and beautiful brochures to explain them, and inventors themselves need nothing less.

Since dreaming up and licensing new products is my business, over the years I've made hundreds of presentations; more than I can count. Regarding the material you need to be prepared with, I have a clear idea of what works and what doesn't; what a prospective investor wants to hear and what will make his eyes glaze over. Everything I know you'll know as well—in just a few pages ahead.

Mistake No. 8: Avoiding Face-to-Face Selling

Although I have this tucked away as Mistake No. 8, it is arguably the most common mistake made by inventors hoping to license their ideas and the single most important reason why more of them aren't successful. As suggested earlier, inventors like to create; that's their pride. "I get a million ideas a day," they say, wanting to impress me with their creativity. What they don't tell me is what they do with the idea after they get it—but they don't have to; I already know. As Kit Carson said, referring to the Great Trek westward, "The cowards won't start and the weak will die along the trail."

In this instance, the cowards who won't start are the inventors who do nothing. Some time later, upon seeing "his idea" in a store, the inventor will say, "Hey! That's my idea! I had that idea years ago!" It's what I call Slacker's Remorse. We can just wave goodbye to these poor souls as our wagons roll westward.

The weak who die along the trail are the inventors who will rush out to get their ideas patented and then send out a bunch of letters to companies that they think might be interested. Seldom do these companies even bother to answer, although the poor inventor waits by the mailbox every day. Other inventors are swayed by the siren call of invention promotion companies, and we all know what happens to them. Others might create a web page for their idea, hoping an interested manufacturer will miraculously come along and strike a deal. Others (for all I know) put their patent into a bottle and send it out to sea, hoping it will fall into the right person's hands on some distant shore. Whatever scheme it takes to avoid a face-to-face meeting will get a full hearing by many inventors. Get out the Bible, pardner. We have to bury these poor souls and move on.

I've worked with thousands of inventors over the years and am not aware of anyone who was able to launch his or her idea through letter writing, getting involved with invention companies, putting up a website, or any other avoidance techniques. I'm not claiming it's impossible, only that I don't know of any. What I *do* know is that successful inventors are the ones willing to go out and ring doorbells.

Many years ago, so the legend goes, there was a beautiful young girl sitting at the soda fountain in Schwab's Drugstore in Hollywood, where she was noticed and approached by a famous director who wanted to put her in his next movie. The girl, Lana Turner, went on to become one of Hollywood's biggest stars, and the legend refuses to die. However, although that was way back in the 1930s, rarely has anyone has been discovered "by accident" ever since. Whether you're an aspiring starlet or an inventor with the next big thing, you have to go out there and get yourself noticed. I know of no other way to make something happen.

The reason most inventors try to avoid these encounters is because they're afraid they won't know what to say and will make fools of themselves. If you have the same problem, you can relax. I know how to fix it. Knowledge is courage. In a subsequent chapter I fully explain what these meetings are like, the questions you're apt to be asked, the precise way to answer them, and how to close the deal. To me, going out to sell the idea is the best part of this business. After you know what I know, you might feel the same way. Henry Ford said that one of man's greatest discoveries, one of his biggest surprises, is to find that he can do what he was afraid he couldn't.

Mistake No. 9: Underestimating the Financial Requirements to Launch Your New Idea

There are essentially three ways to turn your million-dollar idea into a big payday: You can license it or sell it to another company, you can produce and market it yourself, or, depending on the nature of the idea, you can perhaps franchise it to others around the country. Each method takes a certain amount of money, and inventors unfailingly underestimate what they need. Nothing will doom a project or bankrupt a business more surely than lack of funds to see it through. I've been there myself earlier in my career, so I know what it's like.

It's impossible to put a general dollar figure on the amount needed to launch a manufacturing or franchising business because of all the variables involved. However, there are formulas to help you arrive at an intelligent projection. Licensing, on the other hand, is simple enough so that some dollar figures can be proposed.

My best estimate is that it will take from $5,000 to $20,000 to create and polish your idea and carry it to the office of a couple of potential licensees. The reason for the wide spread is that much depends on whether the idea should be patented or not, what it would take to build a working prototype, and how far you have to travel to find the right prospect for it. If you live in Chicago, your chances are better than if you live in Butte, Montana. Sorry, Butters, Butites, or Butians, but that's the fact. That might sound like a lot of money, and I know for some of you it is, but I can think of no other (legal) business venture where the entry fee is so small in relation to the possible payoff. There's a little guy on my corner who sells soft pretzels from a handmade cart. He wouldn't sell you his business for that sum of money.

Yes, certainly it's possible to skimp on many aspects, but I think you'd come to regret it. You can skimp by not patenting your product idea when patenting is called for. You can skimp on not making an impressive prototype or not preparing first-class presentation materials, and you can skimp by not traveling to the prospect's office. Yes, that might cut your costs way down, but to what end? If you fail to find any takers for your idea, for the rest of your life you'll be wondering if it was the idea or the way it was presented. Is that worth it? Spend the dough, I say—even if it's on a wasted effort, at least you'll have the satisfaction of knowing that you gave the idea your best shot—and now, with a clear conscience, you can move on.

Inventions *do* have to be sold, so how they look is important. An impressive presentation commands respect—and if someone respects you, you're already rounding third base. So, even if you've done everything right and still found no takers, it's not the end of the world. If you can come up with one idea, surely you can create another—and that might be just the blockbuster you're hoping for. Inventors often fail with their first idea and, having learned from the experience, succeed with their next one. Lots of my own ideas don't make the grade, and I just shrug them off and move on because I know that one great idea can make up for lots of near misses.

Mistake No. 10: Not Understanding the Talents and Aptitudes Required to Enter the Business World

There are some drawbacks to opting for licensing as the way to cash in on your idea, not the least of which is that the money you can earn is substantially less that if you successfully market the product yourself. However, one of the principal advantages of licensing is that it requires very little from you in the way of experience, aptitude, brilliance, time, or ambition. The product idea itself is the star, and just showing up with it under your arm is 90% of the battle. Whatever you need to know, this book will teach you—and if you follow the steps, and if your idea is a great one, there's no reason why you can't turn it into a success.

However, self-marketing, being an entrepreneur, putting your own money on the line, meeting a payroll, is a whole different matter. I can show you what techniques work and which ones don't, but you, *and only you*, can determine if you have the aptitude for the work. Some folks are born entrepreneurs and immediately find themselves comfortably at home in the business world. Other folks, just as smart, find their talents and interests lay elsewhere. That's no disgrace; Albert Einstein probably would have gone bankrupt trying to run a pizza shop.

What *is* a disgrace is not taking the time to understand what's at stake and what it takes to succeed—and not being truthful with yourself before embarking on any venture. If the work doesn't suit your talents, ambitions, enthusiasm, and interest—no matter how much money you have and no matter how wonderful the idea is—you will probably not achieve success. No entrepreneur in the world would tell you differently.

Mistake No. 11: Not Securing the Advice of Disinterested Others

Inventors send me their ideas, telling me how much their family and friends love it, or, perhaps with a game, telling me how much fun it is to play it with their children. "Everyone tells me that they'd buy this product if it was available. There are 100 million motorists in America, and every one of them could use a great new accessory like this!"

I take all that in with a knowing nod. Of course friends and relatives are going to tell the inventor how great the idea is; why wouldn't they? Even the inventor's dog, looking at him with loving eyes and wagging tail, would tell him the same thing if she could speak.

Many inventors, believing what they're being told without questioning the source, will then plunge full steam ahead—patents, prototypes, invention companies: the works. Finally, somewhere down the line, the inventor finds himself in front of someone actually in the industry where his own product idea is intended to compete and hears the sad truth: The product already exists, or it has already been tried and failed, or it has been superseded by something better and cheaper. Or, frankly, it's just a plain dumb idea.

Through friends or acquaintances, you should be able to network yourself into meeting someone in the business—and without revealing details of your idea, a few questions should let you easily determine if you're on the right track. It's very difficult simply to pop into an unfamiliar industry with a product idea that would be excitingly new to folks who have spend their careers in that business. That's why most successful inventors stick to industries in which they already have firsthand familiarity. It's that insider knowledge—knowing what products exist, knowing what similar products have existed in the past, knowing the direction in which the industry is heading—that enables successful inventors to uncover the niches that can be profitably exploited. If you're not an industry insider, at least talk to someone who is. Inventing is often the easy part; the trick is to know what needs to be invented.

Mistake No. 12: Trying to Sell an Unrealistic Business Plan or Marketing Plan

If your purpose is to get someone to invest in your new company or to lend you money for it, you need a business plan. It doesn't matter in you're asking the Chase Bank or your rich aunt Minnie: Anyone being asked to part with money wants to see how it's going to be spent and how they can be assured that the money isn't just going down a hole. The plan serves to give structure to the inventor's own thinking about the business he intends to run, and it shows the proposed investor or lender how the money will be spent and what reasonable returns can be expected.

If your aim is to get someone to pay you a royalty for your new idea, you need a marketing plan to show the licensee why the product is worth the investment. It doesn't matter if you're showing it to Procter & Gamble or Sal's Fancy Frocks: Anyone being asked to take on the legal and financial responsibilities of a licensing contract wants to know what the competition is, why your product would be better, and the basis for expecting enough of these products to be sold to earn them a profit.

Either with a business plan for a lender or investor or with a marketing plan for a licensee, in the final analysis you have to put a persuasive, intelligently prepared document into the hands of the person being asked to invest in your new product idea. That's what he wants; what he expects; and what he's entitled to. No matter who it is, you are probably talking to a professional who can spot a phony a mile away. If you try to puff the sales figures, you'll be caught; if you try to puff the profit figures you'll be caught; if you try to puff the size of the potential market you'll be caught; and if to try to minimize the competition you'll be caught. Cheat me once, shame on you; cheat me twice, shame on me. The person you're dealing with will spot the false claims and will begin to have doubts about the project in general and you in particular. When doubts make their appearance, deals fly out the window.

I understand that any inventor might be nervous and anxious when trying to present a product or plan to someone who can turn dreams into a reality—and the desire to offer the idea in the best light certainly is a strong one. I see it myself; some inventors will make such preposterously inflated claims that I immediately become dubious, suspicious, and hesitant about moving ahead with a relationship. Simply tell the truth as you believe it to be, and you won't have to answer to anyone. Einstein might not have known how to run a pizza shop, but he knew what he was talking about when he said that whoever is careless with the truth in small matters cannot be trusted with important ones.

Product Licensing Is a Favorite Path to Riches for Many Inventors; Is It the Right One for You? Here's All You Need to Know to Make Your Choice, and Here Are the Critical Licensing Steps Taken by Other Successful Inventors

When you come to a fork in the road–take it!
–Yogi Berra

As I mentioned earlier, when someone is struck with a great new product idea, he has several choices to cash in on it: He can license it, sell it, make it himself, or, perhaps, franchise it to others. One of these success routes is the right one for you, depending on your personal circumstances, talents, ambitions, goals—and the nature of the idea itself. For instance:

Should you create your own business or turn your idea over to others in exchange for royalties? Some points to consider:

- If you're already launched on a satisfying career or profession, or if your life is fine just the way it is, you'll probably be more interested in licensing or selling your idea as a means to provide an extra income source. Conversely, if you're idle, drifting, or stuck in a dead-end job, marketing the product yourself might be a perfect career choice—the opportunity you've been waiting for.

- If you're risk-averse, or if a frank assessment of your skills and talents shows that you don't have the kind on entrepreneurial traits needed to run a business, then you certainly shouldn't take that route. However, if you're confident of your abilities, hugely ambitious, and willing to take risks to achieve your goals, then not only does self-marketing or franchising provide substantially better profit opportunities, but being your own boss might be a thrilling prospect, and the choice could change your entire life.

- Licensing or selling your idea takes very little money and very little of your time. You create the product, license it, and go on with your life. Self-marketing and franchising, in contrast, are life-changing decisions requiring all of your time and perhaps all of your money. Further, successful licensing can provide almost immediate profits, whereas even a successful new company usually takes three to five years to become so. Since the lack of funds is a principal reason for business failure, unless you have a clear idea of the amount of money needed, and unless you have the ability to raise it, then the self-promotion options are probably not the right ones.

- Often the nature of the new idea itself will be the determining factor in deciding one's appropriate course of action. Many new product ideas simply cannot support a full-time business, but they might support part-time ones. And many product ideas, even good ones, don't have the qualities to make them candidates for franchising, although they might be a natural for licensing or self-marketing. A reality check will go a long way in helping to decide on a proper course of action.

- And finally, if you dream up an idea and fail to find a licensee, it's a simple matter to put it aside and move on. If you can come up with one idea, you can probably come up with another one that will be better than the first. However, bouncing back from a failed business is clearly not for the faint of heart.

This book is dedicated to exploring all of these matters to help you make the right choice and is designed to review the steps needed to help ensure that your choice is a successful one. For many reasons, product licensing is the choice of many inventors, and it is the main topic of this chapter. But first a few words about selling your idea for quick cash.

Selling Your Idea

For some inventors, particularly for those in tight financial situations, selling the product idea seems like a fast fix for their problems. Unfortunately, it's very hard to find any takers; and if the product isn't patented, that makes it even harder. The problem is that it's almost impossible for the manufacturer to determine the value of the idea. What the inventor feels the idea is worth and what the manufacturer is prepared to pay for it are often so far apart that one might think they're not both talking about the same product. A purchase price would logically be based on a sales projection over the life of the product, but who'd be bold enough to make and defend that kind of prediction? If the manufacturer is enamored with the idea, and if the inventor is willing to accept a fire sale price, then certainly a deal can be made. However, since the buyer (the manufacturer) is usually the more seasoned negotiator, the inventor often winds up with the short end of the stick. Here are a few true-life examples.

In 1898 a chap named Joshua Lionel Cowen invented a product called an "Electric Flowerpot." It had a battery and bulb built-in, and when you pushed a button, the flowers lit up. Not surprisingly, he had no success with the product and wound up selling the patent for a few dollars to his dear friend, Conrad Hubert. Hubert, no fool, immediately threw away the pot and the flowers. He kept the battery and the bulb and made a wholly new product called an "Electric

Hand Torch" and started a company (Eveready, Inc.) to market it. One can only guess what Cowen thought when he saw what his electric flowerpot became. Incidentally, if that name is familiar to you, it's because he's the one and the same Joshua Lionel Cowen who, a few years later, started the Lionel Train Company.

In 1962 an inventor named Stan Weston had what later proved to be a brilliant idea. He believed that boys would like to play with dolls just as girls did, if an unfeminine doll could be created that appealed to them. He developed a 12-inch male doll, dressed it in a military uniform, added some moving parts, called it "The Lieutenant," and sold it to what later became the Hasbro Company for $100,000. That was a great deal of money in those days, and so Weston probably though he made an incredible deal for himself. After all, there was no way to prove his theory about boys playing with dolls, no matter how they were dressed up, and the toy company was taking a big risk. The Lieutenant, of course, became G.I. Joe and in its current shrunken stature has sold (and continues to sell) billions around the world, not to mention all of the GI Joe tanks and planes and guns and everything else that are sold along with it. A great deal for Hasbro; not so much for Weston.

A Definition of Product Licensing

Companies gladly pay out millions of dollars every year to folks who bring them great new products to sell. That's called licensing. The company gets a great new product and the inventor gets a percentage on each one that's sold. The company's happy. The inventor's happy. Everybody's happy. Think of it like renting a house. You still own the house, and the tenant pays you for its use. In product licensing, if your product is patented, you also still own the property (the patent), and the licensee pays you rent for its use, only the rents are referred to as royalties. Just as you have a lease with your tenant for a specified period of time that describes what she can and cannot do with your property, so you have a licensing agreement with the manufacturer that spells out what he can and cannot do. Instead of being the homeowner, in licensing you're the licensor—and the renter is now the manufacturer, or the licensee.

This analogy works to explain the concept in general, but there are important differences. As the homeowner, the rent that your tenant pays is an exact amount of money every month; but royalties, of course, are based on the sales of your licensed product. And whereas a tenant's lease can be terminated periodically, a licensing agreement usually continues indefinitely if the contractual terms continue to be met. However, those are simply details. Most important; whether you're renting a house or renting an invention, both are intended to achieve the same happy result—a check in your mailbox every month.

The Harvey Reese Famous C.R.A.S.H. Course in Successful Product Licensing

In a previous book of mine, devoted exclusively to product licensing, I introduced my C.R.A.S.H. course to show readers the steps involved in achieving licensing success and to demonstrate the importance for the inventor to proceed in a logical, sequential manner. Or as Attila the Hun probably had to keep reminding his marauder hordes: "Idiots! Pillage first, *then* burn!" Then as now, my goal is not only to inspire you to turn your exciting new idea into a wonderful moneymaker, but to provide the road map to show how to make it happen.

C. as in *Create*

This step shows the inventor how to dream up moneymaking ideas, one after another. There actually is a proven system to make this happen.

R. as in *Research*

Is it really a good idea? Is it original? Can it be done? Will it sell? Does it need a patent? This step shows you how to find the answers to these crucial questions.

A. as in *Action*

Research completed, now's the time to swing into action. Here's everything you need to know about creating your prototype, preparing your presentation, and lining up your appointments.

S. as in *Show and Tell*

It's make-or-break time, when you meet with prospective licensees or prospective investors. This step explains how to make a presentation that will get the person on the other side of the table to extend a hand and say "YES!"

H. as in *Harvest*

You worked hard, the licensee or investor is ready to move ahead, now's the time to reap the harvest. Here we review the kind of contract that's designed to give you all the rewards that your talent deserves.

Good News–Bad News

Which do you want first? When I get asked that question, I always ask first for the bad news. Figuring you're like me, here goes. The bad news is that even under the best of circumstances, companies instinctively hate to sign licensing contracts. They don't like the restrictions that a licensing agreement places on them, and they *hate* paying royalties to outsiders. They'll only go for a licensing deal, kicking and screaming, if the idea is unique, exclusive, fully developed, and offers the promise of big sales and big profits. If the idea doesn't make the manufacturer say "WOW!" as he sees dollar bills floating before his eyes, it's a virtual certainty that he won't sign a licensing agreement.

The good news is: So what? If you *do* offer a product idea that's unique, exclusive, fully developed; something that *does* offer the promise of big sales and big profits, a manufacturer *will* sign the contract. Sure, it's true, he might do it kicking and screaming, but that's his problem. When you take the check to the bank, the teller doesn't ask about the mood of the signer.

Knowing all that, your job as the inventor is simple: All you have to do is come up with something that's brilliant, something that has never been done before, that's cheap and easy to make, and that folks will stand in line to buy. What's that I hear? You say you already have such a product? Well, let's see if you do.

"Success Is When Preparation and Opportunity Meet"

That was an observation by the late Bobby Unser, the great racing car driver, and it's so sensible that you'd think everyone would embrace its logic. But, alas, I'm afraid not. Over the years I've seen literally thousands of ideas sent to me by inventors, and my best guess is about 40% of them are ideas for products that already exist or that have long been made obsolete by newer, improved versions. Amazing, isn't it? Amazing but true. My company charges a fee to evaluate product ideas and report back to the inventor with our impressions, suggestions, recommendations, and estimations as to the idea's commercial value. One inventor was definitely not happy with us when our report back included pictures of virtually identical products already on the market. He felt he wasted the fee and that

Step No. 1.
Before doing anything else, make sure your idea is truly original.

our website should have some sort of warning, cautioning inventors not to send in their ideas until they did the research to see if they were original. Well, *duh!*

Typically I can look at an idea and mere common sense tells me that it's simply too obvious to be new and original. Usually, thanks to the Internet, the Patent Office files, or directories I use, within about 10 minutes I can find the identical product. That's not because I'm a genius: Any inventor could (and should) easily do the same thing. The problem is that these inventors don't make the effort; either they don't want to know, or else they think that just because their neighborhood store doesn't have it on their shelves, the product doesn't exist. However, if they won't do the search, you can be sure that the manufacturer they're trying to license to will. You can call some of these manufacturers all sorts of names, but "stupid" isn't one of them.

Not too long ago I came up with a product idea that I thought was genius—pure genius. The idea was to put a chip with a speaker inside a dog's collar that would be activated by a control built into the leash in the owner's hand. The idea was that the chip would contain several cute, flirty remarks, and when the owner had his dog out for stroll and an attractive young woman walked by, with the push of a button that naughty dog would have some slightly risqué or bawdy remark to make. But, hey! It's just the dog! Who can blame the dog? I almost hurt myself by trying to pat myself on the back.

I took the idea to a well-known company I work with that makes novelty products, and the new product committee was so enthusiastic after seeing my presentation that we did the deal on the spot. (I always have a licensing agreement in my briefcase—you never know.) The company president actually called his wife to tell her what a great gag idea just walked into his office. A done deal, advance check in hand, and I'm off to new adventures. Or so I thought.

A few weeks later I received an e-mail from this company president simply suggesting that I visit a certain website, which of course I did. The website was owned by some small, obscure novelty company in someplace like Frozen Nose, Canada, that I had never heard of.

In addition to their current product line (rubber chickens, handshake buzzers, and things like that), they had some closeouts to offer. Yes, you guessed it. One of the closeouts was almost an identical twin to the product I thought I invented. Naturally the deal was off. I didn't care about the money (no, really) but I was terribly embarrassed; after all, I'm supposed to be a professional. The point is, of course I did do a search before presenting the idea, but the company did a better one.

If I was a salaried employee of that company instead of an outside inventor, and presented the same idea with the same information about the Canadian manufacturer, the company probably would have still gone ahead with it. After all, this large company could easily outsell that little Canadian company, and lots of companies compete with virtually the same product (Coke and Pepsi, Budweiser and Miller, etc.); they do it with better packaging, better pricing, or better merchandising. However, when the same idea comes from an outside inventor, with the demand for thousands of dollars up front, minimum guarantees, and a royalty to be due every time one of the inventor's products leaves the factory, the bar is raised much higher. When it comes to licensing, the magic words are "new" and "exclusive." Without those components to put on the table, getting a licensing deal is almost impossible.

"Utterly Original Is, of Course, Out of the Question"

That quote is from Ezra Pound, the poet, and of course he was utterly right. I can almost guarantee you that whatever your product idea is, it's been thought of before, maybe dozens of times. However, probably none of those folks who did think of it did anything about it. If you're the one who does, that makes you the idea's rightful owner, entitled to receive whatever awards your originality might obtain. Years later, when one of those other folks sees "his" idea in a store, he'll slap his forehead and say, "Damn! That's my idea! I thought of that years ago!" Tough apples. It's your idea now. However, first you have to make sure that they were all the slackers we think they were.

There are several ways to conduct a search, and thanks to the Internet, you probably can do it without leaving home. Visit the Patent Office website (www.uspto.gov), where you can do your own search for existing patents and patent applications, or you can pay a professional searcher to do a search for you. If it's a simple idea, you can probably do at least the initial search yourself. However, if it's complicated, scientific, or technical, you might be better off using a professional; they're trained to uncover what you might overlook. Here are the e-mail addresses for a couple of them:

www.PatentSearchExpress.com   www.PatentMetrix.com

www.PatentSearch.net   www.PatentSearcher.com

Patent attorneys don't do patent searches on their own; they'll use one or another of the firms that you can hire yourself. The quality of the search is the same, the only difference is that you won't have to pay the the attorney's markup. Also, the patent office has depository libraries around the country. The difference in physically going to one of these libraries to do your search rather than doing it online at home is that they're staffed by trained, knowledgeable personnel who can probably help you get better results than you can on your own. There's a list of these libraries in Appendix C.3.

There are, of course, lots of other ways for you to search to see if your product idea already exists. You can search ThomasNet.com, which is the *Thomas Register* website. It has the names of just about every American manufacturer and what they make. Also, just about any industry I can think of has a trade magazine or a trade association that publishes a directory of all the manufacturers and distributors in that specific field and the products they sell. For instance, if your new product idea has to do with sporting goods, you'd go to www.sporting-goods-industry.com, and if your product idea has to do with plumbing products, you'd go to www.plumbingnet.com. A simple search is all it'll take to locate the directory for the industry in which you're interested. And of course there are plenty of other ways for you to search: other Internet sites, wholesaler sites, stores, catalogs, and so on. However you do it, just make sure that you don't have a talking dog collar on your hands.

Aside from searching yourself through patent files and directories, another approach many inventors use is to get the opinion of an independent expert who isn't a friend or relative and isn't trying to sell them something. Your personal involvement makes you less than impartial; your friends and relatives are going to be flattering, no matter what; and you can't depend on your lawyer, your accountant, or your prototype maker to tell you your idea stinks out loud, even if it does. Why would they? And your dog is going to love you, no matter what—so who's left?

As already mentioned, I perform this service for inventors, but there are other reliable and legitimate services as well. Visit the various sites listed below. No matter which one you select, you'll get value for the money spent. As I'm sure you know, you should avoid any company that offers you the come-on of a "free" evaluation. You'll be told that your idea is brilliant, no matter what, and you'll be pestered night and day by pushy company salespeople wanting to sell you a variety of useless services. I can guarantee that none of the following organizations would do anything like that. None of these organizations (including my own) have other services they're trying to sell you, and therefore have no self-serving reason not to tell you the truth about your idea, even if the conclusions are not what you hoped to hear.

Invention Evaluation Services

Organization	Fees	Contact
The Innovation Institute	$200	www.Innovation-Institute.com
United Inventors Association	$300	www.uiausa.org
Wisconsin Innovation Service Center	$595	www.academics.uww.edu/business/innovate/
Washington State University	$795	www.cb.wsu.edu/iac
Innovation Assessment Center, Baylor University	$150	www.baylor.edu/business/entrepreneur
Patent Café	$199	evaluation.patentcafe.com
Harvey Reese Associates	$175	money4ideas.com

"When Is a Door Not a Door?"

Ask any eight-year-old and of course she'll reply, "When it's ajar." Ha-ha, very funny. But then ask, "Oh yeah, big shot? Well, when is an invention not an invention?" And as she gives you a dirty look and starts storming out of the room, yell after her, *"When it's just an idea for one!"*

It always surprises me how little some folks think they have to do before the royalty checks start rolling in. They have an idea, something that usually starts with "Darn! Somebody ought to come up with a _____ to do _____ !" And they think they've really done something. Off the idea goes to the Jones Manufacturing Company and our "inventor" waits, I suppose hoping for an excited call from the company wanting to know where to send the checks. You and I know that's not going to happen, but more "inventors" than you might imagine can't seem to grasp the essential concept of this business: The inventor is supposed to invent the product. Period.

> Hello Harvey: I'm reading one of your books. My question is, I know of a product out there, but I have a unique and original use for it. Can we license this? Thank you!
>
> —John, Elko, NV

That's an exact quote of an e-mail I received the other day. Sadly, I had to inform John, as I inform all the others who send similar questions, that the answer is probably no; as clever as this discovered new use might be, it's probably not licensable. Some people use the products of manufacturers in ways that the manufacturer never dreamed of—and if you inform the manufacturer of this amazing new use, even if it actually is a perfectly reasonable suggestion, the most that will happen is that you'll receive "thank you for your suggestion" boilerplate reply number BT-216 initiated by some clerk assigned to handle such matters. The company would not see a reason to pay you a royalty for each product repackaged to sell for this other use. Perhaps it should, but it's not likely that the company will. It is, after all, still the same product. However, if you can materially alter the product so that it's obviously now superior to the competitors, and if you can patent the alteration, then you do have something that would be licensable. A couple of our inventors whom you'll meet later did just that.

The third and final part of determining if you have a product invention that a company will pay you for is if it has enough profit potential to pique the firm's interest. There are lots of clever, interesting, and useful products that are offered to manufacturers for licensing and are turned down, either because by their nature they're not capable of producing enough new profits to spark the manufacturer's interest or because they'll simply switch sales from one product to another with no net gain.

Let's say that you invented some cute little key holder. Let's say it has a little LED light in it, and let's say it's heart shaped. A nice little product, and certainly some could be sold. Novelty little key holders like this have a general retail value of somewhere between $0.98 to $1.98. Let's say, for example, that your own version would retail for $1.79. That would make the wholesale cost (on which royalties are based) about $0.80 to $0.85. Using an average royalty of 5%, that might earn you $0.04 on each key ring sold—not a fortune by any means. But more important, what's in it for the licensee? The company won't make out much better. It not only has to pay you a royalty, but in order to do so, it has to set up an accounting system just to keep track of sales for this one little item.

Also, since certainly no new company is going to enter the novelty key ring business simply by having access to your design, any likely licensee would come from the ranks of those already in the business. But what's in it for any of them? The folks in the business already have dozens of their own novelty key rings in their product line—so what's one more? Since adding your key ring to the manufacturer's line is not likely to add more sales, but instead would, at best, simply divert some sales from one of its own key rings to yours, where a royalty payment is required, the deal would likely cost the manufacturer money rather than earn the company more.

A few years ago a friend of mind came up with an idea for a new picture hanger, and since he knew I was in the business, he asked if I could get it licensed for him. It was a modest but cute idea, cheap and simple to make, and although I knew what the end result would be, I promised to give it a try. I took the idea to six companies that make picture hangers and was turned down by all of them. Sure, they said, it's a nice idea, but why bother? The tooling costs would be a few thousand dollars, and none of these companies could see how that would be money well spent (and frankly I didn't blame them).

The thing is, if a shopper happens to need a picture hanger, she'll buy what she sees on display with little more thought than she'd give to shooing away a fly. She's not going to shop from store to store to look for the best hanger. Also, the company that supplies picture hangers to any of the major retail chains sells lots of other gadgets to that chain as well. The retailer picked that company as the supplier because its prices were reasonable, the quality and packaging was good, and the delivery was prompt and dependable. Having a better $0.98 picture hanger hanging on the retailer's pegboard would not even make a blip on the store buyer's radar. It's not that the store doesn't want to offer the best products to their customers, but some are simply too insignificant to worry about. As I had to explain to my friend when I reported my failure, a swell product, but no one cares.

Most successful new inventions are need-driven. The inventor uncovers a problem crying out to be solved or an issue that has not been satisfactorily addressed and invents a product to answer the call. That usually happens to inventors who invent for industries they're already familiar with. It's that insider knowledge that lets them uncover the niches waiting to be filled and that lets them know if they're on the right track. That's why most professional product developers work in the one or two industries in which they have become experts.

Pop Quiz! Pop Quiz!

As part of my evaluation report to inventors, I include two worksheets; one addresses factors relative to the idea's potential for licensing, the other for self-marketing. Here are 20 questions selected from the licensability worksheet. Although these questions are intended to be answered by someone with no personal or financial interest in the results (like me), you can take the test to see how well you do. Award yourself 5 points for *Very High*, 4 for *High*, 3 for *Average,* and 2 for *Low*.

	VERY HIGH	HIGH	AVERAGE	LOW
1. Degree to which this is a fully developed and proven new product idea.	❑	❑	❑	❑
2. Probability that this product will do what's claimed for it.	❑	❑	❑	❑
3. Probability that this idea will be viewed by industry companies as new and novel.	❑	❑	❑	❑
4. Probability that this idea addresses issues that the industry has heretofore been unable to solve.	❑	❑	❑	❑
5. Probability that this product idea has not been done before nor has already been considered and rejected by company management.	❑	❑	❑	❑
6. Probability that this product would immediately be recognizable as being superior in function or benefit to existing products.	❑	❑	❑	❑
7. Probability of this product idea creating new profit opportunities for the licensee rather than simply switching sales from already existing products in the company's line.	❑	❑	❑	❑
8. Probability for this product to achieve a level of sales and profits to pique the interest of potential licensees.	❑	❑	❑	❑
9. Probability that there are no competing products or similar products on the market intended to perform the same function.	❑	❑	❑	❑

	VERY HIGH	HIGH	AVERAGE	LOW
10. HOW RECEPTIVE THIS INDUSTRY IS TO THE idea of licensing new product ideas.	❏	❏	❏	❏
11. Degree to which this idea meets current market trends.	❏	❏	❏	❏
12. Degree of ease by which the product's benefits and advantages can be recognized by the consumer.	❏	❏	❏	❏
13. Degree to which this product idea can be marketed through regular channels rather than through specialty methods.	❏	❏	❏	❏
14. How receptive major retailers would be in stocking and selling this new product.	❏	❏	❏	❏
15. Probability for this product idea to open up new yet allied distribution opportunities for the licensee.	❏	❏	❏	❏
16. Probability that this product idea can be the genesis for a full product line rather than a one-shot, short-term product.	❏	❏	❏	❏
17. Degree of success this product can enjoy without benefit of licensing famous characters, logos, athletic endorsements, or sports team affiliations.	❏	❏	❏	❏
18. How does this idea rate for its "WOW" factor?	❏	❏	❏	❏
19. Probability that the demand trend for products like this is moving in an upward direction.	❏	❏	❏	❏
20. Probability that this product can be marketed at a price commensurate with its promised benefits	❏	❏	❏	❏

I'd be mighty surprised if you didn't ace this exam—after all, you wouldn't be reading this book if you weren't convinced that you had a million-dollar idea. I'm not saying you don't, but self-administered tests like this are hardly reliable indicators. Nevertheless, simply by answering each question, you get a sense of the factors that any company would consider when doing its own evaluation of your idea. The one very crucial unknown is what, as already mentioned, is called the WOW! factor; some product ideas just seem to have it and others just don't. Executives, echoing what judges say about pornography, can't describe it, but believe they know it when they see it.

Tough Nuts to Crack

One issue worth mentioning is the use of licensed characters or sports logos to enhance the value of the inventor's product. Some products I see from inventors are based solely on that factor. An inventor might offer, say, a desk set that has pens sticking into a stock car. "It would be great with a NASCAR logo!" he'll add. Maybe so, but if the product won't sell on its own merits, it's almost impossible to license. The inventor can't license what he doesn't own—in this case the use of the NASCAR logo—and so he's left with very little. The prospective licensee would have to go to NASCAR to try to get a license (very difficult and expensive to do) and, assuming he was successful, he'd then be subjecting himself to the payment of two royalties: one to NASCAR for the use of the logo and the other to the inventor for the suggestion its use on a stock car desk set. That's not likely to happen.

Similarly, it's very difficult to license a product based on the claim that it's going to be the next big fad. W. Somerset Maugham, the writer, said that there are three rules for writing a great novel. Unfortunately, he went on, no one knows what they are. The same could be said for fad items: If anyone had the formula, he or she would be a millionaire many times over. Maybe there is a formula—but so far no one has been able to find it. Products intended to perform some useful function—like a kitchen gadget or a gardening tool or a sewing aid—are easy for someone in that particular business to evaluate in terms of their potential commercial value. However, a novelty product whose success depends entirely on the whims and caprices of the intended customer is much more difficult to gauge. Companies in the business understand this and are therefore reluctant to license gag or fad products from outsiders. The risks are too high and the chance for a payoff is too small.

Since I'm in the business, having myself created some hot fad items (among many duds), I tried to study this fad phenomenon to see if I could spot any common traits among the few winners that the hundreds of losers didn't possess. But alas, I quickly realized it was futile. It's impossible to fathom what mysterious forces are at work to make one item become a national craze and another one just sit on the retailers' shelves gathering dust. That's why products like this are so difficult to license. I invented inflatable furniture many years ago, and Santa's Reindog Antlers more recently (with a few others in between) and when they went on to be huge sellers I had no more reason to understand why than I did when other just as clever products failed. If that's what you have, something that you think will be the next hula hoop or Pet Rock, my best and most sincere advice is to put it aside and move on, unless you want to take the chance and market it yourself.

Another difficult category for licensing is what are collectively called *cut-and-sew* products, generally meaning articles of clothing. This type of product is notoriously difficult to license because of the ease with which articles of clothing can be duplicated. Some fabric, an operator, and a sewing machine are all it takes to be in business, with popular styles being copied in cheaper versions seemingly overnight. Design patents offer virtually no protection because a tweak here or there can easily circumvent them, and the styles themselves fade so fast that any particular one is gone even before any legal action can be initiated. That's why famous designers can license their famous names but don't even attempt to license their individual style garments; those are already being knocked off as the models strut down the runway.

And finally, the most difficult category for licensing is made-up characters intended to adorn T-shirts and lunchboxes and notebook covers and so on. Making cute characters is easy; companies can do that all day long. What makes a character licensable is the fame and prestige it adds to the product. Research constantly shows that a lunchbox manufacturer, for instance, can command a premium price for his product if it has Spiderman or Sponge Bob on it, but not for an unknown character just as brave or just as cute. Since individual inventors usually don't have the resources to turn their characters into media stars, I'm afraid they're of no value to any company being asked to pay for the license.

And so, in conclusion . . .

I don't want to end this chapter leaving you with the impression that your idea has to be utterly brilliant in order to get it licensed. None of my own licensed products, I must confess, could justifiably be described in that manner. Clever, perhaps; but brilliant, no. However, I do create products for industries that I'm familiar with, and I know the kinds of products that are being sought. When I present a product to a manufacturer, I'm already pretty sure it's something that the company will be interested in because it fits into the product assortment and it's easy to make, easy to understand, and easy to sell. Brilliance doesn't enter into it. Inventing for profit is like any other business: Customers will buy what you're selling, but only if they see that it's to their advantage to do so.

The first product I ever licensed, many years ago, was almost too stupid for me to tell you about—but I will anyway (I have no shame) because it illustrates my point. There was a company near where I lived that imported expensive artificial roses from China. They were made of dyed red wood shavings and were quite realistic to the eye and to the touch. My idea was to take one of these roses, attach it to a specially created Mother's Day greeting card, and put it into a gift box like a hanky box, with a clear cover with a bow on it. I was ushered into the president's office and, with trembling hands, put my sample on his desk. It was hardly a stroke of genius, but the fellow who owned the company knew that he could sell it and was happy to pay me a royalty for bringing him the idea. I left with an advance check in my pocket for a few thousand dollars (remember, this was many years ago) and knew that I had found the perfect business! The product sold well for several years, I earned nice royalties, and I had a client to bring more new products to for many years after. That's what this business is all about.

If I can do it, believe me, you can do it too, but when you start out, you must first take these three easy steps:

1. **Make sure that your idea is fully developed and proven to work.**

2. **Make sure that nobody thought of it before and that similar or identical products aren't already on the market.**

3. **Make sure the product has enough profit potential to make anyone want to bother with it.**

In this chapter, our focus was on product research from the perspective of licensing. In Chapter 3, where we discuss the self-marketing and franchising options, the value of the idea changes. In licensing, where the inventor has little money and little effort at risk, the product idea is everything. In self-marketing and franchising, the value of the idea itself is less important since other equally important issues must be considered. The next chapter will reveal all.

THREE

Marketing Your Product Idea Yourself Might Be the Perfect Decision—or Might Not. Here's Everything You Need to Know about Your Idea, Your Goals, and Yourself to Make the Right Choice

> *The critical ingredient is getting off your butt and doing something. It's as simple as that. A lot of people have ideas, but few do anything with them now. Not tomorrow, not next week, but today. The true entrepreneur is a doer, not a dreamer.*
> —Nolan Bushnell, inventor of Pong, founder of Atari

I started Chapter 2 with good news—bad news, so let's try it again. The bad news is that of the approximately 800,000 new businesses started every year, half of them are gone within 5 years and 80% of them are gone within 10. But wait, it gets worse. Of those that survive, about half of them are producing only marginal profits. With statistics like this, I wouldn't blame anyone for being disheartened about going into business for themselves—but wait, don't despair, here's the good news:

Research has shown that the *overwhelming* reason for these failures is mismanagement on the part of the owners, most of whom shouldn't have been in business for themselves in the first place. Intelligent folks like yourself, simply by virtue of reading this book among other steps you might be taking, are doing the research to determine if this is the right career move for your own ambitions, circumstances, and talents. And if it is, your personal chances for success are quite high. First we need to review your idea to see if it could support a business, then we need to examine your personal goals and ambitions to see if this is the right move for you, and, finally, we need to examine your own personal traits to see if this is work that you'd be happy with. That's a lot to cover, so let's get started.

There are two ways for you to be in business. One is to keep your job and work at it on weekends, and the other is to quit your job and give this new venture your full attention. This is not a decision you have to struggle with; the nature of your product idea will pretty much make it for you. If what you have is some sort of craft or hand made product, or if it's a specialty item that can best be sold at trade shows and fairs like home shows, pet shows, trading card shows, or any of the many other special events like this, your almost certain choice is to keep your job and work at it on weekeneds. The financial risks are small, so not to try would be a shame. Don't go into production. Make a couple of pieces, get a table or booth at the right venue, put your product up front, and see what happens. If folks want to buy it, and if you can make it and sell it profitably at a price these folks have shown a willingness to pay, then you're in business. That's all the research you need. *Just do it!*

I hear from lots of artists and craftspeople who make and sell products at craft fairs and want to know if we can license these crafts to companies for mass distribution. However, as I explain, what folks are buying is the craft—the handmade quality of the item. Once it's mass produced in China and thrown into a box, it's just one more little *tchatchke* for a dollar store to sell with all the other tchatchkes.

However, if what you've invented is a serious product or line of products, something that requires a tooling investment and mass production, and if you hope to hire national sales representatives, maintain inventories, and sell your products to the major chains and other large retailers, then trying to do this part time will almost certainly lead to failure. This kind of venture requires such a major commitment in time, money, and energy that no amount of research is too much.

First Things First ...

1. Can Your Product Idea Sustain a Business?

If your product is not of sufficient retail value, or if it can't be developed into a full product line, then it probably can't sustain a business and a better choice would be licensing. For instance, if you've invented a better type of screwdriver, something that might sell for $1.98, no company like Lowe's or The Home Depot or Kmart would buy one little product like that from a new vendor. I don't care how great it is; it's still just a $1.98 item. Adding new vendors into the system is expensive for these big retailers, and none of them would do it for an incidental single item.

Similarly, you can't build a website or mail order venture around this one new screwdriver and expect to sell enough of them to turn it into a business. So, while it's doubtful that any retailer would buy a single screwdriver from you, it might be of great interest to an established screwdriver manufacturer that's already selling to all of these outlets. In this instance, the product itself, regardless of your personal desires, dictates whether you should think of self-marketing or licensing. You can't start a business called the One Alone Screwdriver Company.

However, if your product is expensive enough and exciting enough to make it worthwhile for large retailers or big catalog companies to stock it, or if it's better or cheaper than similar products that sell in high volume, then full-time self-marketing might be the perfect choice. Before printing your letterhead, though, there's another matter to consider.

America has a very fast-moving, highly competitive marketplace, and the life cycle of new products is very short. If your product is a fad item that you're hoping will catch on and become the next big thing, you need a quick exit strategy because fad items have the life span of a gnat. And like a gnat, they don't have long, lingering deaths; they go fast. Or, if your product is more basic, like, say, a new barbecue grill, competition will quickly come along with something equal, better, or cheaper, taking market share away from you. That will happen as sure as the sun will rise in the east, whether your product is patented or not. That's OK; you'll do the same thing to them when you get the chance. That's free enterprise. However, before launching yourself into the life of an entrepreneur, before running with the big dogs, you have to know in your heart that you have the skill and creativity to keep coming up with new products. Not being able to come up with the next product after the first has run its course has been the downfall of many new companies, so it's something to consider before seeing about a second mortgage on your house. Paraphrasing the comic Sid Caesar's observation, inventing the wheel was OK, but the real genius was in later coming up with the other three. Before spending your money, make sure that you're a three-wheel kind of a guy.

In the last chapter I presented 20 questions selected from the Licensing Worksheet we prepare as part of our invention evaluation; here are 20 from the self-marketing one. Let's see how you do:

	VERY HIGH	HIGH	AVERAGE	LOW	NOT APPLICABLE
1. Level Of Perceived Value In Relation To Tooling And Production Costs	❏	❏	❏	❏	❏
2. Likelihood that this product can be mass produced efficiently	❏	❏	❏	❏	❏
3. Level of exclusive patent protection applied to this idea	❏	❏	❏	❏	❏
4. Importance of patent protection in determining this idea's marketing success	❏	❏	❏	❏	❏

	VERY HIGH	HIGH	AVERAGE	LOW	NOT APPLICABLE
5. Level and degree of competition offering similar products that may affect market entry	❏	❏	❏	❏	❏
6. Extent to which design and engineering work have been done and proven versus the need to seek outside professional assistance	❏	❏	❏	❏	❏
7. Degree to which the perceived value is high enough to generate profits sufficient to justify the needed risk capital investment	❏	❏	❏	❏	❏
8. Degree to which this product suggests other complementary products to create a product line versus being a single, stand-alone product	❏	❏	❏	❏	❏
9. Difficulty in locating and hiring a national sales rep force	❏	❏	❏	❏	❏
10. Degree to which competition situation, display and size difficulties, profit margins, or any other factor would create retailer resistance	❏	❏	❏	❏	❏

	VERY HIGH	HIGH	AVERAGE	LOW	NOT APPLICABLE
11. Level of safety issues that must be addressed	❑	❑	❑	❑	❑
12. How well this product meets current market trends	❑	❑	❑	❑	❑
13. How easily consumers will recognize price advantages, superior quality, and/or new features with this product over existing ones	❑	❑	❑	❑	❑
14. Level of dependence on outside professionals to provide expert product design, expert packaging, and point-of-sale display to achieve success	❑	❑	❑	❑	❑
15. Level of advertising and extra marketing activities needed to explain product's concept to consumers	❑	❑	❑	❑	❑
16. Level that product depends for success on acquisition of licensing rights to sports figures, logos, cartoon characters, and the like	❑	❑	❑	❑	❑

	VERY HIGH	HIGH	AVERAGE	LOW	NOT APPLICABLE
17. Degree to which this idea can be launched by one person, operating initially on a part-time basis	❑	❑	❑	❑	❑
18. Degree to which this is a need-driven product, solving a problem that has long needed a solution	❑	❑	❑	❑	❑
19. Degree to which this product can create new markets and/or new distribution channels	❑	❑	❑	❑	❑
20. Degree to which the industry in which this product must compete is overcrowded and/or dominated by a few well-established sources	❑	❑	❑	❑	❑

Yes, you can award yourself five points for every "Very High" circle that you fill in, and maybe ace the exam—but frankly, self-tests like this have about as much validity as taking a popularity test in one of those teen magazines. Better, I suggest you forget the grades. Ponder each question and try to honestly viasualize how your own product idea rates. Is it *really* solving a problem that folks care about? Is it *really* significantly superior (not just different) to the already existing products it has to compete with? Go slowly from question to question, answering each as honestly as you can, and by the time you reach the twentieth, I think you'll have a realitic impression of your idea's worth.

Do You Have the Personality Traits that Entrepreneurship Demands?

This is a tough question to answer because successful entrepreneurs get a lot of glamorous press (Donald Trump, Bill Gates, et al.), and we all like to think of ourselves in that way. However, many of us have different skills and can make our mark in other ways. I've had several manufacturing businesses in my career, but I finally realized that I didn't have the enthusiasm and focus needed to run them as successfully as someone else might. I don't have the personality to deal with the minutia that business owners must address, and so, while most of my businesses were successful moneymakers, none prospered as much as they could. After a near bankruptcy, with the fate of more than 100 employees in my hands, I did a personal evaluation and determined that what I loved, and what I did best, was creating new product ideas.

Leaving the manufacturing world behind, I invented a new career for myself; creating new products for other companies and collecting a royalty on each one they sell. It was the right move for me, and I've been happy as a lark ever since. I haven't worn a tie in years and I only shave when there's a full moon. I work at home, and while my neighbors are rushing off to work with their briefcases and iPods and cell phones and laptops and BlackBerries and Blueberries and Raspberries and everything else, I'm relaxing, reading the sports pages and enjoying my second cup of coffee.

I don't look at myself as an inventor—I'm a product developer. I create products that I know are salable based on my experience, and I license them to companies that have the manufacturing and marketing skills to sell them. I'm perfectly content with the fact that the manufacturer gets 95% and I only get 5% because he has 95% of the problems. I'm delighted to let him worry about inventories and worry about sales, and worry about competition and worry about cash flow, and worry about everything else entrepreneurs have to concern themselves with. I just take my 5% and move on, not a care in the world. It was the smartest move I ever made.

Others, sitting in their corner office, running the manufacturing company they created, can just as justifiably say that starting their own business was the smartest move *they* ever made. Money alone should *not* be the determining factor. Enjoying what you do trumps money every time. Only after having experienced the results myself did I come to appreciate the old advice to do what you love and the money will follow. I'm living proof of its veracity. An honest appraisal of your abilities, interests, and ambitions will put you on the right track too; I'm sure of it.

Having been through all of this, I have a good handle on what it takes to be an entrepreneur, and I've listed the 10 most important attributes. You can give yourself a test to see how you rate.

As with the previous test, here too I suggest you just think of yourself honestly as you read each question, without worrying about a

	YES	NO	SOMEWHAT
1. I enjoy selling and do it well.	❏	❏	❏
2. I am a talented manager and easily handle people.	❏	❏	❏
3. I'm an innovator, always thinking up new ideas.	❏	❏	❏
4. I'm naturally organized.	❏	❏	❏
5. I like business and am interested in all its facets.	❏	❏	❏
6. I can handle stress and have high tolerance for risk.	❏	❏	❏
7. I'm a self-starter and don't mind working alone.	❏	❏	❏
8. I'm an instinctive decision maker.	❏	❏	❏
9. I can sweep the floor and close a deal in the same day.	❏	❏	❏
10. I have the self-confidence to call the shots.	❏	❏	❏

score, and try to envision how you measure up. These are the traits that a successful entrepreneur should have, and you're the best judge of whether you have them or not. It's not great if you do, it's not terrible if you don't. Some of us are wonderful at some things, others at something else. Some folks are risk takers and some are not. If there were no risk takers, to paraphrase the playwright Neil Simon, Michelangelo would have painted the Sistine Chapel floor.

A start-up entrepreneur has to be ready to mop the floor and close the deal, all in the same day.

The "WOW!" Effect

When I review an idea for an inventor, I talk about the WOW! effect—something about certain ideas that makes manufacturers say "WOW!" as they rub their hands together in greedy anticipation. It can't be measured and it can't be described, but some ideas have it and some don't. There's also a WOW effect when it comes to deciding on whether to go into business or not—and that has to do with your level of interest or love for the type of products and the industry in which you'd be engaged. For instance, if you love everything about automobiles, and if you go into the automotive accessory business, your chances of success are quite good even if you don't get a 10 for every entrepreneurial trait. Zeal and enthusiasm count for a lot. If anything that has to do with automobiles bores you, however, no matter how great your skills are, you probably won't have the focus needed to make the company soar.

Does Self-Marketing Meet Your Career Goals?

In no particular order, here are the seven best things and the seven worst things about using your brilliant new product idea to go into business for yourself. Think of them in terms of your own goals and ambitions, and the decision whether to proceed or not will easily come to you.

Best Things about Owning Your Own Business

1. **Money**   The best thing, of course, is the unlimited amount of money you might make. If you license your product, your returns might be 3%, 4%, or 5%, and you have no say in how effectively the licensee markets your product. If you're running the show yourself, and if you're good at it, profits might go up, up, up.

2. **Creativity**   Creating something from nothing can provide a level of satisfaction, pride, and accomplishment that's hard to achieve in any other endeavor.

3. **Independence**   Free at last! Free at last! You have no bosses to answer to, no time card to punch, no stupid company rules to abide by. You're in charge of your own destiny, ready to soar as high as your skills can take you. That's heady stuff for anyone thinking of making the move.

4. **Challenge** When we were kids, our pals would challenge or dare us to do certain things. Some of us were eager to accept the dare and some of us weren't. If the thrill of a challenge is still there, starting your own business is about as big a one as they get.

5. **Leaving Something Behind** If you're a family man or woman, one of the best motivators in starting a business is that you have something to leave to your children to ensure their future. Or, if you have a profitable business, you can sell it, take the money, and retire early to your new villa on some Greek isle or in the south of France.

6. **The Perks of Ownership** You might not think of this when you start out, but when your business becomes profitable (and assuming you have a clever accountant), there are any number of wonderful and perfectly legal perks that you can enjoy at the company expense that a salaried person will never have.

7. **Doing What You Love** As already discussed, nothing beats doing what you love—being excited and enthusiastic for the start of each workday. That rarely happens as an employee, but it often happens when people have created and are running their own successful business.

As bettors like to say, there are horses for courses. Not every horse is right for every track, and not every one of us has the mind-set to run our own business. It has nothing to do with brains or ambitions; it has to do with our goals and our individual perceptions of the quality of life that we hope to achieve. You might already be enjoying a satisfactory career or profession, satisfied with your professional advancement and happy with life just as it is. Taking on the risks, drama, and uncertainties of business ownership might not be for you.

Just as you weighed the seven best things about proprietorship, you should also consider the seven worst things.

Worst Things about Owning Your Own Business

1. **Failure** Just as the No. 1 best thing is the chance for high profits, the No. 1 worst thing would be business failure and the

loss of everything. Most small business people have to pledge their personal assets in order to secure loans, and if the business fails and loans can't be met, those assets are gone. Some have the confidence to take the chance, and some don't. You have to look deep inside yourself to make the choice.

2. **Family Problems** When you're running your own business, responsible to pay back loans from friends and relatives, responsible to meet a payroll and responsible to make a profit, you are probably physically and mentally at work all waking hours. Your kids are growing up without you around, and your wife or husband has to throw away dinner more than once because you didn't come home when you promised you would. Some will find the sacrifices worth it and some won't; it's not an easy call.

3. **Loneliness** When you were a salaried employee, you had a great deal of professional and social contact with fellow workers. However, particularly in the beginning when you're doing everything yourself, running your own business often means being alone. If you're accustomed to bouncing ideas off others and being part of decision-making committees, doing everything in solitude is a hard adjustment.

4. **Burden of Responsibility** Big companies can, and often do, make huge financial mistakes, but are able to still remain afloat, going merrily on their way. Small companies, especially startups, don't have that financial luxury; one misstep can close the doors forever. All entrepreneurs have this fact in the back of their mind as they make one major decision after another. Some folks thrive on the challenge; others don't. Now's the time to determine into which camp you fall.

5. **Unlimited Hours** Aside from the family problems that might result from a full-time business preoccupation, the surrender of a personal lifestyle might not be worth the sacrifice to some people. The regular golf game, or regular vacation or pursuit of hobbies and other interests, the socialization with friends and relatives, can all be too important in a person's life to surrender them to the business.

6. **The Long Profit Wait**   If you license your new product idea, you can start receiving your financial awards almost immediately. Upon signing the licensing contract, you'll get some money in advance, and monthly royalty checks will follow shortly thereafter. Start-up businesses often take years before they start to show a profit—usually resulting in lifestyle sacrifices that not everyone is willing to tolerate.

7. **Boredom, Disinterest**   I mentioned before the value in doing work you love. If you have a job and hate the work, you probably can find something more to your liking. However, if you have all of your money tied up in a business that you find boring and dull, with lots of loans outstanding, I'm afraid you're stuck for a long, long time.

There is one other worst thing that's not insignificant. If you fail at running your own business, it's very difficult to go out and find a job. Most employers don't like to hire former entrepreneurs because they're afraid the employment is simply a stop-gap to enable the person to marshal his or her forces for another try at the brass ring. Also, they fear that someone accustomed to being his or her own boss will have a difficult time adjusting to being a salaried worker and a part of a team.

My purpose is not to encourage you or discourage you, merely to point out the essential factors that deserve your attention. If you go into business for yourself and fail, the financial loss and mental anguish can be enormous. Ah—but if you succeed: Seeing the money rolling in and knowing this it was all because of your brains and skill can be a heady experience.

Franchising

Just as some new product ideas would most logically deserve to be licensed and others to be self-marketed, some new inventions might be perfectly suited for franchising. Most franchises are predicated on the franchisee performing a service: baking a pizza, fertilizing a lawn, preparing tax returns, and so on. However, sometimes it's the invention of a new product that allows the service to exist.

For instance, let's suppose you invented some special new plastic molding equipment that enabled a person to make instant, inexpensive fancy electric signs for home or business: happy birthday signs, Christmas signs, special sale signs, what have you. And let's also suppose this special equipment costs $25,000. No individual or independent retailer would make the investment, but any one of them might be interested in getting some signs made for a special party or sales event. It's a perfect idea for franchising! Using this newly invented piece of equipment as the centerpiece, the inventor can create hundreds of independently owned little sign shops all across the country—and collect a royalty on each sign sold. How can you beat that?

Or, for instance, recently an inventor sent me an invention that consisted of a special vacuum system to clean out gutters and downspouts. The equipment is too expensive for individual homeowners, but in the fall, with roof gutters and downspouts clogged with dead leaves, many might gladly call in a service to address the problem: another franchising opportunity. Similarly, I see lots of elaborate car customizing product ideas that would be beyond the skills of most motorists to install, but they might be willing to drive somewhere to pay to have the work done. Of course we all know of the big franchisers like McDonald's, but there are many others that you or I would have no knowledge of. Get this: Even the crews that come in to clean up murder and suicide scenes are franchised operations. Think I'm kidding? Check out http://www.servpro.com/services/biohazard.htm.

There was a time when franchising was the natural hunting ground for crooks, sharks, and swindlers, with the poor franchisees being robbed and conned out of the gold in their teeth. However, thanks to strong government intervention and strict disclosure rules, the industry has cleaned up its act and is now the darling of the business world. It is a known, proven fact that people owning and running franchised operations have substantially lower business failures than independently owned companies. Thousands of men and women would like to be in business for themselves but don't have the singular business idea, experience, or know-how to get themselves launched. If you have the proven idea, proven profits, and if you can provide the proven know-how, any number of these folks might be interested in knowing more. You're probably familiar with those franchise and business opportunity shows that travel across America with booths manned by franchisors explaining their programs. It's not by accident that these shows are always mobbed. If you'd like to know when the next one is coming to your area, visit http://www.franchiseshowinfo.com/.

If you think that your new product idea might work for franchising, here are the important points to consider.

You Should Have an Already Existing Business

Any potential franchisee being asked to invest thousands of dollars would naturally expect to see an operation already in business, running in a smooth, effective way, making impressive profits. On the strength of your personal reputation, you might be able to sell franchises to some friends and relatives based on the idea alone, but arm's-length prospects will want to see visible evidence that they're buying in to a proven moneymaker and that the franchisor has the hands-on experience to guide them every step of the way.

You Need Proof of Profitability

Not only should you have at least your own business up and running, but you are legally bound to open your books to prospective licensees. If your profits aren't impressive, or if you're operating at a loss or break-even, it's not likely that you could get prospective franchisees on board—unless you have a convincing story to explain why the figures are what they are. Total openness and honesty in making claims to franchisees is not only the morally right thing to do, it's against the law not to.

Your Business Has to Be Teachable to Anyone with No Special Skills or Talents

I know two entrepreneurs who tried franchising and both lost hundreds of thousands of dollars because they couldn't teach their business to others. Each of these folks has the kind of verve and skill to be successful, but as to their sorrow they learned, that's not transferable. They could teach the mechanics of their business but not the magic element that made them personally succeed.

One of these entrepreneurs had a home decorating business that he was able to franchise, but because decorating requires a certain level of aesthetic talent that can't be taught, the franchisees quickly got into financial trouble and wound up suing the franchisor, eventually putting him out of business. Later he was able to reinvent his franchising business and became quite successful at it. He got rid of all the fancy decorating features and stripped his business down to one simple element: selling mini-blinds that are custom made to fit any window and that come in a variety of hard-to-find colors to go with any décor. Now calling his company "Mr. Mini-Blind," he easily found franchisees and just as easily was able to teach them how to work the franchise successfully and profitably.

The other entrepreneur was not so lucky. He has a very successful kitchen cabinet refacing business, operating within about a 100-mile radius of his shop where the facings are made. One of the appeals of franchising is the ability to grow fast, with a minimum capital investment. Using that as his incentive, he hired a franchising consultant and set up his business. Everything started off great, with this new division signing up one new franchisee after another.

Unfortunately, signing people up is one thing; teaching them to be successful running their businesses turned out to be something else again. The refacing business turned out to be too complicated to operate as a franchise, requiring a combination of skills that few franchisees have. Some were good salespeople and could get the orders, but couldn't price the job properly and didn't have the mechanical skills to do the work in a profitable and trouble-free manner. Others were craftsmen at heart but didn't know how to go out and get the order. What a mess!

Our poor franchisor wound up hiring one consultant after another, pouring many thousands of dollars into one training concept after another, but was still unable to teach his franchisees how to run their businesses at a profit. People who invest their life savings and go into debt to acquire a franchise properly expect the franchisor to be able to teach them everything they need to know to be successful. Since this franchisor couldn't, as hard as he tried, closures and lawsuits followed, driving him to the brink of bankruptcy. If you don't have a no-brainer business, or if you can't turn it into one, think twice about franchising.

Your Business Must Be Able to Be Systemized

Franchisees come as a blank slate, expecting to be taught *everything*. Successful franchises leave nothing to chance. Franchisor management is able to provide their franchisees with thick operational manuals telling them what to do and how to do it hour by hour, day by day, situation by situation. In order for the system to work, the business must be reduced to routine and be so easy to duplicate that the franchisee in Waterloo, Iowa, operates her franchise in precisely the same way as the franchisee in Bangor, Maine. For example, if you walk into a Dunkin' Donuts shop anywhere in America, it will offer you precisely what you expect to find when you open the door.

Your Business Needs a Unique Selling Proposition

There has to be something about your business that separates it from others that might be performing the same service. Either your business has some little extra service or twist that the others don't have, or your business name is better known, or your business has a unique marketing plan, or you have better service or better pricing. Selling a franchise is like selling anything else: You need to give customers a unique selling proposition to make them buy.

One other point worth mentioning . . .

There is almost always a bank loan required for the franchisee to swing the deal. It's therefore important to be able to structure your offering so that the franchise price and the profit potential are sufficiently in line to present the investment as a prudent one for both franchisees and the banks that will be lending the money.

Why Franchising?

While the requirements might seem stringent and the start-up costs high, you have to consider these factors in relation to the potential payoff, which can be quite substantial. It's not by accident that so many companies have successfully structured themselves as franchising operations. Here are the four principal reasons why this is such an alluring prospect:

1. Franchising enables a company to use other people's money to fund growth.
2. Franchising enables a business to grow faster than it could otherwise.
3. Franchising spreads the risk to individual franchisees.
4. Since branch offices are staffed by motivated owner-mangers, effective staffing is easier than with company-operated branches.

Although the start-up period is a long one because of all the legal requirements, and although the start-up costs can be high—$50,000, $100,000, $200,000, and up—the payoff can make the effort and investment well worth while. If this type of venture interests you, the place to start for more information is with the International Franchise Association in Washington, D.C. (www.franchise.org). This is the trade association for the industry and offers a great deal of information about the industry in general as well as names of many franchisors and franchising consultants and specialists. The other important information source is the William Rosenberg International Center of Franchising at the University of New Hampshire (http://franchising.unh.edu/). William Rosenberg, by the way, a University of New Hampshire graduate, was also the founder of Dunkin' Donuts.

Whether your best move is licensing your product idea, selling it, franchising it, or using it to start your own business, you still have to determine the amount of legal protection the product idea deserves. Read on. The next chapter reveals all.

FOUR

Think Someone Might Steal Your Idea? Here's Everything You Need to Know about Patents, Trademarks, and Copyrights (When You Need Them and When You Don't)

> *Although no one can go back and make a brand new start, anyone can start from now and make a brand new ending.*
> —Carl Bard, author

There's an inventors' newsgroup where folks go to exchange views and opinions (http://groups-beta.google.com/group/alt.inventors/topics) that I visit from time to time to see what aspiring inventors are talking about. Every once in a while someone will post a question about how to make a prototype or how to approach a certain company or to ask what kind of presentation material is needed, and others in the group seldom reply. Eyes glaze over and the questions just drift off, unanswered, into the ether. However, when a person, especially a newbie, asks a question about patenting, no matter how arcane or esoteric it is, suddenly the answers flood in from all directions. Everyone has an opinion, everyone is an expert—everyone knows everything. The knee-jerk response is so predictable that I can't help smiling. The presumed common goal of helping each other achieve financial success with their product ideas is not what holds this group together; rather, a shared interest in the United States Patent and Trademark Office (USPTO), with its insider lingo, endless laws, provisos, documents, and mind-numbing regulations, provides the glue. Visit this site sometime, and you'll see for yourself.

For whatever the reason, many inventors have an intense, almost fanatical interest in the holy grail of the patenting process: the patenting laws, the definitions, the procedural systems, and the entire patenting bureaucracy. You can almost see whiffs of white smoke rising from the headquarters when a new director of the USPTO is appointed. The "how" for these inventors has become more important than the "why." As a practical matter, the "how" is easily grasped on a need-to-know basis, but it's the "why" that truly deserves our attention. How to patent, as it pertains to your individual idea, is not hard to grasp. More important: Why do so at all? Why spend the thousands of dollars that applying for a patent will cost? Very often patents have very little to do with the chances that a new product idea will earn money for the inventor. Visit your local department store and pick up products at random, turn them over, and you'll see that very few are actually patented.

I don't mean that patents are never necessary; sometimes they're critical—but that's the case much less frequently than you might think. The overwhelming majority of issued patents do not earn the patent holder even enough money to pay his or her expenses in filing for it. Some say that figure is 95%— but whatever it is, it's high enough to serve as a caution not to run out to get a patent if it's not necessary to do so.

Notwithstanding these grim statistics, and despite the great expense ($5,000 to $15,000 and more) and the long wait (now running about two years), many inventors still rush headlong into the arms of the patent attorney. One reason is the fear that any company to whom the idea is being presented will plot to steal it; and the other, for those intending to market their idea themselves, is the belief that a patent will keep the competition at bay.

Here are the facts. First, no company that you present your new idea to is plotting to steal it. That's not because the company executives are such honorable and trustworthy people—it's merely that, luckily for you, stealing your idea is not in their best interests. And second, if you're planning to market your idea yourself, think again about how much protection your patent will really provide in America's tough, competitive marketplace. If your idea's any good, I can almost guarantee that you'll have all the competition you can handle, patent or not. In some industries, patents are not even speed bumps to competitors hell bent on copying a winning product. "Sue me," they'll say, knowing that when you see how much a suit would cost, you'll back off. However, while a company might not think twice about knocking off an existing product, they'll think twice about doing so when it's just an idea being presented by you, asking for royalties. Here are some reasons why.

Four Reasons Why Companies Won't Steal Your Idea

Don't get me wrong, I don't mean that it's *impossible* for a company to try to steal your idea, but the chances of that happening are so slim that it's just not worth all the worry and fret that many inventors devote to it. A few simple precautions (which I'll explain in a moment) are usually all it takes to keep companies on the straight and narrow. Again, it's worth stressing that I'm not asking you to depend on the honesty and kindness of strangers, because then you'd really be in trouble. Lucky for us, however, and the reason I urge you to breathe a sigh of relief, is that stealing your product idea is simply not in the company's best interests and doing so would frankly be more trouble than it's worth. Here are some reasons why.

Reason No. 1. You'll Sue Their Pants Off

Any company wanting to steal your idea will likely tell you, when you show it to them, that it's an idea that they're already working on. If you have reason to believe the company is lying, when "your product" starts appearing in stores, you might bring the company to court. If they're sitting with a warehouse bulging with merchandise, with advertising booked and paid for, and suddenly you appear with a lawsuit under one arm and a restraining order under the other, yelling "Hey, you stole my idea," that's not a situation that they'd want to invite; particularly since avoiding it is so cheap and easy. If you follow the steps that I'll outline in this chapter, you'll have full and honest proof when you dreamed up the idea and when you showed it to the company. If the manufacturer did in fact steal your idea, he would have to create phony records to substantiate a defense and would probably need to get some employees to perjure themselves on the witness stand. That is so risky with such potentially dire consequences that I can't imagine any manufacturer would be foolish enough to try it. Paying you a royalty for your idea is so cheap and painless that only a brain-dead executive would choose the other option.

Reason No. 2. Being No Fool, You'll Take Your Idea to a Competitor

If you take your idea to a manufacturer, yes, it's possible that he might lie to your face and say "Nah, we're already working on something like that." Being the honest person you are, you might take him at his word, simply say "Thank you," and leave. However, what will the manufacturer have accomplished? Yes, certainly he'll save a few dollars, but he's running the risk that you'll now take the idea to his arch-competitor. After you climb down from the window ledge, deciding not to jump off after all just because you were turned down, it's perfectly logical for you to start to think "Hmm, just because the Ajax Company doesn't want my product doesn't mean that the Consolidated Thingees wouldn't like it." And so you take the idea to that company and, sure enough, they think you're a genius! So now, instead of Ajax simply paying you the royalty money you deserve, thus giving them the exclusive on your wonderful new product, its archrival Consolidated Thingees will have it as well. How dumb is that?

That actually happened to me (sort of). I had a product idea that I showed to a major bedding company. The product manager truthfully informed me that her company was working on the same idea—and in fact showed me their prototype. It was so close to my own that we could almost have switched with no one noticing. I left the office depressed and disappointed because I knew the idea was a good one, but I obviously wasn't the only one to think of it. It didn't take me long, however, to cheer up. Just because this wasn't a new idea to this company didn't mean it wouldn't be new to one of the other companies in the business.

I licensed the idea easily to the next company I showed it to—and to ease my conscience, I told a little white lie. I didn't tell the second company that I had already shown the idea to the other one, but I did tell them that, "through a friend," I learned that the first company was working on the same idea. I thought it only fair that executives here have this information so that they could cancel our deal if they wanted to. The way it turned out, however, is that my licensee, knowing that the other company was working on the same product, rushed through the process and was on the market first. And the first company, the poor chumps, never did introduce its own version. As I say, that's not exactly the same situation since the first company wasn't lying, but it still illustrates the point of why it doesn't pay to send the inventor away.

Reason No. 3. Sorry, but the Truth Is, You Can Be Bought Cheap

If the product you've invented is a gift item or any other type of product that has slow sales but high profits, you might be entitled to 6% or 7% royalty. Most new products, however, earn royalties of 3%, 4%, or 5% of the wholesale selling price (not the retail price)—and that payment is viewed as simply another cost along with the cost for the plastic or the wood or steel or any other labor and material expenditures that go into producing the product. The manufacturer then adds up all of the costs—10 cents for this, a dollar for that. Included in that long list is the royalty amount the manufacturer is obligated to pay you for each product sold. The manufacturer then totals the costs, applies a markup to earn a reasonable profit, and offers your product for sale. Since the royalty is simply another entry into the cost of the product, not only does the manufacturer recoup that cost when selling your product to customers, but he makes a profit on it besides! Since the royalty expense is passed on, costing him nothing, any manufacturer looking for a way to swindle you, if he gave even a moment's thoughts to the consequences, would quickly abandon the temptation. He may still be a lousy crook, but that doesn't make him stupid.

Reason No. 4. Cheat You Once and They'll Never See You Again

If a manufacturer tries to steal your idea, or in any way treats you dishonestly, you'll not come to this company again with your next idea. That's their loss, not yours. The product currently under your arm might be good, but the next one you dream up might be sensational. There are *lots* of companies but only a few people who can do what you do. Don't sell yourself or your talents short. If you've shown that you have the creative ability to dream up the kind of products that this manufacturer can profitably sell, you can be a great asset. You've demonstrated that you have the creativity to give him great new products that neither he nor his own salaried staff might come up with on their own, so it's all added profit.

The manufacturer's not a fool; he understands your potential value, so instead of chasing you away with a lie, he'll probably want to bolt the door to keep you from leaving. When I make a product presentation to a company, even if they decide not to take it, I am unfailingly told to keep them in mind when I come up with something else. How many salespeople do they tell that to?

Having said that, it doesn't necessarily mean that it's *impossible* for you to run into some manufacturer who will look for a way to cheat even when honesty better serves his interests. The next section details a couple of cheap and easy ways to thwart bad intentions that I and most other professionals take. After all, you never know.

Two Prudent Steps to Keep Your Idea Safe
Step No. 1. Keep a Diary

Keep a diary of your notes and sketches as you go about from day to day inventing your product. It might be useful if the patent office questions any of your claims or if you have a legal dispute with another inventor, or if you're suing a company for infringement. You can buy a diary expressly for this purpose through Amazon.com or other sources for about $15, or you can use any bound notebook that you can buy in a drugstore for a few dollars. It must be a *bound* notebook (not loose leaf) because there can't be any suggestion that pages have been added or deleted. Each page should be dated, numbered, and witnessed by someone who has no interest in you or the product you're working on. If the page isn't full with notes and sketches, draw a diagonal line from where you stopped to the bottom of the page, thus avoiding any suggestion that material was later added. You'll probably never need the diary, but if you ever do, you'll be glad you kept your records so meticulously.

One short note: There is such a thing as a "poor man's patent," meaning that you send invention notes to yourself and you don't open the envelope when it's received. The concept is that the cancellation date on the envelope and the sealed contents will have proof-of-invention value. That's fine in theory, but in practice it has very little legal strength since envelopes can so easily be steamed open and resealed. However, the only cost is for a stamp, so why not do it anyway? Yes, alone it has little value, but in combination with a well-kept diary and a paper trail, the preponderance of evidence is virtually irrefutable.

Step No. 2. Establish a Paper Trail

If you speak to Ms. Kelly, marketing VP of Ohio Amalgamated Company, to make a date to show her your idea, drop her a note or send her an e-mail to confirm the date and time, and say how much you're looking forward to showing her your new invention. After you visit with Ms. Kelly, drop her a note again to say how much you enjoyed the meeting.

Dear Ms. Kelly:
I certainly enjoyed meeting you today and appreciate your interest in my new wagon brake interlock system. I think it would be a natural and profitable addition to your product line and hope that you and your colleagues will agree. Enclosed, as promised, are the picture and specifications. I'll call you next week to answer any questions you might have. Thanks again for your courtesy.

When you present your idea to Ms. Kelly, don't leave your materials. Tell her that you'll send them along, which gives you an excuse for writing the note. And then later, when you do call Ms. Kelly, and if she has questions for you—even though you've given the answers on the phone, follow up with a note anyway.

> Dear Ms. Kelly:
> Confirming our telephone conversation earlier today—yes, I agree that if your engineers move the framus forward, it would more easily fit into the whosis to let the terabon spin in a concentric circle. That would certainly increase the cerbus, which, of course, is the desired effect. It was astute of you to notice that improvement. I'm glad that your evaluation process is going apace and, as you suggested, I'll call you next Monday.

Ms. Kelly is not an idiot. She knows that you're establishing a paper trail to document when you met with her and when you spoke with her and what those meetings and telephone conversations were about. She knows what you're doing, and that's fine—you *want* her to know what you're doing. It's the polite way to let Ms. Kelly know that you're no one to mess around with—and I can assure you she won't.

An Invitation to a Gunfight: The Sad Truth about Patents and the Law

Let's say you have a patented product and you've set yourself up in business to market it. Suddenly discovering that some evil fiend has started to market a product virtually identical to yours doesn't mean you can call the cops and have the rat arrested. All your patent gives you is *the legal right to sue.* "I'll see you in court!" you yell out to him, shaking your fist. But not so fast. Sure, you can sue the bum, but you might not realize what you're letting yourself in for.

Even small litigation trials, according to the American Intellectual Property Law Association, run about $750,000—and up, up, up into the millions from there. Not only is the cost prohibitive for many small business owners, and not only does litigation and the preparation for it remove the owner's focus from running the business, where it belongs, but the association goes on to report that even when small businessperson litigants win, they are rarely awarded enough even to fully cover their legal costs. *Bummer!*

The company that knocked off your product might have done it unintentionally, and so a stern warning letter from your attorney perhaps will do the trick. Or, the other company might also be small, unable to afford the cost of a lawsuit any more than you can. If you can convince your competitor that you're dead serious about suing, that might do the job. What usually happens is that the competitor calls and suggests that the two of you sit down to settle the matter. The result is often a royalty deal, which is what your competitor was really after in the first place. He's got a great product to sell, and paying you a few percentage points is a cheap way to get into the business. And you didn't really do too badly. You saved the cost of a lawsuit, you have an extra source of income, and, although you might not believe me as you read this, competition makes you sharper and having a competitor often broadens the market.

Unfortunately, there is always a worst case scenario. Some companies won't be frightened off, so then what? Larger companies, particularly if they think they have even a slim chance of winning, and knowing that the smaller company doesn't have the same financial staying power, are tough adversaries that won't go away. A bad lawyer can delay a trial for a month or two, but a good one can delay it for a year or more. By then you're gasping for air, circling the drain, ready to sell your firstborn to keep up with the legal bills. And if you think you can get your lawyer to work on a contingency basis, forget it. These guys aren't slip-and-fall attorneys; they want cash on the barrelhead. Let's see—a thousand hours at $400 per hour. How much does that come to? Hmm.

And finally, one other thought to consider: If your product has a short life cycle, it will probably be ancient history before the suit comes to trial and you'll just wind up making some sort of settlement. That happens frequently in the toy industry, where products come and go after one or two seasons and companies knock each other off with gleeful abandon. As mentioned, the company doing the knocking off figures that at some point it will probably be forced to make a settlement with the one that originated the product and will build a reserve fund into the selling price. Pay me now, pay me later: It's all the same to them.

But wait! Getting a patent is not *all* bad news. The good news is that your patent might turn out to be worth every penny that you paid for it. If you do sue, and even if your award barely covers your legal bills, just getting rid of your competitor might be award enough. And other would-be competitors, seeing that you're not afraid to sue, might think twice about messing with you. Also, lots of legitimate companies will respect your patent and will look elsewhere for new products. It's doubtful that your product will last for 20 years—the life of a patent—but for as long as it does last, your patent number on the package might serve you well. As I say, most companies are legitimate and would think twice about investing money in tooling, packaging, and production for a product that might get them in trouble as soon as they ship the first one.

And finally, and perhaps most important, a patent is referred to as "intellectual property" because it's just that—*property*—and like any other property, it can be bought, sold or licensed. If you license a non-patented product, as soon as the first production models reach the stores, your product no longer can be licensed to anyone else if your first licensee bungles the job. Once you offer a nonpatented product to the public, it's fair game for any company to knock it off, either identically or with their own version. That being the case, after dumping the first licensee, you'll find that no second company would pay you a royalty for permission to manufacture something that they're free to make anyway.

If your product is patented, however, it's the patent itself that's being licensed—and you can license that time and time again for as long as it has commercial value. Licensing it simply means that you are, in effect, *renting* your property (intellectual) to the company and can take it back to rent elsewhere if the first renter didn't live up to the terms of the rental agreement. And if you market the product yourself, build up a nice business after a few years, and decide to sell the company, the intellectual property that your company owns is an asset that can have a positive impact on the selling price.

Certainly having a patent will never do you any harm. The question is: Will it do you any good? Is it worth the investment? As you read through all the material in this chapter, I believe you'll have the information you need to make a correct, informed decision.

Everything You Need to Know about Patents, Trademarks, and Copyrights

The first question that inventors almost always ask is if they need a patent. "Show me your idea," I say, "and I'll be able to tell." Here's my general rule of thumb.

If the product is cheap, fast, and easy to make, with a low retail price and little tooling investment, and if it's destined to have a short life span, then usually patenting isn't necessary. Typically these would be gift items, toys, games, novelties, kitchen gadgets, fad items, lawn and Christmas ornaments, cut-and-sew products like tote bags and articles of clothing, and the like. Companies in those businesses rarely patent their products because a season or two is all they expect out of them, and they can get that without legal protection. By the time competition comes along, most of the major business will already have been achieved, and the newcomers will have to fight over the leftovers.

If the type of product you intend to market yourself or offer for license fits that description, any money spent on patents would almost assuredly be wasted. If licensing is your goal, no company will turn you down simply because your idea of that type isn't patented. And if you want to sell it yourself, no retailer would turn you down for that reason. Most of the products that I dream up fit that description—simple, fast-selling products. If I patented every one of them, over the years I would probably have invested more than $1 million in unnecessary legal fees. My patent attorney would have a statue of me on his front lawn with fresh flowers placed at the pedestal every day. I don't license every product I dream up, but no company has ever turned me down because my product wasn't patented. A patent is as useless to them as it would be to me. What matters—*all* that matters—is being first.

Also, if you plan to market your product yourself, and you need investors, if your product is the type just described, no educated potential investor would turn you down because your idea wasn't patented. I don't mean that having a patent would hurt, but I don't think it would help. If investors are knowledgeable, they'll be more interested in what you have planned for an encore than whether your first product is patented. What they want to know (and what you'd have to prove) is that you have a plan to grow the line and establish a niche for it in the marketplace.

However, if your new product has some importance, if it would carry a high retail value, or if it requires a major tooling invest-ment, and if it's intended to be around for years to come, a staple on retailer shelves, then patenting would be expected and neces-sary. A prospective licensee would not agree to pay you a royalty, invest in expensive tooling, and build a market for a product that his competitors can freely duplicate after all of the pioneering work is done. In fact, many larger companies won't even look at a new product idea that isn't patented. Small companies, which usually are more agile, can quickly be in and out of the market with a product that's expected to have a short life, so patenting is not that important for them. They jump in, gain quick distribution and quick profits, and jump out. Because they usually move much more slowly, large companies can't handle short-lived products; they need products for the long haul. Big companies are prepared to spend the money to build acceptance, and the only products they're interested in are ones that they hope will be around for a long time and have full patent protection.

If you plan to market the product yourself, your concerns would be the same as any other manufacturer. If a big investment is required, and if the product is intended for the long term, patenting will probably be a better course of action, if only to frighten off the faint of heart.

Patent or No Patent? First Do the Research

Whether you intend to patent your product or not, the first step should *always* be to search the files of existing patents (commonly known as prior art). Even if you don't intend to patent your idea, a patent search can at least tell you if you're inadvertently trespassing on someone else's. And of course, if you are intending to file for your own patent, this preliminary step can save you lots of money and lots of potential grief. As previously discussed, you can do the initial search yourself. If you turn up nothing to interfere with your own plans, I suggest that you next hire a professional search organization. Professional searchers are just that—trained professionals—so I'd be surprised if they didn't uncover a trove of important information that your own searching overlooked.

If you intend to market your idea yourself, and if you do find prior art that's similar, that doesn't necessarily have to be the end of the world. First, even if competitive patents exist, that doesn't necessarily mean that any products were actually manufactured and offered for sale. And second, even if they were, you're clever! You can design around it and still launch your own version. In fact, a case could be made that it's easier to capture a share of business that already exists from the efforts of established competitors than to create a new market for a product that has never been seen before.

However, if your plan is to license your product to another company, finding similar, already patented products will almost surely be the deal-breaker. When presenting your idea, you're honor-bound to tell the prospective licensee what you found, and that will probably be the end of it. He'll figure that he already has enough problems of his own to deal with without paying some stranger a royalty just to inherit more. Companies typically plunge into the marketplace with all sorts of internally developed products: old ones, new ones, exclusive, nonexclusive. . . . It all depends on the needs and goals of the marketer. Sometimes a company will add an old item to a line just because one of its big customers asks it to. However, when it comes to licensing, paying out thousands of dollars to some crazy inventor, the magic word is "new." If what you're offering is something already known to prospective licensee, something he can do anyway, it's unlikely that you'll get a signature on a licensing agreement.

What Can Be Patented, and What Can't

The patent office describes a patent as

> a property right granted by the Government of the United States of America to an inventor to exclude others from making, using, offering for sale, or selling the invention throughout the United States or importing the invention into the United States for a limited time in exchange for public disclosure of the invention when the patent is granted.

There are three types of patents covered by this general description: design, plant, and utility patents.

Design Patents

Again quoting from the patent office, a design patent is

> a government grant of exclusive rights in a novel, non-obvious, and ornamental industrial design. A design patent confers the right to exclude others from making, using, or selling designs that closely resemble the patented design. A design patent covers the ornamental aspects of a design; its functional aspects are covered by a utility patent. A design patent and a utility patent can cover different aspects of the same article, such as an automobile or a lamp.

In other words, a design patent covers what the product looks like, not how it works, and provides this protection for 17 years (unlike a utility patent that lasts for 20). Rarely does the precise way that a new product looks have significant value. The design might be beautiful, but other companies are capable of making equally beautiful designs. Design protection is so difficult to defend, and so easy to circumvent, that you should give considerable thought to the matter before making this kind of investment. Invention promotion companies that promise to get "a patent" for their inventor-customers often just get them design patents because it's easier to do and often the inventors' ideas wouldn't earn the more desirable utility patent. Only later do the poor inventors realize how little value design patents offer.

However, having said that, there are indeed some situations where the nature of the design is a significant factor, and legal protection for it can be money well spent. Here's one example:

Do you know those little cardboard air fresheners that hang from a car's rearview mirror? One company has a design patent on fresheners that look like an evergreen tree, which for some reason has become the gold standard for car air fresheners. Motorists like the way they look and buy them by the millions. Other companies in the business come out with one fancy new air freshener after another, but that little evergreen tree keeps selling and selling. Without the protection of the design patent, I think it's safe to say that the fortunes of this company would be considerably different.

If you believe a design patent fits your needs, the application form is in Exhibit B.3.

Plant Patent

The definition commonly used for what is covered by a plant patent is any new variety of a cultivated *asexually* reproduced plant (as opposed to naturally found ones). The example often offered is of Henry Wallace, our country's one-time Secretary of Agriculture and later Vice President in the Roosevelt administration, who developed hybrid corn, thus making him and his heirs quite wealthy.

Utility Patent

This is the type of legal protection that most inventors mean when they talk about getting a patent. The patent office states that a utility patent might be awarded for

> a new, non-obvious and useful process, or machine, or article of manufacture, or composition of matter or an improvement on any of these items or processes.

What cannot be patented are laws of nature, physical phenomena, and abstract ideas or artistic creations, such as literary works, dramatic plays, movies, songs, TV shows, and the like (all of which can be copyright protected). Inventors also cannot get a patent for nonuseful inventions (like a perpetual motion machine) or for "articles deemed offensive to public morality" (whatever the heck that might be). Utility patents provide protection for 20 years. If you have any doubts as to whether your product idea fits into one or the other of these categories, call 800-PTO-8189. The patent application is in appendix B(4).

Provisional Patent Application

Although many inventors think a provisional patent application is a patent, it's not. It is, as the name suggests, an application to the patent office to hold your place in line for a set period of time to allow you to determine whether investing in a true utility patent is worth the cost.

This type of patent application was enacted into law fairly recently (1995) and is expressly intended to help small inventors by simply and inexpensively providing a degree of temporary protection for a period of one year to give inventors time to determine the true worth of their ideas and whether a formal and expensive patent application would be necessary and prudent. The United States is a "first to invent" country, meaning that if two inventors file for a patent at the same time, the inventor who can prove that he or she invented the product first is the one awarded the patent. That's why I suggested that you keep a documented diary, signed, witnessed, and dated.

Many people dream up similar ideas and figuratively find themselves staring at each other in the patent office waiting room. If you have a provisional patent, for a period of one year, by which time you will have filed for a regular patent or let the provisional patent lapse, you come first in the eyes of the patent office, even if the other guy shoves his way in front. The patent office does not examine your provisional patent application, so theoretically you can write anything you want and still earn the right to say "patent pending" on your material. However, if you *do* ultimately decide to apply for a utility patent, the description in your provisional application has to justify the specific claims made in the utility patent application. Otherwise, you might forfeit the early filing date for the utility patent claims that the provisional one was intended to earn.

As I say, if, by the end of a year, you have not converted this provisional application into a utility patent application, it automatically expires and that's the end of it. Yes, you'll have spent some money, but lots of inventors think it's worth it, as do I. Here's why:

First, as discussed, it gives you priority if you decide to make a regular patent application. Also, the provisional patent application gives you the right to place "patent pending" notices on all of your material and prototype, so that you can show it to others with a degree of assurance that it won't be copied or stolen. Of course, patent pending status does not make it illegal for someone to copy your idea, but they're less likely to do so if they believe that you'll be awarded a regular patent in short order and will then come after them. Patent pending is patent pending—it doesn't say whether it's for just a cheap, temporary provisional patent or for the real thing.

While the application for a utility payment by using a patent attorney will probably be $5,000 to $15,000, filing for a provisional patent application, again by using an attorney, will probably be around $1,000 to $1,500. Also, since a provisional patent application does not require that you make the explicit claims required in a utility patent application, many inventors feel capable of doing it themselves. Without attorney fees, the only out-of-pocket cost is the $100 filing fee. Cheap enough. If you decide to go ahead, and if you decide to do it yourself, the application form can be found in Appendix B(2). If you do decide to proceed on your own to submit the application, there are books to guide you through the process, along with several excellent software programs that offer to make the process fast and simple. These are among the best:

Name of Program	Publisher	Web Site
PatentPro	Kernel Creations, Ltd.	www.patentpro.us/
PatentEase	Inventorprise, Inc.	www.inventorprise.com/
PatentWizard	PatentWizard, LLC	www.patentwizard.com/

Trademarks (and Service Marks)

The patent office describes a trademark as a word or phrase or symbol or design that identifies and distinguishes the source of goods from one party to another. A service mark is the same as a trademark except that it identifies and distinguishes the source of a service rather than a product. In other words, "Coke, "Bud," and "Dell" would be trademarks, while "FedEx," "Roto Rooter," and "Orkin" would be service marks. Trademarks and service marks don't prevent other companies from making the same product or offering the same service; however, they can't copy the name or use a name so similar in sound and appearance that it might confuse customers into thinking that they were dealing with the original company. For instance, if some little bottling company tried to sell their soft drink under the name "Koka Kola," it would be in for a world of hurt.

If you intend to self-market your product, a trademark might be important as you go about establishing your brand. This is something you can do yourself; the filing fee as of this writing is $375.

A trademark can last indefinitely (renewable in 10-year intervals) if the owner continues to pay the fees and provides the required affidavits stating that the mark is still in use. If you're licensing your product, a trademark probably would not have any value unless the name you came up with for your product is so clever, novel, and appropriate that the name itself has value. If that's the case, then certainly you should get a trademark for it.

I can't stress enough the importance that companies place on the names of their products, so if you have a great one, by all means protect it. No one can challenge the statement that a great product name can improve sales and a lousy name can hurt them. (I wonder what ever happened to the U. Stink Perfume Company?) Years ago I did work for the founder of Hooked on Phonics. One of his first official acts was to pick up the phone, dial 1-800-222-3334, and make a deal to buy the number for thousands of dollars from the fencing company that owned it. He didn't care about the numbers, he cared about the letters they represent (1-800 A-B-C-D-E-F-G), and he built a multimillion-dollar company around it.

Many companies take product naming seriously enough to hire professionals to address the matter. In fact, there's an entire industry devoted to product naming, with a dozen or so companies in business expressly for that purpose. They're professional linguists, and their list of clients includes many Fortune 500 companies. Here are the websites for some of the leading ones if you'd like more information:

www.AHundredMonkeys.com   www.IgorInternational.com

www.NameBase.com   www.TheNaming Company.com

Copyrights

Copyrights automatically protect any artistic effort (literary work, musical works, dramatic works, artwork, motion pictures, sound recordings, etc.) from the time of the creation. Even if the artist does nothing, the protection is automatic. Doing nothing, however, can have consequences. The advantages of formal registration are important, and the filing fee is so small (currently $45) that the minor effort involved is quite worthwhile. Formal registration establishes a public record of your claim and gives you the right to file an infringement suit if such action becomes necessary. Prompt filing also gives you the right to ask for statutory damages and attorney fees (in addition to actual damages) if you have reason to bring suit against an infringer. An official "C" in a circle is all it takes to stop problems before they begin. Because the trademark is intended for artistic achievement, the protection remains valid for the life of the artist and for 70 years thereafter. That's why properties like the Beatles and Elvis still have monetary value to their heirs.

Could You—*Should* You—Do the Legal Work Yourself?

If you're going to apply for a design patent, you probably could and should do it yourself. The application is simple, and it's the design itself that does most of the talking. If you're going to make a provisional patent application, you probably could and perhaps should do it yourself. As mentioned, the application remains unexamined, earning you the right to put "patent pending" on your material regardless of what you write. The application has significance only if, sometime within the year, you decide to apply for an actual utility patent. And yes, certainly if you're applying for a trademark, you could and should do it yourself. Why pay a lawyer to do what you can do just as well? And finally, if you're applying for a copyright, you certainly could and should do it yourself. Filing for a copyright is cheap, fast, and easy, so why not?

A patent attorney can do all of this for you—he can file for a design patent, he can file for a provisional patent, he can file for a trademark for you, and he can officially make your material have copyright protection. If you're uncertain about proceeding on your own, be assured your attorney is keeping a line open for your call. However, I think you should at least first look through the applications to see what it's all about. The process might be simpler than you imagine it to be.

However, if you're going to apply for a utility patent, maybe you could do it yourself, but in my opinion, you definitely should *not*. I do encourage you to file for the other protections on your own, but a utility patent is quite a complicated matter. I don't say that you're not bright enough to do it yourself, and I don't say that if you're willing to learn the methodology, you can't get a patent awarded for your efforts. However, smart as you are, it's not likely that you can get the quality that an experienced, professionally trained patent attorney can get for you—and when it comes to a utility patent, *quality is everything*. A talented patent attorney can craft the claims in a way to give you a level of protection that you'd probably not be able to get on your own. It's not that you aren't just as smart (or maybe smarter), but that's what the lawyer has been trained to do—and has probably done it many times over. For you it's just a one-shot deal, and the time it takes to master the craft might be better spent elsewhere.

If you're still interested, there are books to help you do it yourself, the most popular being *Patent It Yourself* by David Pressman. The author is perfectly legitimate and the book is carefully and intelligently written, but all it did for me was to convince me that this type of patent application is best left to the experts. I do, however, recommend that you read the book if you have the time—but only because knowing the process will make you a better client for whomever you appoint to do the work.

How to Find a Patent Attorney

If I was strolling past a fancy hotel and a chunk of concrete fell on me, or if I was hit by a FedEx truck exceeding the speed limit on a quiet residential street, and if, while lying bandaged in the hospital bed, I looked in the Yellow Pages phone book for an accident lawyer, I'd find them by the gross, page after page with full-color, full-page ads, their smiling, eager faces promising me that I will pay nothing until my case is won. In fact, as I look down at my bandaged torso, I see that a few of them have already left their cards.

However, if I needed a patent attorney, I'd probably find them all huddled together in a corner section of one page, listed one after the other in small, discreet type; no big display ads here. Even in the big city I live in, there probably are no more than a dozen or so. However, that's still enough to let me pick and choose.

Some might advise that the way to start is to get recommendations from other inventors, but I frankly don't believe that would be particularly productive. Your personality is different and your invention is different from the other inventor's, so the lawyer who might have been perfect for her might be a disaster for you. No, I think the only way to do this is to look these guys over face to face and pick the one that best suits your own needs, not someone else's.

The logical place to start, of course, is by looking for "Patent Attorneys" in the yellow pages of your phone book. When you do, you'll probably also see a listing for "patenting services" or "patent searches" or some other innocent-looking title—but beware, that's where the invention marketing companies lurk. I know I mentioned them earlier, but since these companies draw thousands of innocent inventors into their clutches every year, fleecing them for millions,

I figure mentioning them again can't hurt. Here's a quote, in part, from a Federal Trade Commission bulletin:

> —other inventors use the services of an invention or patent promotion firm. Indeed, many inventors pay thousands of dollars to firms that promise to evaluate, develop, patent, and market inventions. Unfortunately, many of these firms do little or nothing for their fee.

The FTC has found that many invention promotion firms claim—falsely—that they can turn almost any idea into cash. But, the agency says, smart inventors can learn to spot the sweet-sounding promises of a fraudulent promotion firm.

The bulletin goes on to discuss the typical come-on lines. The first step, as I previously mentioned (after the inventor has received the "free inventor's kit"), is to offer a "free" evaluation of the inventor's new product idea. The result, of course, is always that the idea is brilliant and that the company is excited to be working with such a talented inventor. The grading system for these outfits starts with "brilliant" and proceeds upward from there. Next, after exclaiming the incredible virtues of the idea and the excitement around the office that it inspired, comes the offer to do an "in-depth" review of the product and the market, usually for a measly $500 to $750. It wouldn't be so cheap if the company wasn't already so enthralled. I've seen these reports and it's so obvious that they're simply a string of boilerplate paragraphs that you'd think the company would be embarrassed sending it out. But no, the poor inventor, now so excited by the glowing praises, is prepared to believe anything. If the check for the research isn't promptly forthcoming, the inventor is given urgent advice: "You need to hurry and patent your idea before someone else does!" And on it goes, step by step, with thousands of dollars pouring out of the inventor's bank account and into the company's.

I won't bore you with the rest of the grim details: The inventor is charged for patent research that's rarely done or is cursory at best. The inventor then pays for a patent that is almost always useless and is then urged to pay the company to find "willing licensees." It's easy for the inventor to be strung along, step after step, until the promotion company has $10,000 or $15,000 of his or her money, maybe more. If you'd like to read the entire FTC bulletin, you can find it at http:// www.ftc.gov/bcp/conline/pubs/services/invent.

Also, if you go to the FTC main site (www.ftc.gov) and enter "invention companies" in the search section, you'll find a great deal of information about these companies and what the FTC is doing to shut them down. The patent office also publishes complaints from inventors, naming names, which you can read at www.USPTO.gov/ web/offices/com/iip/complaints.htm. There are also two privately run websites that I'd like to call to your attention:

www.inventorfraud.com A website run by an independent patent attorney who lists invention companies that have lawsuits against them by disgruntled clients

www.inventored.org Owned and operated by Ron Riley, an inventor who has made it a personal crusade to expose the malevolent practices of some of these inventions companies

There are many other sites addressing these issues, so it's not difficult for you to identify which companies to avoid—but for now, let's go back to the important task of finding you the right patent attorney.

When you start out, you'll quickly see that, like so many other things in life, patent law firms come in three sizes: small, medium, and large. Frankly, most of the large firms don't want your business, and they kind of groan when they see you come in. It's been my experience that they're not embarrassed to tell you that the match wouldn't work and please don't let the door hit you on the way out. Large firms are accustomed to dealing with large corporations where they can hold fancy meetings and charge big hourly rates. Most private inventors can't afford the fees. Charming and delightful though you might be, you're more of a hassle to a big firm than your business is worth.

However, if they haven't beaten you off with a stick, and if money's no object, there are some advantages. Large firms have lots of experts and subexperts, so you'll probably have someone working on your patent application who really knows what he's doing. And if litigation becomes necessary down the road, these are the guys best equipped to handle it. However, even if you are willing to pay the fees, I believe the attorneys in these large firms will still view you as a loss leader deal, and I'm afraid they'll treat you as such.

Most individual inventors center their search on small and medium-size firms. The small firm, often a single practitioner, will probably have a lower hourly rate, and you'll be dealing personally with the man or woman who actually will be preparing the application. However, since he or she has to personally do all the work, the end savings might not be much. Attorneys in a medium-size firm will surely have higher hourly rates, but since they have lower-rate paralegals to do much of the work, the end costs might be near to the single practitioner's. If you're thoroughly confused by now, then I've done my job because other factors are more important than size or hourly rate.

The first consideration is to find a lawyer whose training enables him to fully understand the nature of your invention. All patent attorneys, in addition to their law degree, are required to have an undergraduate degree in a technical field. The patent office divides utility patents into three main categories: chemical, mechanical, and electrical. Attorneys can be separated in the same way (with many subspecialties). Even if the first attorney you meet with is cheap, charming, and located around the corner from your house, if his specialty is in chemical products, you don't want him working on your new mechanical robot.

Make some calls and get some appointments. First appointments are usually free, and you'll be able to determine if the lawyer you're visiting is someone you can work with, and if his fees are manageable. Once he sees the nature of your invention, an experienced attorney with the right educational background should be able to give you a reliable cost estimate for doing the job. If he won't, you have a right to be wary. Since the application process can go on for a year or two, with lots of back-and-forth between you and your attorney, it's important that you choose one that you're comfortable with. If you like one particular lawyer in particular, and if his fees and pay schedule are in line with those of most of the other attorneys you talked to, and if his experience is in the kind of product that you've invented, then quit looking: He's your guy (or woman)!

One word of caution about lawyer billing practices. For a simple patent filing, your attorney will probably quote a flat fee. If instead he's going to charge you an hourly rate, he will certainly tell you what that rate is—but there's more for you to know. Most attorneys now bill in 15-minute segments. If the lawyer's hourly rate is, say, $300, then each segment is worth $75. If you talk to your lawyer for 5 minutes, you pay $75. Client 2 goes into the office as you're leaving, talks to

Never sit and tell jokes to a lawyer who bills by the hour.

the lawyer for 6 minutes, and leaves; client 3 calls on the phone, has a 4-minute conversation, and hangs up. For that period, the lawyer "legitimately" charged all three clients for the same 15 minutes, earning $225. That's how the billable hours—the holy grail of the legal profession—become astronomical. That's all well and good, as long as you understand how the game is played. When you sit down with your attorney, be as mindful of the clock as he is. Come prepared, ask your questions, get the information you need, and leave. If you pause to tell some long-winded joke or how well your kid did at the soccer match last Saturday, I can assure you you'll have a rapt audience, but when you get the bill, you'll never do it again.

Now that you've selected your attorney and settled on the cost, before reviewing how the process works, this is a good a place to address the matter of co-inventing or co-ownership of the patent you're about to apply for.

A Word about Patent Partnerships

Sometimes an inventor needs the help of an expert who has the kind of specialized skills needed to turn the product idea into a reality. Instead of paying the expert for this work, it's not uncommon for the inventor to make the expert a co-inventor. This is not a good practice and should definitely be avoided. You can make a side arrangement with the expert that gives him a certain share of any profits, if that's what he's entitled to, but don't make him a co-inventor or joint owner of the patent. That can only lead to no good. The problem is that the patent office doesn't offer half shares in the patent that it awards. If two inventors are named, they each own the patent, free to do whatever they wish with it. There's no such thing, in the eyes of the law, as a junior inventor and a senior inventor. In other words, your co-patent owner can go off and make whatever deal he pleases without your consent or even your knowledge. He can sell the patent and doesn't even have to give you a share of the proceeds unless the two of you have a separate contract covering this event. It doesn't require much imagination to envision the kinds of problems that can be created under a relationship like this.

Sometimes, when both of you are true co-inventors, say two scientists working side by side in the laboratory, joint ownership of the patent is unavoidable. If that is the case, now that you're about to walk into the attorney's office to start the patent application procedures, explain the situation to so that the attorney can prepare a separate contract between you and your co-inventor to avoid any unnecessary conflict.

The Patent Application Process

Step 1. The Initial Attorney Meeting

Your first meeting with the patent attorney, where you discussed rates, fees, and estimated costs, will probably not involve a bill. However, now that you've made your selection and you are sitting in front of the lawyer you chose to do the work, the clock is ticking (if you're on an hourly rate). Knowing that, you will have beforehand reviewed and sorted through all of your material, separating the critical from the commentary, so that you can present to the attorney what he needs in a prompt, crisp, businesslike manner. Your attorney doesn't need to know the fascinating story about how you stumbled upon this idea, and the critical role your Aunt Bertha played in guiding you along the path of your discovery, and the miracle of seeing your Uncle Henry in a dream that unlocked the clue to how to make your invention work. Save all of that for the TV cameras when you become famous. Tell the story now, in the lawyer's office, and it'll cost you a fortune.

What your attorney needs are your specs, drawings, plans, or whatever else you have to explain your invention. The attorney will probably ask a few questions to make sure he fully understands the idea and then will offer his legal opinion as to whether the idea is patentable, whether the patent would be meaningful, and what kind of patent would apply, utility or design. Good attorneys usually can find something patentable on every idea they see, but if they are honest (and almost all are), they'll tell you if the patent would be meaningful or simply a gesture. Question your attorney closely about this, and make sure you understand the answer and are comfortable with it.

Assuming the attorney's comments are positive, you move on. Remember: The attorney is in the business of selling patents, so asking his opinion about your idea's commercial value has no bearing on anything. What does he know? His opinion about the commercial value of your idea has even less weight than that of the guy who parked your car in the garage down the street. At least the guy in the garage isn't selling you anything.

Step 2. The Patent Search

Hopefully you've already done your own patent search, but if you haven't had a professional search on your idea, your attorney is going to recommend that one be conducted. While doing so is not a mandatory step on the way to making a patent application, it's a perfectly sensible suggestion. As already discussed, a professional will look in places that you never dreamed even existed; and who knows what she'll find? My advice is to let her look. Better now than thousands of dollars and six months later.

Your patent attorney can arrange to have this done, but I suggest that you arrange to have it done yourself, before even meeting weith the attorney. I say that for three reasons:

1. Your patent attorney doesn't conduct the search personally; he uses the same type of professionals you yourself can employ. Finding these companies on the Internet is easy, so you can hire the same caliber of searchers as the attorney. The quality of the work doesn't suffer and you will have saved the attorney's markup.

2. If you hire the professional searcher yourself, even before meeting with the attorney, what the professional uncovers might preclude you needing the attorney at all. Why pay legal fees when you don't have to? Or, if the professional finds something that might be a problem, you'll already be able to discuss that on your first meeting with the attorney. It skips a step, skips a meeting, saves some time, and can save you hundreds of dollars.

3. While I don't for a moment suggest that patent attorneys are dishonest, the fact is that they *are* in the business of selling patents. On principle, I don't think it's a good idea to leave the patent search in the hands of a person who has other patenting services to sell you. Professional searchers in your employ get paid the same regardless of what they find.

Step 3. The Invention Drawings

The attorney hires the patent artist. The patent office has very specific, stringent requirements for patent drawings, and it's a craft that not all graphic artists are familiar with. Your attorney has a list of patent artists and will select the one that he feels is best suited to illustrate your specific invention. You and your attorney will meet with the artist to decide how many drawings are needed to fully explain the idea, and the artist will go to work.

Step 4. Making the Patent Application

This is the critical step, where the attorney writes up the application, including the reasons why your idea should be considered new, novel, and useful and why it therefore deserves to be patented. Also, and most critical, the attorney will carefully and specifically lay out each facet of your invention that deserves patent protection. These are called the claims, and an application can have one or dozens, depending on the invention's complexity. It's in the writing of the claims that we would expect the attorney to do a better job than a layperson, and since it's the approved claims that determine the strength of the patent, logically we would want the best case made.

After the claims are written up, the completed form, signed by you and your attorney, and along with the drawings and fee, is submitted to the patent office.

Step 5. The Patent Office's "First Office Action"

At some point after your application is submitted—three months, six months, a year later—the patent office examiner will report back with his or her findings, called the first office action. Even though you and your attorney did your own search, the examiner also will search to see what prior art exists. Based on the findings and his or her own expertise, the examiner will state which claims are determined to be patentable and which aren't (and why). Rarely are all claims rejected or accepted in the first office action.

Step 6. Your Attorney's Response

Your attorney will write back to the patent office examiner, addressing each rejected claim individually, offering new reasons, new facts, or a new perspective as to why these claims should be accepted after all. The examiner might agree on some, none, or all. If the examiner has turned down a particular claim twice, he or she has the authority to deem that a final action. There might still be some back and forth (with the examiner's approval), and if the claims remain rejected, your attorney has the right to appeal to a higher authority; a committee of supervisors established for that purpose. However, rarely are appeals made; they're protracted and seldom successful.

And then, finally, after the back and forth is completed, with the accepted claims now a settled issue, the patent is officially awarded and published in the patent office gazette for the world to know of your singular accomplishment.

One warning: When your patent is officially issued and published in the patent office gazette, you will be inundated with mail from every smarmy, slick company in the invention business trying to sell you their products or services.

The appeals are quite compelling until you dig deeper, so be on your guard.

Patent Agents

In your search for a patent attorney, someone might mention patent agents. There's nothing wrong with using a patent agent rather than attorney, but there are some differences. In order to work with the United States Patent and Trademark Office as a professional, people are required to pass a test to confirm their qualifications. Patent agents have to pass the same test as attorneys, so in the eyes of the patent office, they're just as qualified. However, patent agents are limited to just that: filing patents. They're not attorneys, and they cannot prepare legal documents, initiate lawsuits, offer legal advice, and so on. The patent agent's fees are almost always lower than those of attorneys, so if all you want to is file a patent and don't expect the person to help with other legal needs, you might want to consider that type of professional.

Foreign Patents

Sony and Microsoft and Panasonic and other heavyweights routinely file for international patents whenever they create a new product. However, you're not in that league (not yet, anyway) and so this is not a step to be taken lightly. Foreign patents are *very* expensive and seldom necessary. America itself is such a huge market that for most smaller companies, that's enough protection for their purposes. For instance, if you're either of America's neighbors, a Mexican or a Canadian, filing for a patent in your homeland would probably be a waste of time. No offense Canadians and Mexicans, but what you really need is a genuine, official U.S.A patent. The reason is the size of America's market in relation to its neighbors to the north and the south. A Canadian company or a Mexican company usually gets double protection with an American patent. The reason is that if Canadian Company A has a U.S. patent, unless the product's really cheap to make, it's not likely that a potential competitor, Company B, would tool up just for the local Canadian market.

Most of the world's industrialized nations belong to the Paris Convention, a patent treaty that gives a citizen of one member country the same filing rights (for one year) in any of the other member countries. For instance, if you invented a new garden tiller, for up to a year after being awarded your U.S. patent, you have what amounts to a patent pending in France, Germany, England, Japan, and all the other member countries. If the Stuttgart Gardening Company, for instance, sees your new tiller at a gardening trade show in Chicago, it can't rush back to Germany to file patent on it. If you were awarded your U.S. patent on January 1, and if the German company filed a German patent on it in April, you would have until the end of December to decide if you want a German patent yourself. If so, your filing takes precedence over the Stuttgart company's filing.

There are other options. For instance, if you license your product to an American company that has a strong international business, it might apply for foreign patents in your name, and you would assign the marketing rights to them. Or if you license your invention to a distributor or manufacturer in another country, one of the licensing provisions might be that that company must file for a patent in your name in its native country. My point is: Don't rush into making this expensive investment. You have a year to decide, and chances are it'll prove to be unnecessary.

———————————

If your lawyer was a good one, he was successful in getting you approval for the invention claims that matter, and you're now ready to go out and meet the world. What to do next? Read on!

FIVE

Getting and Keeping Everything That's Coming to You. All about Proprietorships, General Partnerships, Limited Partnerships, and Corporation Structure Options

> *I'm proud to pay my taxes. The only thing is, I could be just as proud for half the money.*
> —Arthur Godfrey, entertainer

As I mentioned earlier, there's a fellow at the corner of my street who sells soft pretzels from a home-made cart. Every morning he goes to the Federal Baking Company on Federal Street, or DePalma Bakery on Bustleton, or any one of a number of other bakeries that make this Philadelphia specialty. He buys his pretzels for $0.75 and sells them for $1.50. His only other costs are for mustard, napkins, and the street vendor license he has to pay to the city. At the end of the day, after he's sold his last pretzel, he goes home with the money in his pocket and uses it, presumably, to buy more pretzels the next day and to pay his rent and feed his family. This man is undoubtedly a sole proprietor; he *is* his business and is personally liable for his own debts and potential lawsuits. Lawsuits? Let's be realistic. Who's going to sue a pretzel vendor? The pretzel man buys and sells for cash and has no business assets other than his vendor license, his homemade cart, and the stick that slathers the mustard on. He operates almost totally under the radar, and whatever city, state, and federal taxes he pays are probably more linked to the phases of the moon than to any true financial facts.

That might sound appealing to you as an inventor, but alas, you're not buying and selling pretzels for cash and your personal assets are probably much more substantial than my vendor friend's. If you've licensed your product to another company, the money you receive will be in the form of checks, and at the end of the year, your licensee will issue a tax statement to you and to the federal government showing exactly how much money it paid you. It's all there for anyone to see. Plus, suppose the wonderful new product you invented seriously hurts someone. Yes, the injured party will go after the manufacturer, but any good lawyer will also go after everyone else who has a say

The right legal structure can protect your assets and minimize your taxes.

in the product's design and its quality—meaning, of course, you. A lawyer won't sue the pretzel man, but you're another story.

So yes, you can remain a sole proprietor, take the checks, deposit them into your regular bank account, pay your taxes, and be done with it. If the products you're licensing or selling have no risk factor, and if the chances of you being sued are negligible, then starting off as a sole proprietor might be the smart move. You can graduate up, depending on how things go. However, if you do have assets or income to protect, and if there's even the slightest risk attached to your invention, you might want to consider the advantages of incorporating, with your corporation (not you) being the owner of the patent and/or licensing agreement. I'm not an accountant or an attorney and so I would urge you to get professional advice, but in general terms I can point out the advantages.

Advantages of Incorporation

Less Taxes

If you don't incorporate, your royalty income is regular income and, being commingled with your other income might place you in a higher tax bracket. However, if the royalty or sales income goes to the corporation, taxes paid will be on that *net* income alone (gross income minus expenses and depreciation associated with the business), with no tax impact on the money you're earning from a job or any other sources. Also, since the corporation is set up to create and license products, all expenses attached to that activity—an office at home, supplies, part of your car expenses, part of your telephone expenses, and the like—can all more easily be charged against royalty income than if everything is in one commingled jumble.

More Prestige

Prestige in this case is not an incidental matter. If, as a corporation, you're approaching another company to license your invention, it becomes a business-to-business dealing, which is more palatable to the licensee than an inventor-to-business arrangement. You and the licensee, perhaps both presidents of your respective corporations, will meet on a more equal basis than if you came in as a sole inventor.

Easier to Find Investors

Marketing your invention yourself and looking for investors are easier and more logical with a corporation. Investors like to receive stock for their investments, and as a corporation, issuing stock is a simple procedure. As an unincorporated individual, giving a "piece of the action" to an investor, while obviously possible, is more cumbersome. Also, corporations are structured to have advisors or directors who may or may not be investors, but who might have the knowledge and expertise you can use to grow your business.

Estate Planning

An estate planner can guide you, but in principle, by giving shares in your business to your children, you lessen the tax burden on them should you die. Also, as your tax expert will explain, there are other tax saving issues, such as paying yourself dividends and setting up a deferred profit-sharing plan. It's all about the money and how to keep it. And as Woody Allen observed, it's always better to have the money, if only for financial reasons.

Minimizing Liability

If the corporation owns the patent and/or product license, and if it's the corporation that's conducting the business, then it's the corporation that is responsible for all debts and lawsuits that might arise out of failure to meet notes, product liability suits, or other issues. There are negating factors, however. While this protection can work for routine, everyday vendors, banks and other lenders almost assuredly will demand that you sign personally for loans to the business. Also, if there is a product liability lawsuit, and if the opposing lawyer deems that you structured yourself as a corporation only for liability protection, she might attempt to "pierce the corporate veil" in order to include you personally in the suit. Whether she'd be successful remains to be seen. However, that's an extreme circumstance.

Ordinary vendors who sell materials and supplies to the corporation would seek recourse from the corporation alone.

The sections that follow list the full range of options for owning a business along with their advantages and disadvantages.

Sole Proprietorship

As already discussed, the sole proprietorship is one-person owner-ship; you alone are calling all the shots, answering to no one, rising or falling on purely your own personal actions. The advantages are that to be a sole proprietorship, you needn't do anything; that's what you are by default. There are no big (expensive) meetings with lawyers, no partnership agreements to hammer out, no corporation papers to file—with all of the restrictions and reporting procedure attached to it. The sole proprietorship and general partnership are by far the most popular types of structure for folks going into business, repre-senting almost 75% of all business entities. The essential appeal is that it doesn't require any sort of fancy organizational procedures, and you and the pretzel vendor are not under the same kind of official government scrutiny that filing corporation documents will bring. If this is your decision, I say congratulations! I'll take two pretzels.

General Partnership

This is the same as a sole proprietorship, except there are now two (or more) of you to share the decision making, share the workload, share the financial obligations, and, of course, share the profits. Maybe you're good at some aspects of running the business and your partner is better at others. Together you're invincible! Some men and women are more comfortable embarking on a new venture if they have someone by their side to bounce ideas off of; such people are naturally attracted to this type of structure. There are, however, certain drawbacks that should be considered. Your partner might be a lifelong friend, but he or she might have a totally different perspec-tive about running a business than you do; the partner might not have the same zeal or judgment, and perhaps he won't be willing to work the long hours that you're putting in. In a small company where so many decisions are made jointly, partners frequently disagree, fight, and often split up in an ugly manner. Smart partnership agreements already have a buy-sell agreement in place before the name is put on the door.

I've seen it and experienced the ugly side of partnerships, both from a personal perspective and seeing company clients break apart for that reason. One partnership company that I created products for reached such an impasse, with neither partner willing to talk to the other, even to negotiate who would buy the other out. The attorney for one of the partners came up with a plan. Each partner would come to an arranged meeting with a sealed envelope containing a cashier's check made out to his partner, with the sum being what he'd pay the other partner to leave. At the appointed time, both partners opened their envelopes. The lawyers examined the checks and took the higher check from Partner A and gave it to Partner B. Some already prepared papers were quickly signed, Partner B left with the check, and Partner A kept the company. To this day, as far as I know, the former partners still haven't spoken to each other.

Twice in my business career I had partners, and both times we split up. It's not that my partners were bad people, but the strains on a partnership in a small business are often hard to overcome. Partnerships seem great when first starting out, but rarely do they stay that way. How long do you think the Pep Boys, Manny, Moe, and Jack, remained partners?

Limited Partnership

In a general partnership, both partners usually invested equally and both are equally responsible and liable for the company's debt. And, of course, they usually share equally in the profits. In a limited partnership, there's a general partner and one or more limited partners. Limited partners are liable only up to the sum of their investment, and the profits are also, usually, proportionally divided. If two general partners split up, that's a major upheaval. Limited partners, however, can come and go with no business interruption.

General C Corporation

Larger companies are all C corporations—it's the perfect entity for their requirements and growth ambitions. The corporation can have an unlimited number of investors, executives come and go, and the corporation remains a viable enterprise. A C corporation is a legally created business with strict reporting procedures, structure, and rules that must meet federal, state, and local government requirements. The principal advantage of a C corporation is the limited liability exposure it provides for its investors. If you buy a hundred dollars' worth of stock in General Motors, and if it loses a billion dollars, no creditor is going to come knocking on your door. The corporation is the entity that incurs the debt, and the corporation is the entity responsible for paying it. The corporation earns its own money and pays its own taxes. The taxes on any dividends paid to investors are paid by the investors themselves. So, in other words, there are two taxes: one that the corporation pays on the money earned and the other that the investors pay personally on any profits that are distributed to them.

Subchapter S Corporation

The subchapter S corporation, which has its own benefits and drawbacks, is a structure intended for smaller companies. It is similar to a general corporation in regard to the limited liability exposure, but instead of the corporation income being taxed by the government and then taxed again when you take money out as dividends, the profits are not taxed by the federal government but flow directly to you as personal, taxable income, thus avoiding the double taxation. The drawback is that the subchapter S corporation can have a maximum of 75 stockholders. Regular corporations, particularly if they're publicly traded, normally have stockholders numbering in the thousands.

Limited Liability Corporation

The limited liability corporation (LLC) is the most popular formation for small companies, and you'll frequently see "LLC" after the company name. For tax purposes, this is very much like a subchapter S corporation, where the income flows directly through to the owners without paying corporate taxes. However, a limited liability corporation can have an unlimited number of investors. Most small companies will start out as a sole proprietorship or subchapter S or LLC and graduate to a regular C corporation as they grow.

As mentioned earlier, if you decide to start out as a sole proprietorship, waiting to see how things go before deciding on a more formal structure, you needn't do anything except maybe get some licenses. However, when you do reach the point of partnership or incorporation, you'll need an attorney, an accountant, and, if you have employees, probably a payroll service provider. Your attorney will draw up the partnership agreement or advise on the right corporate structure for you, and will file the articles of incorporation with the appropriate government agencies. The attorney will even get you an official corporate seal. Your accountant can help you determine which structure is best for tax reasons and, of course, can set up your books and records. If you already have employees, then you know how time-consuming it is to pay the payroll taxes and keep in compliance with the ever-changing laws. A professional payroll specialist can be a godsend.

If you'd like to know more about the various corporate structures and organizing your new business, these sites might be interesting:

www.businessfilings.com Includes many interesting articles about the various options: C corporation, subchapter S, and LLC. It also offers incorporation packages.

www.corporate.com The leader in online corporation filings in all 50 states; provides checklists to help you decide which structure is best for you.

www.smartonline.com Offers software packages to help you organize your new company as efficiently and productively as possible.

Whatever course of action you take, you can now order the business cards and letterheads. And while you're waiting for delivery, I suggest you read the next chapter about where to find the money you need. I believe it will be interesting.

SIX

Need Money? How Much? Here's How to Figure What You Need, Where to Find It, and How to Get It. All about Working with Angels, Bankers, Investors, and Your Rich Uncle Louie

I've got all the money I'll ever need–if I die by 4:00 o'clock this afternoon.

–Henny Youngman, comic

There's an old saying about how to make a million dollars—first get a million dollars. Ha-ha. I know that's not very funny, but it's not far from the essential truth that it almost always *does* take money to make money. One of the principal exceptions is if you decide to license your product to another company. I can think of no other business endeavor where the investment is so small and the potential is so large. That's not to say that you don't need *any* money—but one hopes that it wouldn't be that much that if you lost it all (which is quite possible), it would change the quality of your life. While it's impossible to pick a number because of all the variables, I think an investment of about $10,000 is what the typical motivated inventor will have made before either achieving a licensing deal or giving up on it. The key word is *motivated* since many "inventors" never get beyond the idea stage, hoping for . . . what? I have no idea.

If you decide to market your product yourself, building a company around it, you'll find that you'll need a great deal of money—and whatever you calculate you need, you'll probably find that you should have gotten more. It has been proven time and time again that the principal causes of business failure are lack of capital and lack of business skills. Unless you're sure you have both in abundance, you might want to turn back and reexamine your options. No one would have blamed Christopher Columbus for turning back. (Of course, no one would have heard of him either.)

The first obvious step in acquiring money is to calculate how much you'll need and when you'll need it. It's not likely that you'll need all the money the first day you open for business, so why pay interest today on money borrowed that you won't need for several months? As to sources: I'll pass on to you the advice that some wise guy once gave me. Try to borrow from a pessimist because he won't expect to be paid back. However, if you don't have access to rich pessimists, here are the other options.

Money Sources

Option 1: Bootstrapping

If you're able to start your business in a small way, you might be able to finance the costs out of your own pocket, which is called bootstrapping, either alone or with a partner. That's the genesis for many businesses; the inventor starts small, using her own funds, and after she's proven that her product will sell, that the market potential is substantial, and that she has the skills to run the business, she then goes to outside sources for growth funding. By then her chances of raising money are far better than trying to do it right off the bat. Or also, quite typically, the inventor with the idea will team up with a partner who has the money to get it launched. That's not my favorite arrangement, but I can't deny its popularity.

The first words of advice any counselor will offer is to not rush to quit your day job. There's a great deal of preparation work that you can do in the evenings and on weekends while still earning a living. Why dip into savings until it's absolutely necessary? Not only will that save you money, but it'll give you the time to marshal your own financial resources so that, we hope, you can launch your business without needing to borrow or take on partners and investors. You might be able to borrow on your insurance, or use your retirement money, or take a second mortgage on your home, or use your credit cards for money. I know these are all scary things to contemplate, but that's what entrepreneuring is all about. It's not for the faint of heart. One cautionary note: If your employer had you sign any sort on noncompete clause when you were hired, you should let your attorney look it over before making any financial commitments to your new business.

If you can swing it, nothing's better than bootstrapping as a way to get started; you have no creditors, you have no partners, and your rich uncle Louie is not looking over your shoulder. If you have investors, they're probably with you for the duration—in fact, depending on the arrangements, they might be able to get rid of you easier than you can get rid of them. Also, aside from your continuing reporting and decision-making obligations, since they legally own part of the business, they have certain rights. They have the right to participate and maybe even approve major decisions; they have the right to share in any profits the company makes; and they have the right to share in company losses (for tax purposes).

I don't mean to suggest that having investors is the end of the world—far from it—but if you can do it yourself, it's worth considering. You'll probably operate your business more carefully when using your own money—and later, when your business has grown a bit, you'll probably be a far more interesting prospect to lenders and investors than you were just starting out. Many highly successful entrepreneurs started in this manner. Michael Dell of Dell Computer started with $1,000; Steve Jobs and Steve Woznik started Apple with $1,350. Of course, no one ever reports about all the zillions of guys who started out with a few thousand dollars and lost it all in about five minutes, but that's a story for another day. We're only interested in successes.

If you can't bootstrap the launch of your business, you'll have to look elsewhere for financing. Before making any commitments you might later regret, this might be the perfect time to pause and look around for a mentor. If you don't have a wise counselor to turn to among your friends and relatives, a good place to find one is at www.score.org. This is SCORE, a nonprofit organization made up of retired executives whose sole mission is to help folks like you succeed. If you have a great idea and don't know what to do next, SCORE will match you with a volunteer executive who will happily be your mentor and guide. I urge you to visit the SCORE website, if only to take advantage of the abundance of information it contains.

Option 2: Money from Outside Sources

If you don't have the personal financial resources to support a successful launch, or if you prefer using other people's money, there are two basic ways to get it: equity financing and debt financing. Equity financing is just that—you give up part of the equity in the business in exchange for money. Debt financing is also obvious—you borrow the money personally; you go into debt, and the lender expects to be paid back. Each method has a few options.

Debt Financing

Banks

Banks are not interested in being your partner or owning a part of your business; they don't want to own your inventory, and they don't want to own the building that you run your business from. All banks want is their money back, on time, along with a profit for lending it to you. Period. Borrow $10 and pay it back on time; the next time they'll lend you $15. The more comfortable you can make a bank feel about you personally and about the nature of your new business and your ability to repay the loan, the better your chances are of getting that loan. Entrepreneurs just starting out are compelled to personally collateralize any loan that they might ask for. If you want to borrow $100,000 from the bank, you'd have to give the bank the right to seize certain personal assets to recoup its money if you fail to make your payments. If your personal assets only add up to $50,000, getting that $100,000 loan is probably not in the cards.

If you can't quite meet the bank's standards, you might be able to get your rich father-in-law to cosign for the loan, or you might qualify for a Small Business Administration loan. The SBA doesn't actually make the loan itself, but it becomes your guarantor to the bank that you'll repay it. You can visit the SBA on line at www.SBA .gov for information about all its loan programs and other services it provides to start-up entrepreneurs. Or, if you'd like to speak to a representative in person, a list of locations of all the SBA Business Development Centers is in Exhibit C.2.

Friends and Relatives

The good thing about borrowing money from friends and relatives is that they are, after all, your friends and relatives. The bad thing is that, yes, that's what they are—your friends and relatives. These folks are happy to lend you money. Well, maybe "happy" is too strong a word, but probably they'll come through for you. However, if they do, you have to be prepared to start each conversation with a full business report, at least until the loan is repaid. Also, you'll never suffer for lack of advice from folks who love you and believe in you, but who know as much about your business as the man in the moon. It's almost inevitable that relations will get strained, so it's important

Relatives can be an excellent source for funding, but there are consequences.

that you structure the loans in as businesslike a way as possible. Make sure the terms and conditions of the loan are documented in writing, and be sure to give friends and relatives a reasonable interest along with the payback. And for your own good, stay away from family get-togethers.

Equity Financing
Angel Investors

An angel investor is usually a wealthy, retired individual who likes to stay involved and is always looking for new investments. If he's impressed with you as an individual, and if your business is one that he's already familiar with, he might be just the angel you need. There are lots of these guys around, and if you hit it off with one, that might be the only connection you need. Not only are angels sources for financing, but they usually have the right connections as more funding is required. Also, since angels typically are smart, successful entrepreneurs in their own right, having done it themselves, they can be mentors and guide as you go from step to step.

Since you can't find angels in the telephone directory, you'll have to do some networking with friends and relatives—angels might be anywhere. You should also ask your lawyer and accountant if they have clients looking to make investments. I'd be surprised if they didn't. You might even pick up the phone and ask the business editor of your local newspaper, who is certainly wired into the business community. Also, since angels sometimes congregate in informal groupings—maybe they're golfing buddies or play gin rummy together at the club—you might ask the chamber of commerce or your local banker for leads and suggestions. Angels, by definition, are looking for deals, so why not make them happy?

Family and Friends

Sometimes a friend or relative, instead of simply lending you the money, will be interested in investing in the business by providing money for equity. The same problems exist as if the money was lent, with one important distinction. If you think cousin Herman was butting in before when he lent you the money, just imagine what it'll be like now that he's a part owner. However, if that's the price you have to pay, then you'll just have to suck it up.

Joint Ventures
If the new business you're starting is in an industry in which you're already known and respected, you might be able to find a manufacturer of similar products who'd like to invest in your start-up. For instance, if you formerly worked for a company that made gardening tools and, say, you're now going into business manufacturing a new type of gardening shed that you invented, you might be able to secure an investment from your former employer, since you're not in direct competition; or maybe you can get funding from a garden fencing manufacturer you know from being in the same industry. Or, if your shed is going to be made of steel, why not approach your steel supplier?

Venture Capitalists
Venture capitalists are the least likely source of money for a start-up situation. Not only is competition for their dollars fierce, but venture capitalists usually come along later, after management has proved that they know what they're doing and the business concept has proved workable. Venture capitalists like to enter the picture in the second round, after all the bugs have been worked out and the company has shown itself to be ready for a major launch into the big leagues. Also, venture capitalists are seldom in it for the long hall; they want to take their profits and move on. When pitching to them, remember that they'll be as interested in your exit strategy as in anything else.

There are some realities about venture capitalists that you should know before devoting too much time to them. First of all, as I say, the competition from other entrepreneurs is fierce. On average, a venture capitalist will go through more than 2,000 business plans to find 10 deals. Also, with all due respect, you might be too small for them. Few venture capitalists are interested in deals for $100,000 or $200,000;

they take up just as much time as deals for $1,000,000 or $2,000,000. Also, since venture capitalists are usually hands-on investors, they ordinarily don't make long-distance investments. If your business will be located in Boston, you're probably wasting your time trying to interest venture capital groups in Palo Alto. These organizations also tend to specialize in industries that they're familiar with. If your business is centered on a new gardening tool that you've invented, it's a waste of your time to approach a venture capitalist who's looking for the next big software application. And finally, as indicated, most of these companies like to come into the picture in the second financing round, after the start-up has proven its viability.

Comforting Numbers

If the thought of borrowing money seems daunting, these numbers will surely supply some relief. *Inc.* magazine has a yearly feature listing its choices for the 500 fastest-growing companies of the year. Some of the statistics about the owners of these companies are interesting.

- 41% of these owners launched their business with $10,000 or less.
- More than a third started with less than $1,000.
- 20% began with $100,000 or more.
- 62% of the owners started with partners.
- 87% used personal assets to start their companies.
- 28% got seed money from cofounders.
- 19% of the owners got seed money from family and friends.

Another interesting statistic is that by the time these entrepreneurs needed a second round of financing to put them on a fast-growth track, almost all were ready to turn to more traditional sources, such as banks and venture capital groups. They almost all started small, using their own money or their own money along with a partner's or sometimes with an assist from a parent or relative. And then, when they proved the viability of their business and their own management skills, they could pretty much pick and choose from a variety of large-scale lenders and investors. If you can launch your own business in that manner, that's the model to copy.

"Show Me the Money!"

Let's suppose that Fat Jerry, your brother's son with all the tattoos, comes to see you one Sunday afternoon while you're trying to watch the game. "Hey, Unk," he says, standing directly between you and the TV screen, "hows about lending me $ 5,000? I got this great idea for a business." Since you're the one in the family who wound up with most of the brains, that stirring presentation will not likely cause you to strain your wrist as you leap for your checkbook. "Sit down, Fat Jerry," you say in a wise, calm voice. "I have a few questions for you."

It's not that you absolutely refuse to lend Fat Jerry the $5,000—after all, he *is* your nephew—but nephew or not, you need a lot more information before you start handing out that kind of money. "Tell me what this is about, Fat Jerry. Is there a product? What does it look like? How does it work? What does it cost? Are there others selling the same thing, or is this one of your own inventions? How much can you make it for? How much can you sell it for? How many do you think you can sell? How will you do it? Why do you think you can sell that many? Who's going to be in this with you?" And on and on and on. Before you give Fat Jerry $5,000, you want to be assured that he's thought everything through, that he knows what he's doing, that his plan sounds reasonable, that, hopefully, he's smarter than he looks—and that there's a good chance you'll get your money back with some interest.

In the real world, you have to assume that you're Fat Jerry—with a couple of differences. First of all, you're not asking for $5,000; you're probably looking for $50,000 or $250,000 or maybe even $2,500,000. And second, whoever you're asking for the money, perhaps an angel or a bank manager, is not going to be as patient and kindly as you were with your nephew. That person is not going to sit you down and calmly take you through a thousand questions; she's going to expect you to put a report in her hands that gives her all the information she needs to make an intelligent decision. That report is called a business plan—and in it is precisely the information that you wanted from your nephew, Fat Jerry. If the information is for lenders, it's intended to show them how you're going to spend the money that they give you and how that will earn enough profit to pay them back with interest. And if the report is for investors, it will also explain how the money will be spent and how you intend to grow the company so that the investment proves to be a wise one. It doesn't matter who the lenders or investors are: your best friend, your former girlfriend, or the rich cousin that's always picking invisible lint off your jacket. They'll all want to see (and all deserve to see) your business plan.

The Business Plan

A business plan can be any length—a few pages or dozens; it can be informal or structured—tied with a pink ribbon or professionally bound—just so it impresses lenders or investors and compels them to act in the intended manner: with a loan or an investment. Whether you intend to prepare this plan in the prim, structured manner recommended by business plan experts or are more comfortable doing it in a breezy, informal manner, the information that it's expected to contain is pretty much the same:

1. Executive summary
2. Industry analysis
3. Company and marketing overview
4. Management team
5. Financial plan

Executive Summary

Although the executive summary is the first document in the report, it should be written last, since its intent is to provide a concise overview of all the information that follows: a description of your invention, the target audience, what it costs to make, how big the market is, how many can be sold, at what price, by whom, and so on. Remember the old joke about the guy in the circus bragging about all the new tricks he taught his elephant? "Let's see," said his friend, and so the guy goes over and gives the elephant a hard whack on the head with a stick. "What the heck was that for?" asks the startled friend. "Well," the guy replies, "first I have to get his attention." Your executive summary is the whack on the head. If you get readers' attention, they'll wade through the rest of the report. And if you don't, they won't. As already reported, venture capitalists read through thousands of business plans, looking for that one great deal. Seldom do they read beyond the executive summary. They know if that doesn't excite them, probably nothing that follows will either.

Industry Analysis

Let's say that you've invented a marvelous new backpack for school-kids. You have to assume that your rich spinster aunt Mary, although a lovable soul (but tight with her money), knows not a whit about backpacks or schoolkids who use them. Since you're asking her to lend you a fairly substantial amount of money, it's only common sense that you'll want to impress her with how huge this industry is, how many kids of backpack age buy a new one every year, and how much business some of the larger companies do. She'll also be interested in the fact that the population of backpack-age kids continues to grow every year, with no end in sight. The market is big and getting bigger. "Wow! Aunt Mary! What a great time to get into the backpack business!"

Company and Marketing Overview

Often these are separate sections, company overview and marketing overview, but since they're so closely intertwined, I believe it's more logical to put them together. Now that Aunt Mary is impressed with how big this growing market is, this section demonstrates how you intend to muscle in and take a share for yourself: how you're structuring your company, the goals you hope to achieve, and how you plan to achieve them. How is your newly invented backpack better? How do you intend to let the customers know? How do you intend getting space in the retail stores that sell these products? Where will these backpacks be made? What is the manufacturing cost? How much can they be sold for? How many can be sold? What new products will later be added to the line? Harken back to Fat Jerry. What you wanted to know from him, your lender or investor wants to know from you.

Management Team

Your aunt Mary already knows what a genius you are, so you needn't impress her with your credentials, but not everyone you approach for money will have changed your diapers when you were a baby. In this section you have to impress an arm's-length investor or lender that you have a successful record of accomplishment and/or an impressive educational background and/or partners or members of the management team who have the blue-chip credentials to steer this company to inevitable success. The venture capital companies will first look at the executive overview, as mentioned—and if it interests them, they will next go to the management team section to see if the guys running this company have resumes to show that the business is in good hands. No matter how much experts and consultants like to formalize business plans and insist that you indent here and capitalize there, it still comes down to lenders having confidence in the person they're handing the money to. Everything else is details.

Financial Plan

You probably will need an accountant to help you with the financial plan section unless you already have professional experience in these matters. In this section you show lenders or investors precisely how you intend to put their money to work. What are the start-up costs, what are the fixed expenses, what are the production costs, the sales costs, the marketing costs, and so on? What are the projected sales for the first year? The second? The third? Based on these figures and projections, you'll be expected to provide a profit-and-loss statement, a break-even analysis, a balance sheet, and a projected cash flow analysis. Investors understand that these are projections and not firm numbers. However, professional lenders and investors can tell if they're formulated in a logical, defensible manner or if they're numbers just grabbed from the ether. If investors aren't comfortable with what they see, they're not going to be comfortable in giving you the money. How can they trust you when the document in their hands, your business plan, is obviously a fiction?

While I can't stress enough the importance of a business plan in raising capital, I don't mean to imply that it has to be ponderous. Having waded through my own share of business plans, I know how screamingly boring some are and what a chore it is to plow through them. Some inventors believe the best approach is to include every sliver of information they have on the subject and to let the readers sort it out. I'm of the opinion that less is more, and the more briefly you can provide the salient information, the more likely the report will be read and acted on. In any event, there's a great deal of information written on this subject if you care to do more research. In fact, there's even software for sale that guides you through the process.

Not only do I suggest that you keep this business plan as brief and as readable as possible, but whatever you do, don't exaggerate or lie. You might not like your rich cousin Irving, but that doesn't mean he's an idiot. If your report makes wild claims about projected sales, profits, market penetration, or any other issues of that sort, they're sure to be spotted—and the whole plan now becomes suspect (and so do you).

For more information on raising capital, these websites might be of interest:

www.bplan.com Shows dozens of sample business plans and offers business plan software to guide you through the process of writing your own.

www.businessfinance.com Provides more than 4,000 worldwide sources for business loans, venture capital, equity financing, and the like.

www.capital-connection.com/incubators.html Contains the names and contacts for a variety of angels, private investors, bankers, venture capital groups, and so on.

www.morebusiness.com Has templates to help you with your business plan or marketing plan, plus others for a variety of contracts and business agreements.

www.nbia.org The official Web site of the National Business Incubator Association with links to members who offer this service to start-up entrepreneurs. An incubator, as you probably know, is a physical structure devoted to providing office space to small, commonly related start-up companies at a low rent or no rent basis, and jointly offering these companies free business advisory services. A community or town, for instance, might set up a high tech incubator to foster business growth in the local area.

The Value of a Business Plan for Its Own Sake

While the emphasis here has been on the importance of a business plan as a tool for raising money, let's not forget the plan's value in its own right. Even if you don't need to look to outsiders for money, it's still important to create a business plan. A properly reasoned, intelligently and honestly prepared business plan with measurable goals and mileposts will give structure to your venture, sort of a road map as you proceed from day to day. As ancient sailors would say, you have to know what port you're making for, or no wind is the right wind. Also, if you're honest with yourself and use defensible figures, a business plan can help you decide if it's even worth leaving port in the first place.

My own daughter had an idea for a business, but after doing a business plan, she came to the realization that her idea wouldn't work. Her idea was for a service business. By calculating the maximum she could charge for the service times the number of customers she could accommodate, and comparing that figure against the costs of attracting the customers and providing the service, she determined that the business could not generate enough profit to make the venture worthwhile. Yes, she was disappointed, but not as much as she would have been if she had just plunged ahead.

Obviously, if you're not contemplating going into business but are planning to license your product, little of the information in a formal business plan would be of interest to your prospective licensee. You need presentation material of a different sort, which is reviewed in the next chapter. There is one common element, however.

Whether you intend to start a business or take the licensing route, the star of the show is still your invention. Whether you're dealing with lenders, investors, or licensees, you have to be able to put something into their hands that'll knock their socks off. Read on; in the next chapter I tell you exactly how it's done.

How to Create the Kind of Powerful Presentation Material for Your New Product Idea or Invention That'll Knock the Socks Off Whoever You Present It To

> *Successful people are successful because they form the habit of doing things that failures don't like to do.*
> —Albert Gray, author

T his chapter is all about how to prepare your idea and your presentation material, but alas, it's also where we start to separate the folks who have a good shot at making a success of their new invention from those who don't. The reason is that, whether you're looking for a licensee or an investor, all of this preparation work is leading up to the point where you go out, ring some doorbells, and get yourself in front of some grim, pasty-faced executive who looks like he's ready to call security if you even move in a funny way. Many inventors, I'm sorry to say, will avoid this step like the plague, particularly if their aim is licensing. If you fit that description, I have good news for you. This chapter is cunningly designed to change your entire perspective. When you see how easy it is to do this stuff, you'll be saying *"Let me at 'em! Don't hold me back!"* At least that's the plan.

First, it's important to understand and come to grips with the fact that a product idea or invention is a commodity that has to be sold like any other one. You're asking the investor or prospective licensee to make a major commitment in you and your idea, and they're not easily budged. You must construct a prototype, prepare presentation material, anticipate questions, determine facts, offer proof of validity, and develop reasons to buy.

And then, just like any other salesperson, you have to hit the road, get yourself in front of the people who can say yes, and convince them that by doing so, riches will pour down on them and their company. Inventing for profit is a business like any other business; it's all about the money. Show the prospective investor or licensee that he can profit by doing business with you and he'll agree to make the deal. Don't show him and he won't.

If you send some kind of "Dear Sir or Madam" letter to folks who didn't ask for it in the first place (like invention submission companies do) or think you've done something wonderful by making a website to show your idea, you can spend your life sitting by the phone. It'll never ring. The only person who will see your submission letter is the mailroom clerk, and nobody who matters will ever see your website.

Although I'm in the business of acting as the licensing agent for inventors, I have to be candid and say that, as good as I believe I am at doing this work, and as much as I enjoy doing it, no one can do it better than you yourself. You have the most enthusiasm and familiarity with your invention, so you should be the natural person to sell it. I'm happy to do it for folks who won't do it themselves, or because of circumstances, can't do it themselves, but I always say that if they can do it, they should.

Sadly, many inventors, bright and clever though they may be, just don't think they have the skill to effectively present their idea and strike a good deal for themselves—and they're afraid of appearing foolish. I understand that, and felt the same way starting out. Now that I know what I'm doing, it's what I like most about this work. As I stated earlier, knowledge is power. I got mine the hard way, but there's no reason why you should have to go through the same trial and error. My hope is that this book will provide the knowledge that I've gained along the way to give you the confidence to get the job done, and get it done right. Whatever I know, I want you to know as well. And whatever success I've enjoyed at this inventing business, I want you to enjoy it too.

Over the years I've dreamed up and licensed more products than I can remember, certainly more than 100. That's how I have earned my living for decades. I don't say this to be boastful; any one of you might invent just one product with more impact and earning potential than all of mine put together. However, in terms of sheer volume, and in terms of numbers of successful presentations made and agreements signed, I probably have more experience than anyone I know of. This experience has taught me a few things about landing the deal that I'm happy to pass along. Here are three key points:

1. *Great presentation material and an impressive prototype make the rest of the selling job easy as pie.* Great material and a beautiful prototype show respect for the idea and for the inventor him- or herself. Even the most experienced executive will consider a professionally prepared presentation more favorably than a slipshod one.

2. *I have* never *licensed a product to a company except through a face-to-face presentation.* I took the easy way lots of times, sending the idea along through the mail, but not once did that ever pay off. Not once.

3. *I have* never *licensed a product to a company where this meeting was with anyone other than the person authorized to sign the licensing contract.* In smaller companies, it's the president who's also usually the owner; in larger ones, it's the divisional vice president whose income and bonus are profit-related. I wish I could have back the hours that I've spent with engineers, designers, purchasing agents, assistants, and clerks. These gatekeepers all have the power to say no, but not one of them has the authority to make the deal. Furthermore, as I'll later discuss in some detail, these midlevel management types instinctively do not welcome ideas from outsiders because they feel it lessens their own importance to the company. Fortunately for us, top executives and owners don't care where the idea

comes from: If it'll make a profit and if the risks aren't too great, they want it.

Because I know how to get myself in front of the right person, and because I know the kind of reception I'll receive, I'm one of those rare guys who really enjoys going out to sell the products that I or another inventor has dreamed up. I think your attitude will become more positive as the power of your prepared material starts to become evident and if you already know what to expect and what to say as the meeting with Mr. Big unfolds.

First of all, I view this as a business. As I said elsewhere, I'm not an inventor—I'm a product developer. I don't dream up inventions, I create and design interesting new products that a company can look at and see that it can market it profitably. Second of all, I have no personal attachment to any product that I create. Tell me it stinks and I'll say "Thanks for the information." I put the product idea aside and move on. It's just business, nothing more.

And finally, I like to call on companies with my new product idea because I have the attitude that every call is worthwhile—even when the guy I'm meeting with tells me that my product is one of the dumbest ideas he ever saw in his life, I just laugh. Actually, lots of my products can fit that description, but I can usually license them anyway. Dumb ideas can sell too, if they're clever. I figure that there are only four possible results of every personal meeting, and each of them is beneficial. And mind you: None of the information taken away from these meetings would have been obtained by sending letters or opening a website.

1. *If Mr. Big did indeed think my idea was stupid, maybe he's right.* Isn't that worth knowing? Why waste your time on a nonstarter? Move on; if you can come up with one idea, surely you can come up with another one. And that might just be the blockbuster that everyone's looking for. Second ideas are often better than first ones. If you sent your idea in a letter to Mr. Big, if he replied at all, he'd do it formally, saying something about your idea not being right for his company "at this time." Or he might say that it doesn't fit in with the company's marketing

direction. No one knows what that baloney means, even Mr. Big. They're just pat phrases intended to tell you to go away. If Mr. Big thinks your idea stinks, that's what you what to hear, and you want to know why. Anything else is valueless.

2. *OK, so maybe the idea is actually OK, but maybe it's just not for Mr. Big's company.* With a little coaxing Biggy (his nickname) will happily mention the name of a company the idea *is* right for. "That's not for us," he might say, "but I think it's something that Worldwide Amalgamated would be interested in. Show it to Tom Kelly, and tell him I sent you." Now you know what company might be in interested, the right person to see, and a perfect key to open the door. "Mr. Kelly? Hi. My name's Harvey Reese and I'm a new product developer. I was with Biggie the other day over at U.S. Gizmo Sales. I showed him a new product we've just created and he said he was sure that it would be something that you'd be very interested in. Oh, and he said to be sure to give you his regards." How can you beat that? Me and my new best friend Biggie talking about good old Tom Kelly. Try getting something like that going through a letter.

3. *If your idea truly isn't for Biggie's company, he'd usually be quite happy to tell you what kind of products he is interested in.* "Nah, that's not for us," he might say, "but if you could come up with a whosis that could fit into the thamos we're now selling and turn it into a dinkom, then we might be quite interested." My granddaughter is always asking me what to draw and inventors always ask me what to invent. I don't mind giving suggestions to my little granddaughter, but inventors have to find out for themselves. Figuring out what to invent is the whole key to this business.

The inventing is often the easy part; the creativity is uncovering *what* needs to be invented. By personally calling on executives like Mr. Big you'll get that kind of information; and once you do, the rest is easy. It's money in the bank. Picture this scene, three weeks later: "Hi, Biggie, this is Harvey Reese. Remember that whosis idea you mentioned to me?

Well, I've got good new news. I invented it, perfected it, and it works like a charm." "Great! Fabulous!" exclaims Biggie. "I'll send my limo right over for you and we'll start chilling the champagne." OK, a slight exaggeration, but that's how these relationships develop. I've never licensed an invention to a company where I didn't go on to license more. That's the whole secret of this business: First learn what a company wants, and deliver it.

The toy industry relies on freelance professional inventors and product developers more than any other industry that I know of, and it routinely sends these folks a "wish list" telling them the category and type of new products they'd like to see for the coming season. Other industries may not have such a formalized approach, but every company has a wish list even if it's just in the boss's head. Ask him what he's looking or in the way of new products and he'll gladly tell you. Why not? It costs him nothing to give you this information, and who knows what you might come up with?

4. *And of course, the best benefit is if Mr. Big stands up, offers his hand, and says that you have a deal.* Get that the through a letter? No way! Nobody will write you a letter back to tell you that your idea is stupid; nobody will write back suggesting another company to show your idea to; no company will write back to tell you what type of product ideas they are looking for; and definitely no company is going to write back with a contract and check enclosed.

Preparing for the Meeting

Before meeting with our prospect, we need to prepare three things and have one issue settled. We need to prepare the:

1. Invention in the form of a prototype
2. Written presentation material
3. Graphic presentation material

And finally, as we'll discuss in the next chapter, the issue to be settled is getting an appointment with the person that matters. For now, let's look at the meeting preparation material one part at a time.

The Prototype

Someone once said that he could think of no situation where having money made it worse. I can think of no presentation situation where having a beautiful prototype (usually referred to as reducing an idea to practice) wouldn't make it better—and in many instances it's virtually mandatory. As already mentioned, if what you've invented is supposed to *do something* or accomplish some specific task, then you're expected, as the inventor, to prove that your invention will do what's promised; and that means a working prototype. If you've invented a vacuum cleaner that you say will pick up dirt twice as efficiently as any other vacuum cleaner on the market, you are expected to put a working model of this vacuum cleaner into the hands of your prospective licensee for him or her to look at, examine, and try it out to see if it does what's claimed for it. There are no shortcuts. The devil is in the details.

Just showing the manufacturer a pretty computer-generated picture of a vacuum cleaner with some plans and diagrams will not do the trick. Companies know from long experience that what seems so perfect in the inventor's mind's eye has a nasty way of not turning out that way when she's charged with the task of making the darned thing work. If you just offer an idea or product suggestion, presumably expecting the prospective licensee to invest his own money and resources to try to turn it into a reality, he will rightly wonder, since he's the one spending the time and money to perfect the idea, and since he's the one taking the risk, why he's being asked to pay you a royalty. That's your job: you're the inventor. Some folks think that merely offering an idea to some big company is going to start the royalty checks rolling in. They don't seem grasp the fact that it's only the physical inventing itself that might possibly earn them any financial rewards.

Lots of inventors have good ideas for products but don't have the technical background to figure out how to make it work. That's

OK; technical skills can be bought. You can still be the inventor and earn the inventor's rewards simply by causing the product to be invented. You can pay the technical expert for his work, or you can agree to give him a cut of any profits. The licensee doesn't care. All that matters is that you're the rightful owner of the invention, your prototype proves your product works as promised, and it's something that the licensee thinks he can sell. You can be Vlad the Impaler who plundered and stole the invention from some dying inventor in the deep, dark forests of Bulgaria. If it's legally yours and it works and a licensee likes it, the details are of no concern.

What I Know for Sure

What I know for sure is that the essential idea of any presentation is to bring your proposed product as close to reality as possible. The difficulties many inventors have is that they try to sell a dream, but nobody licenses dreams. Businesspeople deal in realities, in hard facts. The closer you can get your product to be viewed in that manner, the less doubts there are—and as doubts dissipate, interest increases. All of your presentation material should be focused on that goal: Nothing is "if," it's all "when." These are the types of phrases that work in presentations:

- Here's a prototype showing what my product will look like when it rolls off the assembly line.

- Here's a mock-up package that shows what my product will look when it's on display in retail stores.

- Here's a drawing showing an in-store display that can be used when special sale deals are offered to retailers.

- Here's information on why this product is superior to products already on the market.

- Here's information on what this product will cost to produce, the retail price it can be sold for, and information on how many you will sell.

You'll add more "whens" appropriate to your own idea, but it's the spirit of the presentation that I want to get across. One reason that franchises are so popular is that professional franchisors are able to anticipate every question or doubt in the franchisee's mind and address them before they're asked. The franchisee's confidence that the franchisor knows what he's doing grows and grows, and striking the deal becomes the logical conclusion.

Of course a licensing presentation is not the same as selling a franchise, but it has many of the same principles. The more you're able to convince the licensee that you have considered and solved every problem that might be associated with your idea, the more favorably it will be looked on—and the best way to start is by placing a beautifully finished, looks-like-works-like prototype into the manufacturer's hands. John Wanamaker, the famous nineteenth-century merchant, said that he knew that at least half of the money he spent to advertise his store was wasted, but he could never figure out which half. Half of the money I spend on a beautiful prototype and professional-looking presentation material might be wasted as well, but like John W., I also can never determine which half. Wanamaker never regretted the waste because his beautiful department store was always crowded; and I don't resent my waste either because I can so often walk out with a licensing contract in my pocket.

There are a great many options for making prototypes: rapid molding, vacuum forming, injection molding, compression molding, rotational molding, sand casting, die cutting, sheet fabricating, and on and on. I see no value in going into exquisite detail on each of these processes. Not only would I risk putting you to sleep, but your own invention will suggest the proper approach. Not every model shop is equipped to do everything, so it's best to shop around to find the one that is best suited to your needs. Or, if you're using an industrial designer, he or she should be able to guide you. If your product idea is simple, and if making several prototypes is not a financial burden (or if you're making them yourself), you'd be wise to do so. You can present the idea to several licensing prospects at one time, and if one of them holds on to your prototype for an extended period, you can still be pursuing your interests elsewhere.

A word of caution: Before discussing your idea with any craftsperson, artist, or model maker, make sure he or she signs your nondisclosure agreement. All of these professionals are accustomed to documents like this and will sign them without question. Otherwise, how could they stay in business? Nevertheless, as a matter of form, get the document signed and file it away. The one I use is in Appendix B, and I invite you to use it.

Once you have your prototype in hand, and assuming it's for a consumer product, it's well worth the money to get a graphic designer to create a mock-up retail package for it. This is so important, yet I have such a difficult time in getting people to do it that it's a source of constant irritation. In support of the tenet that the closer to reality you can make your proposed product, the more willing the manufacture will be to license it, I want to say that *nothing* can advance that goal more convincingly than by placing in the manufacturer's hands a packaged product as it would look in the store and as it would look to the consumer. When you see the impression that this kind of presentation makes on the proposed licensee, you'll thank me for making you spend the money.

When I meet with a manufacturer, I spend surprisingly little time talking about the product; it's value is a given. I spend the majority of my time discussing how I think it can be marketed: what the packaging should look like, what features should be stressed, what kind of store displays would work, what the price point should be. The product is just the McGuffin. "McGuffin?" you might say. "What does that mean?"

I'm Glad You Asked

Alfred Hitchcock, the famous director who specialized in thrillers (*North by Northwest, Rear Window,* etc.), once said that in his movies, the actual crime (the theft of state secrets, the murder of a rich spinster, etc.) was of no consequence. The crime was simply the McGuffin—the excuse to have the baddies chase the goodies and the goodies chase the baddies, and for the hero to wind up with the girl at the end.

To licensees, that's what your product is, the McGuffin—an object to earn some money. If it offers some benefits, that's fine, but it's the profit potential alone that makes it interesting. That's why, when I'm with a potential licensee, I pay so much attention to packaging, appearance, and price points. Granted, I have a great deal of experience in those areas, but the product I put into the manufacturer's hands has been so thoroughly developed and thought through that all the person has to do is nod yes. And most do. The issue of packaging is of paramount importance because if the product can't be packaged to sell itself in a crowded retail store, no one will license it.

I've seen perfectly decent product ideas get abandoned because they were too convoluted and complicated for their "buy-me" aspects to be effectively presented in the millisecond that consumers give it when strolling down the store's aisles. In all my years of guiding a product through from an idea to a product ready for shipment, I can honestly say that frequently as much time and thought are devoted to the packaging as to the product design itself.

I'm not naive enough to think that my prototype and mock-up package will even remotely resemble what the product winds up looking like in final form. That's OK. If the materials help me to land the contract, they did their job. When the licensee turns the project over to his own designers, they will, as a point of pride, change everything. The areas that I've designed to be round, they'll make square; the sections that I show to be yellow, they'll make blue. I understand that and I expect it, so when it happens I just shrug. I take no pride in ownership. In fact, it's good that they've redesigned everything because that gives them the ownership of the idea. That's as it should be. I'm just the guy in the background that they send checks to every month.

If you saw me at work at a presentation, it might seem that I'm almost lackadaisical. I'm not sitting on the edge my chair, pounding my fist on the licensee's desk to emphasize point after point. My presentation material is so professional looking that even if the prospective licensee doesn't already know me, he sees that he's talking to an experienced product developer. I don't mean that I sit there mute; however, but if your presentation material is as good as you can make it, that alone will carry most of the load.

My subtle message to the licensee, supported by my demeanor, my words, and my presentation material is this: "My friend, there is no doubt that this terrific new product will wind up in retail stores all across America. All that remains to be settled is whether you're the one who gets to own it or if it goes to your competitor across town." That might seem nervy (and of course I don't actually say it) but the message is unmistakable—and meant!

The Presentation Material for Investors, Lenders, and Licensees

Although I've been discussing the importance of prototypes and presentation material when seeking a licensee, if your plan is to market your product yourself, they are no less valuable when trying to interest lenders or investors. These folks are no less interested in what your product looks like, how it works, and why it beats the pants off of anything like it already in the market. Only your written material would have to be tailored to this audience's interests.

A prospective investor, lender, or partner is obviously looking for a great deal more information than a prospective licensee. The licensee only needs to have details about the product, but someone being asked to help fund a start-up company wants to know how you are going to spend all the money that's being asked for. Off comes your inventor's cap, and on goes the one of a businessperson—prepared to confidently offer the investor all the financial details he needs to convince him that his investment will be secure and profitable. This written material, when prepared for a prospective licensee, is referred to as a marketing plan. When it's for an investor or a lender, it becomes a business plan. There's a big difference.

For the Licensee—the Marketing Plan

The intent of the marketing plan is simply to support the information that you've already supplied verbally. There are no set components for a marketing plan, just as there are no components set in stone for

A great product presentation shows respect for the product and commands respect for the inventor.

a business plan, regardless of whatever anyone might say. Your own common sense will tell you what information licensees would like to have to help them reach a positive decision about licensing your product. The trick is to supply information that might be helpful but without being patronizing or insulting.

What I mean is, let's say that you've invented a fingerprint lock for bicycles. Bike owners don't need a key and don't have to remember a combination. They just stick a finger into a hole in the lock and *presto!* It opens. The logical licensee would of course be a bike lock manufacturer. In your written material, you're not going to drone on about how many bike owners there are in America and how many bikes are stolen each year and what dollar loss those thefts represent. If the bicycle lock company doesn't already know that stuff, it shouldn't be in business. However, it's a good bet that such a company knows nothing about fingerprint recognition in terms of bicycle locking devices, so that's what your report will address.

Overview of the Field

How far has fingerprint recognition progressed? How is it used in other industries? How foolproof is it? What patents already exist? What do experts project for the future? That's the kind of information that would logically be included in the overview section.

State of Current Competition

Are there other fingerprint bike lock manufacturers in America? Who are they? How much business do they do? How much do the locks cost? Is their business growing? Are any in other countries? If yes, how much business do they do? If there are none now, have their been any in the past? When? Why did they fail? If other products already exist, pictures of them here would be helpful.

Why Your Product Is Better

Compare your product to other finger-recognition bike locks (if any exist). Why is your lock better, cheaper, faster, easier, safer? Compare your lock to conventional locks. What are the advantages, why would customers buy it? If you have a patent on your product, include a copy here. Stress the patent's key elements. If you have test results, include them here.

The Future for Finger ID Bike Locks

Is this the wave of the future? Why? How much business do you estimate the licensee can do the first year? In five years? Use sales of other locks to support claims.

Your own product invention might require more or less information, and you might even make a video of it in action. Prepare the written material expertly without typos; include appropriate pictures, graphs, and other supporting material; add a cover page; and bind it in a spiral or other binding method. Your local Kinko's or Staples or Office Max can do it for you or supply you with the materials to do it yourself.

Who's Your Daddy?

When you're writing your plan, you have to understand who you're writing it to and what his or her needs and desires might be. In this instance, your daddy is the person who signs the royalty checks, and he's the only guy you have to please. It's swell if your product benefits the consumer, the ultimate user, but that's not the motivating factor that might persuade the company to take on a licensing deal with you—just as the absence of consumer benefits might not be a deal breaker.

Other factors are in play.

For instance, if there's a major retooling expense involved, and if all that consumers would do is switch purchases from the licensee's existing product to your improved one with no increase in overall sales, why would the licensee bother to make your product? Why pay out royalties and get no profit in return? Actually, your idea might even be costing a licensee money rather than earning the company any. Since the company doesn't pay anyone royalties for its own product, but now has to pay you royalties for yours, that's more money going out rather than more money coming in. Yes, with your product consumers might get something better, but if there's no profit in it for the licensee, the chances for it to wind up in consumers' hands are not great.

On the other side of the coin, your new product might not be that much different from other products that exist, but it might help the licensee round out his line; it might be something that a major customer has been asking for, or it might be used to dislodge a competitor. Consumers might not notice or care that the product in a store is now from the Jones Company instead of the Smith Company, but Jones might care a lot.

The Written Presentation Material for Investors and Lenders

Of course, anyone lending you money wants to know what the product looks like, how it works, what it does, and why it's so much better than the stuff already on the market. And, of course, they want complete financial facts and figures to allay their fears and to convince them that the money being requested will be wisely spent and pay dividends. How this plan should be constructed and what information it should contain were already discussed in Chapter 6, so I won't repeat myself here. Instead, I'd like to tell you a secret I learned that will help you write this plan (or the marketer's plan for licensees) in a more persuasive manner.

My Brilliant Discovery

Many years ago a friend of mine, a college professor, asked me to take over his marketing class for the day because he had an important appointment. I agreed, of course, but I was plenty nervous. At the time I had no teaching experience and wasn't sure what to say or if I could even keep the class's attention. Just to be safe, I prepared a lot of material.

The dreaded day finally came and I timidly called the class to order. I knew my subject, and, as I say, I had a lot of material prepared. Taking a deep breath, I plowed right in. I thought I had a great deal of interesting and useful information to offer, but one never would have guessed it by looking at that sea of stone-faced students. On and on I went, and nobody moved—they just sat there and stared. Was anything getting through? I had no idea.

Finally, by sheer happenstance, I came to a section in my presentation where I said something like "Here are the eight reasons why marketing the product through independent agents will not produce the desired results." A miracle happened! As soon as I said, "Here are the eight reasons," there was a great deal of shuffling and chair scraping as the students threw open their bags, pulled out their notebooks, and sat there, pencils poised (this was before laptops). At last I was about to say something important! *I was experiencing the magic power of the list!*

Everyone loves lists—rich people, poor people, young people, old people, big people, and little people. Here are five reasons why:

1. Lists are easy to read.

2. Lists seem important.

3. Lists seem factual.

4. Lists seem to the point.

5. Lists seem conclusive.

Look how painlessly you read my list about lists. I'll bet you can now state the five points with your eyes closed. So—trust me on this—when preparing your business or marketing plan, put as much information as possible into list form. If you do so, the plan is more likely to be read and more likely to be accepted.

Five Reasons Why Consumers Will Buy This Product

Four Reasons Why Major Retailers Will Stock This New Product

Seven Advantages This Product Has over the Competition

And so on.

The Graphic Presentation

Since I'm constantly making presentation material for one product or another, I have my own designers and do the work routinely. However, it shouldn't be difficult for you to find a local freelance graphic designer to create a presentation board for your own product. A rough sketch of what it should look like is included in this chapter. The board offers a headline name of the product and clearly shows what it looks like, how it operates, and what purpose it serves.

The board also prominently shows if the product is patented or patent pending, and if a logo or name has trademark protection. Also featured is a brief list of the product's important features with a copy block that might indicate how this amazing new product is superior (better, cheaper, easier to use) than any other competitive products that might already exist. And finally, as a clincher, your product should be shown in a proposed retail package, and if you have in mind any kind of special in-store display, that should be illustrated as well.

Remember, this presentation board is not intended to be a technical manual; that information should be included separately. This board is a marketing tool, straightforward, exciting, and punchy, designed to say, "Look at this great new product I've invented! You'll sell a zillion of them!"

The graphic material should be printed on 16" × 20" photographic paper, mounted on a black presentation board, with an acetate overlay. Yes, that's strictly for show, but don't underestimate the importance of showmanship. Prepare your material in this manner and you'll be amazed how impressive your product looks. "Wow! Did I invent that?" you'll say. A great visual presentation not only will impress whomever you show it to, it'll give you the pride and confidence that your accomplishment deserves. You're now a professional product developer, doing a big favor to the company to which you're offering your amazing new product.

One Last Word about Making Your Presentation

If you're a young man, asking a girl to marry you, you're not going to say, "Shirley, it's true that I asked four others to marry me before you and they all said no, but I'm hoping you'll be different." You would never say that (even if it's true). You'd say, "Shirley, you're the only girl I've ever loved and I want you to be my wife." And if you offer her an engagement ring, you're not going to take it out of a battered and torn ring box that looks like it's been passed around among every one of the 40 Radio City Rockettes (and rejected by all of them).

It's the same with your prototype and presentation material. Even if this is the third company that you're showing your idea to, you have to create the impression that no one except the executive in front of you has ever seen the material before. They won't ask, but they'll know from what's laid out in front of them. If the person you're presenting this product to starts to pick up clues that the material is shopworn, he'll know you're lying through your teeth when you tell him that his company is the first in the world being offered this fabulous product. Touch up your prototype. Replace bent pages in your written material. Reprint and remount your graphic material. Do whatever it takes.

"Ms. Jones," you want to say, without the material telling a different story, "I'm bringing you this product first because it's such a perfect fit for your company, and you guys are such great marketers, that I can't think of anyone else I'd rather give it to. Let me show you what I mean. . . . And that's how your presentation should begin.

OK, great, your prep work is done. You've written lots of checks and spent lots of money, but look what you have to show for it! You have a beautiful prototype that proves your product works and that suggests what it might look like in finished form. You have a beautiful mock-up retail package to show what your product might look like to consumers when they see it for the first time. You have beautiful graphic material that shows your product in use, lists its features, explains the concept, and shows it on display in a retail environment. And, finally, you have a bound presentation that answers all of the potential licensee's or investor's questions and proves why licensing your product will be a great profit move or why investing in your start-up company is bound to pay big dividends.

Whew! The hard work is behind you. Now comes the fun part (no, really)—getting yourself and your material in front of the right decision maker, closing the deal, and claiming all the rewards that your creativity entitles you to. The next chapter explains how easily all of that can be accomplished.

EIGHT

It's Show Time! Lights! Action! How to Get You and Your Great Product Idea in Front of the Right Person at the Right Company Who Can Make Your Dreams Come True

> *Apply yourself. Get all the education you can, but then, by God, do something! Don't just stand there, make it happen!*
> —Lee Iacocca, industrialist

If you recall my C.R.A.S.H. Course, the *S* stands for Show 'n Tell—the time when you gather up your impressive materials and beautiful prototype and find the perfect executive in the perfect company who has the will and the authority to make your dreams come true: to license your product, invest in your newly forming company, or lend you the money to launch your idea on your own. I know what you're thinking: "Sure, easy for you to say, but actually doing it is another matter." Not to worry. I'm going to show you exactly how it's done. If it works for me, it'll work for you. But first, for those of you looking for a licensing deal, here's a little story.

Many years ago when I was first starting out in this business, I dreamed up what I though was a clever gift product, and there was one company in particular, on Long Island in New York, that I thought it would suit perfectly. I called the company and was told that Sarah Jones (fictitious name) was in charge of new products, and I was connected to her line. Sarah Jones seemed like a lovely person, and she was happy to let me come in to show her what I had.

A week later, brimming with confidence, I was in her office. As nice as she was on the phone, she was just as nice in person. She listened to what I had to say, looked at my prototype, carefully asked a few questions, took notes, made some nice comments leading me to believe that making the deal was just a formality, and said she'd call me the following week. I didn't hear and I didn't hear.

Weeks went by and I finally called. "Sorry, Harvey, I should have called you earlier. Everyone here liked the product idea, but I'm afraid it just doesn't fit into our plans at the moment. But please, don't give up on us. Next time you have something that you think might be for us, I hope we'll get to see it." That was long ago when I was young and innocent. If I was told that today, I'd ask the person to explain precisely what their "plans at the moment" are that my product doesn't fit in to. The truth is, there are none—it's just a brush-off—but it's fun to hear the Sarah Joneses of the world try to come up with an answer.

Anyway, about a month later I did in fact have another product that I though would be right for this company. Again Sarah Jones was kind and welcoming, and again I was turned down. I was puzzled. I knew the products I had shown Sarah would be perfect for her company and were, in fact, better than most of the products already in their line. So why the turndowns? Was I never to license anything to this company? One day I came on the answer and have profited from the experience ever since. Sarah Jones and all others of her ilk sufferers from the dreaded N.I.H. disease. Others before me who also experienced negative responses when bringing fresh new ideas to a company gave it the name: NIH, or "not invented here."

As previously mentioned, middle management types, jealous of protecting their own turf, do not welcome ideas from outsiders. Creating product ideas for the company is supposed to be their province, so when one comes from an outsider, it's automatically labeled inferior. To say it's great, in their view, reflects badly on them. ("That's what I'm here for," they silently say). Here's how Wikipedia, the online encyclopedia, defines it:

> **Not Invented Here (NIH).** A pejorative term used to describe a persistent corporate culture that avoids using existing research or knowledge because of its different origins. Not Invented Here sometimes occurs as a result of simple ignorance, as many companies simply never do the research to know whether a solution already exists. Also common is overlooking existing work while believing that one's own work should produce a superior product and more prestige.

The Wikipedia definition refers to research from the outside, but it applies to an invention from the outside as well. In any company, you need to find a champion who will speak up for your idea and push it through. You will never find your champion among the ranks of engineers, purchasing agents, product managers, marketing assistants, or others of that sort. First of all, they don't have the clout to be your champion, and second of all, they don't have the incentive. These people are your enemies; why would the help you? Your luster dulls theirs by comparison. Time spent with engineers or marketing assistants is time wasted, and no good can ever come of it. They'll fill the air with promises and ultimately break your heart.

Fortunately, others in the company aren't similarly afflicted, and those are the folks you have to get in front of. In a smaller company it's *always* the owner. Owners might have underlings with fancy titles, but it's the owners' money and they call the shots. Owners, I'm glad to say, couldn't care less where great product ideas come from. You could be a recent escapee from a Georgia chain gang, for all owners care. They'll just instruct the accounting department to send the royalty checks down to your Mexican hideout. In large companies, it's not the president you want to see, it's whoever is in charge of the division in which your product would be sold. If you've invented a new type of bandage, you don't want to see the president of Johnson & Johnson, even if you could. That person is above the fray. You want whoever is in charge of the Band Aid division.

The people who start these companies or rise to a vice presidency are doers; they're accustomed to making decisions and moving on. If they like what they see and what they hear, it's not uncommon for them to make the deal with you on the spot. (I always have a licensing agreement in my briefcase.) If you talk to someone in the engineering department, she'll let you talk on and on, being careful to nod pleasantly at the appropriate times. However, I promise you: Nothing will come of it. She'll waste your time and kill you with pinpricks ("Don't you think it would be better to use a Phillips head screw here and maybe a cotter pin there?"). Meanwhile, upstairs on the top floor, the big boss is yelling, "We need new products!"

Could/Should Some White Knight Do the Job for You?

Before discussing how you can get the appointment with the right company executive, first you have to decide if you'd rather have someone else do it for you. By "someone else" of course, I mean an agent. I define an agent as someone who has access to decision makers, who will represent your interests in a professional manner, and whose remuneration comes from royalty sharing. The key is in the method of remuneration. Anyone who charges you fees, advances, or retainers for this work is not a true agent.

In the spirit of full disclosure, I should remind you that I myself am an agent. In addition to creating and licensing my own products, sometimes I try to get ideas from other inventors licensed. Nevertheless, as I stated earlier, if you have the confidence, the zeal, the time, and the funds, my best and most sincere recommendation is that you do it yourself. No one knows your product as well as you do, and no one can duplicate your enthusiasm. Why give up part of your royalties if it isn't necessary? Nevertheless, there are a couple of times when I think you should at least consider using an agent (assuming you can find one who'll take the assignment—which is a big "if").

Why Use an Agent?

Reason No. 1

When I discussed the concept of going into business for yourself, I reviewed the personal traits that are usually found in successful entrepreneurs and asked that you measure your own traits against them. "Be honest," I urged. "Don't risk your own money or the money of others if the life of an entrepreneur isn't for you." Here too I urge you to be honest. If going out to sell your idea in person is simply not something that you can bring yourself to do or is something that you are unable to do, for whatever reason, then certainly you should try to find an agent who will do it for you. The worst agent, if he at least makes an honest effort, is better than you sending unsolicited letters, depending on a Web site, or falling into the clutches of an invention submission company.

Reason No. 2

The main asset that agents have to offer inventors is that, because being an agent is their business, they are more likely to have access to the decision makers in any particular industry. In some industries the manufacturers will only work with agents, and some individual companies hesitate to meet with inventors for reasons discussed earlier. Nothing personal, but the hard fact is that most companies will be more inclined to see me than they will be to see you. You might be a lot smarter than me, and you certainly know your product better, but companies know that as a licensing professional, I'm not going to give them any grief and, since I've screened the inventions, I'm not going to waste their time by showing them something that's off the wall. Larger companies in high-profile fields like toys and games will *only* deal with agents. If you contact companies like Mattel or Hasbro, for instance, they'll give you a printed list of agents to show your product to. If one of these agents takes it on, he or she will be invited right in.

Good agents perform a useful function for both parties. For the manufacturer, they prescreen ideas before presenting them, so the manufacturer is less likely to be wasting time. And for the inventor, agents generally have better access to manufacturers.

So, since access is the key, agents work in industries where having connections matters. For instance, if you invented an attachment for a metal spinning machine, you don't need an agent and you won't find any even if you want one. The reason is that if you call a manufacturer of metal spinning machinery, you'll have no trouble seeing him. You might, in fact, be the only inventor who has every called. Why pay an agent if Mr. Jones from the Jones Metal Spinning Company says come right over? If, however, you've invented something in one of the popular categories, such as toys, games, kitchen, or lawn and garden—you probably should at least consider having an agent, since many of the larger companies are more inclined to deal with them.

You May Need an Agent, But Does the Agent Need You?

Since many inventors are happy to give up a share of their potential royalties if an agent will do the chores for them, and since agents essentially work for nothing unless they produce, they're swamped with far more submissions than they can handle. Most product agents, including me, charge a fee for reviewing the idea, but still the product ideas keep pouring in. Of all the submissions I personally see, only rarely do I find one that I'd like to try to get licensed. Most are not fully developed, or have been done before, or don't offer enough profit potential to make the effort seem worthwhile. I always, of course, report back fully to the inventor with my suggestions, recommendations, and estimations as to the idea's commercial value, but most often the report contains the bad news that I don't believe I could successfully represent him or her. I'm quite sure other agents have similar experiences.

The rejection is not personal, of course, and any agent can tell you of the ideas that he turned away that went on to become big sellers. Evaluating the marketability and licensing possibilities for any new product concept is frankly more of an art than a science, and no one can be right 100% of the time in judging their potential. If there was a science to it, every new product would be a hit, when in fact the overwhelming majority are failures. Since there is no perfect formula to follow, the best that an "expert" can do is hope to be right more often than wrong. Also, as discussed earlier, there are many perfectly decent product ideas that might be marketable but don't have the special qualities needed to make them licensable.

What You Want from the Agent, What the Agent Wants from You

What you want from the agent is simple. You don't want to be charged fees or retainers or advances, and you don't want to pay for his or her out-of-pocket expenses. You want an honest effort, and you don't want the agent to sign any contracts without your approval. Further, if the agent does land a deal, you want an honest accounting and the right to see the books. If the agent doesn't land you a deal, you want to be able to fire him or her without any hassle. True agents, not invention submission companies, will readily agree to each of these terms—and if the one you choose doesn't do the job, you can easily fire him. Since he was unable to produce results, he wouldn't want be your agent any longer anyway.

You're entitled to each and every one of those demands, and if you've somehow hooked up with an agent who won't give them to you, keep your hand on your wallet and back out the door.

What the agent wants from you is a bit more complicated, but it's fair. I've attached my own agent contract in Appendix C. My contract is typical, and as you look through it, you'll see that it covers these points.

Agent Agreement

Financial Arrangements

Product licensing agents take a larger royalty share than in most other fields (usually 30% to 50%) for two reasons. The first is because supply and demand dictates they can, and the second is because they're much more than just agents. We product licensing agents usually have to take the inventor's raw invention and turn it into something that a professional executive would expect to see before agreeing to license it. Licensing agents prepare much of the presentation material that you would prepare if you decide to go out on your own. I do the works for my clients, as called for: prototypes, pictures, presentation material, whatever is necessary. My own arrangement is 40% up to a certain figure and 20% thereafter.

Exclusivity by Time

My agent agreement gives me agent exclusivity for a specified period of time. During that period, whatever chain of events causes your product to be licensed, I get my agreed-on royalty share. You might be stuck in a long line at the airport on your way home from Romania and strike up a conversation with the woman in front of you. She turns out to be the president of a worldwide company head-quartered in Shanghai that would be the perfect licensee for your new product. The friendship between you grows and the woman agrees to license your product. Although I'm 8,000 miles away, lounging by the pool, not knowing your new friend from Adam, I still get my cut. Thanks very much. Call me again when you have another new product.

Exclusivity by Place

My agent agreement gives me worldwide exclusivity. Other agents' agreements do the same. If you tell me that you don't have to pay me my share because the company licensing it is in Shanghai and you closed the deal in Romania, I'll just refer you to this clause. The last I heard, both Romania and Shanghai were part of this world.

Length of Payment

I'm your friend for life, or at least as long as the royalty money keeps coming in. There is no end to me getting my share. As long as you get yours, I get mine. Sorry about that.

An unemployed plumber from Allentown, Pennsylvania, invented the game of Monopoly more than 60 years ago. If the plumber's heirs are still getting a royalty check from Parker Brothers, and if there was an agent involved, his heirs are still getting a cut.

Negotiation Limitations

There are some unscrupulous agents (so I'm told) who insist on being co-inventors with the actual inventor. No legitimate agent would ask for that. We are agents and nothing more. My own agent agreement, and those of others, states that while I can negotiate on your behalf, no deals can be set without your signature approval and your name, not mine, is on the contract as the inventor.

Method of Payment

It's not that I don't trust you, but all the money comes to me. I cash the licensee's royalty check, take my cut, and send you my own check for yours. All agents work this way. I've never met one who didn't. Yes, certainly I'm obligated to provide full accounting details, but I pay you, you don't pay me.

How to Find Professional Agents

Professional agents can be found most often in popular consumer product industries like toys, games, housewares, bath, gardening, home office, giftware, software, and so on. Companies in these industries are besieged by inventors with ideas,, and often prefer to deal with agents rather than individual inventors. It's in those industries that agents are active, and the best place to look for them is in industry directories. Most industries, either through the trade association or trade magazines, publish a list of member companies and the service organizations that cater to them. That's where agents are usually listed.

Also, you might join a local inventors' club and ask members with similar products if they have any agent names to offer. Appendix C(1) presents a list of these clubs.

Industries that deal in products for special trades and professions seldom have agents, and if some company tells you that they do work as agents in one of these fields and asked to be paid a fee for their services, you can be sure they're just after your money. If you've invented a product for plumbers or architects or cement contractors, you're probably best served by proceeding on your own.

How to Find Secret Agents

Since access to the right person at the right company is the key to the agent's value, just about anyone who has that access can be your agent. A fellow you met playing golf might the first cousin of a company executive you've been trying unsuccessfully to get an appointment with. If he can use his family connections to get you that appointment, there's no reason why you can't make an arrangement to compensate him for his efforts. Ex-congressmen, voted out of office by angry constituents, often wind up on K Street in Washington, working as lobbyists. Companies are happy to pay old pols big sums because they have access to lawmakers. Knowing and using contacts with special access is all perfectly legal. Knowing the right somebody has more than once earned a person that big house on the hill.

Here's another idea that I've personally used to great advantage. Call the company and get the name of their local salesperson. He's easy to see, and if he likes your idea, he'll gladly put you in touch with the right person at the main office. That helps you and it makes him look good in the eyes of his superiors. He probably wouldn't even be looking for a payment since that might be seen as a breach of ethics. After all, he *does* work for the company. If there's no local salesperson, a local exclusive distributor or even a major local customer of the company can work just as well.

Doing It Yourself

Pick the Right Company

If you don't care to use an agent, or can't find one, there's no reason in the world why you can't do it yourself. The first job is finding the right company. You don't necessarily want the largest company in any industry, since it might be fat and contented. The number 2 or number 3 company might be more receptive and easier to make contact with. Just as you used the industry directory to find potential agents, you can also it to find target companies. Or you can visit stores that would logically sell your invention and look at the products that are closely allied to it. The package or the underside of the product should reveal the name of the manufacturer or importer. Also, many Internet catalogs provide the names of the company or the brand names of the products they sell.

Just about every industry has a trade show once or twice a year. By visiting the one for your industry, you can get the names of the companies that would be appropriate for your product and chat with someone in the booth to learn the name of the person to see. The person you're chatting with will probably give you his business card, and you can use his name to get through to the person you want to contact.

My strategy is to present my idea exclusively to the one company that I believe would be the best prospect for my product. If my presentation to that company doesn't produce results, I then simultaneously show it to as many other companies as I can. I've never had two companies wanting my product at the same time. However, that event is not impossible—and I would just tell one of them that they were too late. Companies aren't embarrassed to tell me that they're not interested, so why should I be embarrassed to tell them that I'm not?

And, finally, if possible, I strongly suggest that your first choice be a company that you can physically get to easily. This is a personal business; you have to put yourself in the face of the person who has the authority to make the deal—and you have to sell him or her on doing so.

Letters, even good ones, don't sell ideas to people. People sell ideas to people. Also, you want to establish a personal relationship because you're a creative person, and if you can come up with one product for this person, you can come up with the second and the third. It gets easier every time—not only because you have instant top-level access, but the more you know about the company, the easier it is to create products for it. That's not likely to happen if you have to spend $700 on airfare every time you want a meeting.

This is easy advice for someone living in a major market, such as Chicago, New York, or Los Angeles, but not so easy for those living in smaller, remotely located areas. If I lived in a smaller market, I'd work this inventing business the other way around. Instead of inventing the product and looking for a company to license it to, I'd first target the companies that I can get to—say, within 100 miles—and create products expressly for one or more of them.

Getting the Appointment

In a previous book I offered my readers a telephone script to follow to get them in front of the right person at the company they want to do business with. Since so many inventors have told me that they used this script and it worked like a charm, I'd be remiss if I didn't include it here. But before I do, here are four ground rules.

Ground Rule No. 1: You Are Not an Amateur

Let's face it, inventors are often characterized as loony, and many executives are hesitant to invite them to their office. They feel it's a waste of their time and that it's going to be difficult to get the guy to leave. You and I know that this is (usually) a bum rap, but why look for trouble? You're not an inventor, you're a *product developer*—and this is not something you do in your spare time, this is your business. If executives are comfortable dealing with professionals, then presto! You are one! In a moment I'll explain what I mean, but for now, consider this a war—and, as they say, a war's first casualty is the truth. Later, when you and the company president have become fishing buddies, you can set things straight, but not now.

Ground Rule No. 2: You Will Go for the Owner/President

I don't care how many design engineers, marketing assistants, and product managers are floating around, in small and medium-size companies, it's the president who makes the final decision about new products. It's the president's money and it's his company, so what the company sells is his major concern. He's the person you want to see, and as I'll show you, getting to him is surprisingly easy. In fact, he's waiting for your call.

There have been times, fortunately very rarely, when I've simply not been able to get to the boss and was constantly switched back to some assistant. I am so convinced that meeting with an assistant is a waste of time that I usually just move on to another company. One time I was actually in the company's office when I turned and left, rather than sitting down with some assistant.

I had an appointment with the president of this particular company and left home at dawn to be in her Staten Island office on time for an 11:00 AM meeting. By dumb luck, since it was a three-hour ride, I arrived precisely on time. My luck changed, however, as I found myself waiting in the small reception area for an eternity. Almost a full hour after the appointment time I was finally ushered into the president's office. As I sat down starting to unpack my material, she informed me that she was terribly busy with unexpected emergencies and wanted me to give the product information to her assistant. "NO," I said, as I stood up. "I won't do that. Meaning no disrespect to your assistant, I came here with an important product to show to you personally, and if that's not possible, I'm leaving. Perhaps we can start again some other time." And with that I turned and left, leaving the president and her assistant too dumbfounded to speak. If I wasn't already furious for being made to wait for almost an hour, after driving for three, I might have finessed the situation better, but I was not in the mood to be shunted about.

In the following weeks I received several phone calls asking if I'd like to reschedule, and I said no, I wasn't ready to do business with them. When I was, I'd call. Actually, to be honest, the product I wanted to show them was not of great consequence and I placed it elsewhere, but wondering what I had in my box to show them was eating them up. And I smile whenever I think about it.

Ground Rule No. 3: You Will Be Brief and to the Point
When you get the president on the phone, you will use the script that follows and say as little as possible about yourself and your idea. The purpose of the call is to get the appointment and nothing else. Once you have it, say goodbye and hang up. If you offer too much information, the chap you're talking to will feel he knows enough

When you call for an appointment, say what you have to say and hang up. Don't blab!

to make a decision then and there. "Nah, I don't think that would be for us. Thanks for calling, but I really don't think that idea would fit into our ongoing plans." Fighting your way back from that attitude to get the personal appointment you're looking for would take more persuasive skills than most of us have.

Ground Rule No. 4: You Will Be Nice to One and All
Before you get the president on the phone, you'll probably have to go through a couple of receptionists and assistants. No matter how snippy they are or how officious they might seem, you must always be patient and pleasant. If you come off as a nice person, the assistant at the other end of the line is likely to do more for you than if you sound impatient or rude. We are still all just humans interacting with each other—and we're all more helpful to those we like than to those we don't. There often is also a niceness bonus. When you do meet with the executive and show him your prototype, he might very well call his assistant into the meeting. "Ruth, you love animals, what do you think of this pet idea?" If Ruth's impression of you from your telephone chat is that you're a nice guy, what she has to say now might be quite different from what it would be if you were rude or hostile. Pleasantness and politeness so obviously produce better results that you have to wonder about folks who go out of their way to be otherwise.

The Magic Two-Minute Telephone Conversation

Here's the script for my widely acclaimed play called *The Appointment*.

The Cast:

HELEN FURY
Receptionist

HECTOR GREENBOTTOM
Vice President

MAX DUBOIS
President, Global Amalgamated
 Things, Inc.

BUSTER BALDWIN
Greenbottom's personal
 assistant

DONNA MADONNA
Dubois' Personal Assistant

THOMAS ALVA REDDISON
Handsome young inventor

SCENE ONE: PHONES RINGING IN CORPORATE OUTER OFFICE.

FURY:

Hello, Global, can you hold?
(Good, a busy, overworked receptionist doesn't have time for
questions.)

FURY:

(Two minutes later)
Global, hello—sorry for the wait. How may I direct
your call?

REDDISON:

That's OK, no problem. Let me have Max, please.
Max Dubois.
(Reddison had called a few days earlier to get the president's name. "I
have to write a letter to your president, can I have his name please?"
will usually do the trick. Fury has had a thousand calls since then
and no longer remembers. Asking simply for Max suggests that
he and Reddison are old friends. Fury asks no questions and puts
the call through.)

FURY:

Ringing

MADONNA:
Hello, Mr. Dubois's office.

REDDISON:
Hi. My name's Tom Reddison. We create new products for companies and have come up with something that I know Max will want to see—so if you can put me through, I'd appreciate it.

Warm, friendly voice using Dubois's first name suggests an already existing relationship. Note the use of "we," not "I," suggesting that Reddison represents a company, not just himself.

MADONNA:
Moment—

DUBOIS:
Yeah. Dubois here.

REDDISON:
Hi, Mr. Dubois. My name's Tom Reddison. Thanks for taking my call. I know you're busy so I'll be brief. We create new products for companies and we've hit upon something that I think can be very special for Global Amalgamated. If I could have a few minutes to show it to you, I promise you won't be disappointed.

This is the perfect 15-second presentation. Reddison thanked Dubois, flattered him by acknowledging what a busy man he is, stated the purpose of the call, piqued Dubois's interest, and asked for the appointment. The use of "we" suggests one company prepared to do a deal with another one. Language Dubois understands. The words "invention" and "inventor" are not used. I like to say "we hit upon something" because that makes it sound like some wonderful discovery.

At this point, Dubois will say one of three things:

1. OK, when do you want to come in?
2. Sounds interesting, what have you got?
3. Oh, you want Hector Greenbottom. He's the guy that handles all new products.

If Dubois's answer is number 1 (When do you want to come in?) Reddison makes the appointment and hangs up promptly, but not before being transferred back to the assistant to leave a contact number. This is important. Reddison doesn't want to drive all the way from Pittsburgh to Cleveland only to learn that Dubois has been out sick for the past few days and his assistant didn't know how to reach him. It happens.

If Dubois's answer is number 2 (What have you got?) Reddison says: "I really can't do it justice by trying to describe it over the phone, but I know your product line quite well and this is a great new product that I know will fit right in. When you see the prototype I think you'll see what I mean. I only need a few minutes, Mr. Dubois, and I promise I won't be wasting your time. I can be there whenever is best for you."

Dubois says something like OK, how about next Tuesday at ten o'clock?

If Dubois's answer is number 3 (Oh, you want Hector Greenbottom), Reddison asks to be switched.

BALDWIN:

Mr. Greenbottom's office.

REDDISON:

Hi. My name's Tom Reddison. We create new products for companies and have just come up with something for Global Amalgamated. I was talking to Max about it and he wanted me to show it to Mr. Greenbottom—so if you can put me through, I'd appreciate it.

When Greenbottom gets on the line, Reddison repeats what he told Baldwin and an appointment is made.

— CURTAIN –

The key is to be pleasant and to the point. The words "invention" and "inventor" are not in your vocabulary. Present yourself as a professional product developer representing a company and don't chat unnecessarily. "Can't you just give me a hint?" Dubois might say. "No [chuckle], honestly, I don't want to spoil it. The only thing I can say is that you're going to love this product when you see it."

Nice guy that you are, and rightly proud of what you've invented, the temptation is to accede to Dubois's request and tell him a bit about your invention. Once you start, though, you won't stop, and the need for an appointment goes up in smoke. "Well, you know—it's really not necessary for you to drive all the way over here. How about if you just put something in the mail and we'll look it over." That's the precise response you want to avoid. Say *nothing*. Executives are always interested in new products, it's the lifeblood of their business. By not taking the edge off their curiosity, you will almost assuredly get the appointment.

OK, so here we are. You have great presentation material and an appointment with the person who can put your name up in lights. Now comes the really easy part: sitting down with the prospective licensee and getting him to say "WOW!" as he rubs his hands together in greedy anticipation. How to get that happy response is all explained in the next chapter. Read on!

NINE

Meeting with the Manufacturer, Licensee, or Investor. What to Do and What to Say to Make Your Talents and Hard Work Pay Off (It's Easier than You Think!)

> *You were born to be a winner, but to be a winner you must plan to win, prepare to win, expect to win.*
> *—Zig Ziglar, sales expert*

When a professional golfer lines up her putt, she envisions the ball rolling along its path from the moment it's hit until the moment it drops into the cup. A professional baseball player doesn't just swing at the ball, he envisions precisely where he's going to hit it and how he's going to hit it. These professional athletes are envisioning success as they step up to the ball or up to the plate. Without envisioning success and expecting success, they are unlikely to achieve it. They've known that to be true from the moment, as kids, they first dreamed of professional careers.

Similarly, any good salesperson will tell you that he envisions success and expects success on every call. He's convinced that what he's selling is good for his customer, and he has the confidence that he can make the point convincingly. Confidence comes from knowledge, and that's where I come in. I've made more presentations to investors, licensees, and manufacturers than I can begin to count. I know what the prospect is going to ask you and I know how you should answer. What I know you'll know—and soon you'll have the confidence to close the deal and earn yourself all the rewards that your talents and hard work entitle you to. As Zig Ziglar, the great sales guru, said, you have to plan to win, prepare to win, and expect to win. The planning and preparation are over; now it's time to deal with the knowledge to give you the winning expectation.

If this is to be your first sales call, remembering my own, you may be feeling fear, nervousness, and doom. I won't simply say "Don't be nervous, don't be scared," because I know how little weight that advice carries. What I will say, however, even though I've said it before, is that *lots* of companies are looking for fresh new ideas, and there are a limited number of creative and innovative people like you to provide them. The person in front of you is *hoping* that you have something great under your arm. The investor *is* looking for something great to invest in, the manufacturer *is* looking for a great new product to license. Half your job is done! In most sales situations, customers are sitting there thinking up reasons not to buy. When you enter the president's office with that mysterious package under your arm, however, she's hoping and praying that what she sees will make dollar bills dance before her eyes. You have a situation that other salespeople would die to have.

The three difficulties that just about all salespeople must overcome are convincing prospects that: (1) they need the kind of product the salesperson is selling; (2) this product is better than the competitor's; and (3) it's worth the price being asked for it. But you have none of those problems! Your customer already has the need for new products, price is not an issue, and you have no competition since your product idea stands alone. How can you beat that?

However, before you're allowed into the executive suite to work your charms, particularly if you've approached a large company, you'll probably be obliged to sign a disclosure agreement. Although reading it can scare years off your life, don't be too alarmed: It's not as bad as it seems. I sign them all the time, usually not even reading them.

The Disclosure Agreement. Do You Sign Theirs or Do They Sign Yours?

If you're a well-known scientist, perhaps dealing with highly sophisticated technology, maybe under the auspices of a great university or research institution, you probably can get a company to sign your nondisclosure agreement before you disclose your information. However, if you're just a regular guy like me, and if what you've created is just a regular little product like a garden tool or a kitchen gadget or a Christmas ornament, it's highly unlikely that any prospective licensee will sign your nondisclosure agreement. You're wasting your time and aggravating the manufacturer by even bringing it up.

People you hire to do a service for you—model makers, product designers, and graphic artists, and the like—will certainly sign your agreement, but your prospective licensee almost certainly will not. That's just a fact of life, and you shouldn't let it deter you from pressing forward; you already have other remedies if the company turns out to be a bunch of crooks (not likely, I assure you).

However, the fact that the corporation won't sign your agreement doesn't mean that you won't be required to sign theirs. Small and medium-size companies seldom have these agreement requirements, but large companies almost always do. Please notice that what you'd theoretically be giving the corporation to sign is your *non*disclosure agreement. Their version, a "disclosure agreement," has no "non" in it because the two agreements have different purposes. Your nondiclosure agreement binds the company to keeping your idea confidential. The company's disclosure agreement specifically states that they do *not* promise to keep your idea confidential. You might call it the dark side of a nondisclosure agreement.

Here's the corporation's attitude: Look, pal, nobody asked you to show us your idea and we're not exactly thrilled that you insist on doing so; we're getting along just fine without you, thank you very much. However, if you *do* insist on showing us what you have, here are our rules:

1. Don't show us your idea unless it's patented or patent pending because that's the only protection your idea will have. We here at the company accept no responsibility for the confidentiality of your idea. Understand this and proceed at your own risk.

2. You are submitting your idea to us on your own initiative and free will. The company has not promised you anything. It's possible that we have already seen your idea from other inventors or are working on the same idea ourselves, thereby making your own submission redundant.

3. You understand and agree to these conditions:

   A. The company does not agree to keep your idea confidential.

   B. The company does not promise to return your materials.

   C. The company doesn't promise to pay you anything for your idea.

As draconian as this sounds, the company is simply saying that whatever legal options having a patent might give you is the only protection you have when you submit your idea to it. Your signature on this agreement confirms your understanding that the company makes no offers, promises, or guarantees whatsoever—so sue it if you think you have a case. Otherwise, don't let the door hit you on the way out. And oh yes, have a nice day.

"Holy cow!" you might logically say (or worse). "How the heck could I sign something like that? These guys are going to steal my idea and run off like thieves in the night!" It's understandable that you might think that way, but fortunately, all is not lost. The fact is that the company *will* keep your idea confidential, the company *will not* steal your idea, the company *will* strike a deal with you if it likes the idea, and the company *will* return your materials after reviewing the idea. There are some crazy inventors walking the earth, or so the urban legend says, so these companies are simply protecting themselves. Bright, smart, sane inventors like you, with legitimate product ideas, need not fear. My advice is to take a deep breath, cross your fingers, say three

Company disclosure agreements can scare the heck out of you. But sign them anyway.

Hail Marys, and fearlessly sign on the dotted line. And anyway, it's not as if you have any options. It's their house, their rules.

Salesmanship 101

The Basics, Part A

It's worth repeating that people are more likely to buy from people they like and trust. This is particularly true if you're looking for a lender, investor, or licensee since any of those activities suggests a long-term relationship. You're 90% there just by showing up so that folks can see what a pleasant, smart, clever gal you are. No one is going to like you and trust you via an unsolicited sales letter. Even if it hurts, your first and most important job is to make the executive like you, trust you, and have the impression that dealing with you will be a pleasant experience. As Sam Goldwyn, the Hollywood studio founder, is reported to have said about the importance of sincerity, "If you can fake that, you have it made."

If you were sitting in the outer office, waiting to be interviewed for a job instead of looking for an investor or licensee, and if an employee walked past you on her way to the inner office, the human resources person who's about to interview you might ask, "What's she like?" He's not asking for your height, weight, and unusual physical characteristics; this isn't a lineup. What he's asking is if you look like you fit in. If the impression is that you can be part of the team and not some oddball who's going to give them trouble, the interviewer immediately has a favorable impression. That's your goal as well—to look like you're part of the team, a regular guy just like them, and not some lunatic inventor who's going to make their lives difficult. And there's no better way to start creating that impression than by dressing the part.

Based on the type of company you're seeing and where it's located—in a downtown office tower or in a rural setting—you should have a good idea how the employees dress, and you should dress accordingly. If the men wear conservative suits and the woman wear the equivalent, so should you. You're not going to show up in shorts and a Hawaiian shirt, looking like Chuckles the Clown. If the dress code is conservative, you dress conservatively; if the dress code is casual, you dress casually. Once I had to meet a prospective licensee in the warehouse of his company where he was supervising an inventory count. I came in casual slacks and a sport shirt, and the guy actually thanked me for not wearing a suit. As trivial as it might seem, what you wear really does matter.

The Basics, Part B

As important as what you wear is what you say. Don't chew gum, don't curse, don't make political or sexist remarks, and whatever you do, don't talk down! If the person you're meeting is much older than you, don't even make the slightest suggestion that he's not up on the latest way of doing things. Conversely, if you're old enough to be his mother, don't talk about the good old days, sonny. The two of you are equals, and hope-to-be friends, and that's the way to view him. We humans form lasting impressions of each other in a matter of seconds, so concentrate on presenting yourself as someone who is pleasant, affable, and easygoing. In other words, look like and act like someone who can fit in and who dealing with will be a pleasant experience. If you come across as rude, arrogant, supercilious, and a know-it-all, I'm not saying that you still won't land the deal since there are plenty of other factors to consider, but you'll have a much higher mountain to climb to get to the promised land.

The Basics: Connecting with Your Customer

Salespeople know that customers buy from people they like, and so they understand that their first job is to establish a personal rapport with customers. For some happy souls, that comes naturally. Others have to work at developing the skill. Either way, it's what you must aim to achieve.

If what you've invented is, say, a new fishing lure, you might say something like "I gotta tell you, Mr. Brown, it's a real honor being here. I can't wait to tell my father that I was actually in the offices of the Brown Fishing Lure Company. He has used your lures for as long as I can remember, he swears by them—and of course he made me a fan as well." Brown will say thanks, and the two of you might chat for a moment or two about fishing before getting down to the business as hand—just two good old fishing buddies about to do some business together. "You can call me Jerry," he tells you, sitting back comfortably in his chair.

If fishing is not the common ground, as you walk into Brown's office, be alert for other clues to his interests. Notice the plaques or pictures on his wall, the trophies on the shelf, the toys on his desk, the magazines on his coffee table; something will give you a clue, and off you go. You can't just say "How are you? Nice day, isn't it?" and sit back, thinking you've done something.

Understanding Your Customer

The more important the executive, the more conscious she is of wasting time, and the less tolerance she has for people who cause her to do so. When you get into your presentation, don't dawdle, don't drone on, and whatever you do, don't sit there reading your material to her. The executive you're talking to is bright and quick to grasp things, so don't insult her intelligence by filling the air with unimportant babble, half truths, inflated claims, and bald-faced lies. The executive will pick up on them instantly, and for the rest of your presentation she won't be listening; she'll be looking for an exit strategy. Here are seven other points to remember.

1. If possible, begin your presentation with a little story, perhaps how you accidentally uncovered the need for your invention. Don't make it a saga, just some short exposition. Everyone loves stories, even busy executives.

2. If you have a written presentation, don't give it to the executive until you've discussed its contents. Otherwise, he'll skim it in 15 seconds while it takes you 15 minutes to tell him what he now already knows.

3. No matter what, the prototype is the star of the meeting. When you unveil it, place it into the executive's hands. The product is not yours anymore; it's hers.

4. Remember to make your points in terms of what *will* happen, not what might.

5. If there are any real or theoretical drawbacks to your product, bring them up yourself without waiting for the executive to point them out. And when you bring up these drawbacks, be sure you have solutions to offer to allay the concerns.

6. If the executive offers arguments, don't argue back. View them as simply requests for more information. Listen carefully to what he's really saying and respond in kind.

7. Sell to the buyer's needs or wants, not just to what she should have. It's what the sales books call benefit selling. All sales managers tell that to their salespeople, and they invariably use the example of do-it-yourselfers wanting ¼-inch holes, not ¼-inch drills. If you keep your antennas out, you might discover openings that can easily be the tipping point in your presentation. For instance, probably you're prepared to say something like "My new product will easily sell 50,000 per year, and you should easily clear $15 profit on each one." More sales and profits are great, who wouldn't want that? But how much sweeter is it if you can show that these gains are coming at the expense of a chief competitor?

Maybe you can say something like "By any standards, this product is far superior to the one being sold by Ajax Nut and Bolt, so you should be able to dislodge them from wherever they have their product placed." That argument—gaining sales and distribution at the expense of a chief competitor—is so much more powerful than the simple claim of more profits that you should look and plan for those opportunities as vigorously as you can.

The Basics: Dealing with Customer Responses

You can be sure that when you've finished your presentation, the executive isn't going to jump up and give you a big hug. Nor is he going to call security to have you escorted from the building. However, it's virtually a sure thing that he'll offer one of these responses.

"Thanks, but This Product Idea Really Isn't for Us"

You're not going to lean across the desk, grab his tie, and say, "Are you crazy? Don't be an idiot! Of course this product is right for you!" What you're going to do is gently ask some questions to find out what he really means. Is he just being polite? Is he really saying that he thinks the idea stinks? If so, what's wrong with it? Maybe it can be corrected. Or is he really being truthful—that there's nothing wrong with the idea, only that it's not right for his company? Who is it right for? Can he give you some names? Can he arrange an introduction? What kind of product *would* be right for him? Perhaps you can come up with it. The professional attitude is to not take rejection personally, but to use the rejection to gain valuable information. Just because the meeting didn't turn out to be a great one doesn't mean that it can't be a good one.

"I Like Your Idea, but I Have to Show It to My People"

You should say that you'll send presentation material along with a letter confirming the meeting. That just lets good old Jerry know that you're establishing a paper trail. Don't leave anything, particularly not original material. You should have copies of everything. Original material can get dog-eared and sometimes even lost. Also, even though you might have a dozen more in the trunk, I suggest that you not leave a prototype, nor should you promise to send one.

Say: "Sure, I understand, Jerry, and I'll have some presentation material and a confirming letter on its way to you tomorrow by express mail. However, unfortunately, I can't include the prototype. I have a couple of tentative appointments next week where I think I'll need it. However, if you can tell me when you want to have a meeting with your people to show the idea, I can make sure to have the prototype here for you."

I suggest that kind of answer for a few reasons. First, sometimes the executive is really trying to say a polite no. A fast way to find out is by making an issue of the prototype. If he couldn't care less about not having it, you can be pretty sure he's not really interested. Second, suggesting mysterious "other meetings" indicates that you're not just sitting around twiddling your thumbs. Third, if he truly does want to show the prototype to his people, if you bring it in for that purpose, chances are good that you can sit in on the meeting. Remember, all of his people are probably your enemies (NIH types), so if you're present you can probably counter any criticisms or doubts.

And fourth, sending your material with a cover letter, preferably by a carrier like FedEx or DHL, elevates it in importance over a sales brochure left by a regular salesman.

"It Looks Interesting but I Need a Little Time"

"That's fine, Jerry," I'll reply. "I don't blame you for wanting a little time to decide. However, let me be frank. Your company is the one that I really want to do work with on this idea because as far as I'm concerned, you're the best in the business. The first appointment I made is with you. No other company has seen this idea. However, I have made other appointments for later, which I don't mind postponing if you can give me a date certain when you'll have reached a decision. I don't mean to rush you, take the time you need, but by knowing your plans, I can make my own." Jerry will probably reply "That's fine, give me a week (or two weeks)." That way you've pinned him down to a date and made it clear that you're prepared to take the product to a competitor. It's important that this exchange simply be a frank, all-smiles discussion. In no way should you pose it as threat.

"OK, You've Got a Deal"

That, of course, is what you want to hear, but you might have to do a little more work to make it happen, especially if your product isn't patented. Here's what I mean:

> Prospective Licensee: So what about knockoffs? How do I know that as soon I start shipping this item, some of my lousy competitors won't start making the same thing?

> You, the Suave Inventor: Jerry, if a pro like you ever worried about knockoffs, you'd never produce your first product. First of all, there's no reason to expect to be knocked off at all. Lots of products I've licensed can go for years before knockoffs come along, and by then, who cares? But anyway—even if someone does knock off the product, by the time they spot it and tool up, you'll have at least a six- to nine-month head start. By then your sales guys will have this product in every decent store in America. All that's left for any competitor are the scraps that

you don't want in the first place. And what the heck, by then I'll have something new for you anyway.

Prospective Licensee: Yeah, well, OK—so what kind of deal are you looking for?

That's it. When the potential licensee asks what kind of deal you're looking for, all else are details. You've got yourself a licensee. You didn't tell Jerry anything he doesn't already know, but sometimes a little stroking is required.

When to Ask for the Order

Whenever sales companies do a survey of executives and ask them why they didn't buy what the salesperson was selling, the overwhelming response is that the salesperson never asked them for the order. Hello? I once knew a buyer for a chain of drugstores who made a vow not to buy anything unless the salesperson asked him to. He later told me that he had to cancel the vow quickly because his store shelves would soon begin to look empty. For whatever the reason, salespeople, both professional and amateur, are reluctant to ask for the order. When you think about it, that's pretty crazy since it's no secret why they're sitting in front of the customer in the first place; and yet there's no one in sales management who doesn't know that getting salespeople to ask for the order is the hardest thing they have to do. Oh well, ours is not to reason why. Ours is to take the information and learn from it.

You Know It's Time to Close the Deal When ...

Knowing when to ask for the order is as important as asking for the order. Knowing when to ask makes the actual job of asking easier. Here are a couple of telltale signs.

- The prototype is in the executive's hands, and the conversation moves on packaging and displays and marketing. You know that the executive is starting to think of the idea as her own. Ask now and ye shall be given.

- The executive calls someone into the meeting who also shows enthusiasm for the product, confirming the executive's opinion. Now it's time to close the deal. If the person called in is one of the assistants that you chatted with on the phone, your friendliness has paid off. However, if it's an engineer or someone like that, you know that person is not your friend. The best defense is to treat him or her with great respect and deference. Flatter the hell out of the person. If you can make him or her look important and wise in front of the boss, you've made yourself a valuable convert.

- Watch your prospect. If she's handling your prototype in a pleased or proprietary manner, and if she's nodding agreeably as you're quoting sales projections, then she's obviously ready to make the deal.

The Basics: How to Ask for the Order

The reason so many salespeople don't ask for the order is that they don't know how. If they knew how to do it without simply saying "So—you heard my pitch, can I have an order?" they'd do it every time and their sales would double or triple. No salesperson I ever met would baldly ask, "Oh, sir, may I please have an order?" Only Girl Scouts selling cookies do that ("Oh, mister, how about buying some of these cookies?"). Actually, maybe they could teach something to the rest of us. In any event, for the faint of heart, there are other ways to ask for the order without having actually to do so.

As a young man I was a salesman on the road. After I made my presentation, I would take out my order book, ostentatiously plop it on the desk, and take my pen from my breast pocket. "I suggest you take two-thirds blue and one-third mauve because that seems the way the sales have been breaking. Is that OK?" Almost always the customer would simply nod and I was on my way. Once in a while a customer would say, "Hey. I didn't say I was ordering anything!" I'd give them a dumb look. "You didn't? Gosh, I'm sorry for jumping the gun. I guess I should have said if you *are* ordering, I think you should take two-thirds blue and one-third mauve." And I'd sit there, pencil poised, waiting for instructions. Almost always the buyer would say something like "OK, but just don't take things for granted and don't be such a smart aleck." Order written, we'd part as friends.

Of course you're not a salesperson on the road and you don't have an order pad, but you have something just as good: a licensing contract (or at least I hope you do). All salespeople should have *something* in their bag to write orders with; and for folks like you and me, that would be the licensing agreement. Looking for signals, when I think the time is right, I'll simply plop my contract on the desk and ask, "Would you like to review my licensing agreement so you'll know what I'm looking for in the way of a deal?" Any executive interested in your product will of course say yes. Naturally she wants that information. Take out another copy, hand it to her, and go through it item by item. She'll see how simple and painless the contract is, she'll ask that this or that be changed, and you're home free! Congratulations—you've licensed your first product!

The trick is to have a contract in your pocket so you can whip it out at precisely the right time, one that's cunningly designed to give you all the rewards and goodies you're entitled to. As the old saying goes, "Forty for you and sixty for me, and equal partners we shall be." Oddly enough, a clever contract just like that is waiting for you in the next chapter.

TEN

Reaping the Harvest. Use My Own Battle-Tested Licensing Agreement To Bring You All the Rewards that Your Talents and Hard Work Deserve

> *The fellow who says he'll meet you halfway usually thinks he's already standing on the dividing line.*
> —Anonymous

In 1936 a young machinist named Henry Phillips patented a new type of screw for the automotive industry that was expressly designed to provide more torque, be easier to use with an electric drill, and prevent overscrewing by the assembly-line workers. If you're a do-it-yourselfer, you know that if you overtighten a Phillips head screw, it will "cam out," or the screwdriver head will slip. That's not by accident, and it's why automobile makers immediately adapted this screw as their own, as did manufacturers of endless other products and, finally, by the consumers themselves. The inventor of this clever product never manufactured a single screw; all he did was license the use of his patent to every screw manufacturer in America.

Similarly, Robert H. Abplanalp did not invent the aerosol can, but what he did invent, in 1949, was the clog-free spray valve. Without it, no manufacturer of spray paint could compete, and so paying a royalty for its use was an automatic decision by everyone in the business.

If you've invented a product like that—something so basic that no company in the industry could afford to be without the manufacturing or usage rights—then you should certainly look into the possibility of multiple licensing. However, if your invention is just some regular little product—say, a new kind of garden tool or golf gadget—then you should understand that multiple licensing is not in the cards. For instance, if you came up with a novel idea for an ice cube tray, you wouldn't be able to license it to Company A, then turn around and license it again to Company B. The second company won't want it, and the first company won't stand for it. The product is simply not important enough or essential enough to either ice cube manufacturer for them agree to a multiple licensing deal. And anyway, particularly if the product's not patented, it's fair game for one and all as soon the first production item appears in the marketplace.

A hot graphic character, however, represents the epitome of multiple licensing. If you created something like SpongeBob SquarePants, manufacturers will stand in line outside your offices with suitcases full of money to plead for a licensing opportunity. Magnanimous soul that you are, you'll award an exclusive license to a manufacturer of metal lunch boxes, another exclusive license to manufacturers of plastic lunch boxes, another exclusive license to manufacturers of vinyl lunch boxes, another exclusive license to manufacturers of fabric lunch bags, and on and on. The owners of popular characters can mince, slice, and dice the licenses in so many ways that it would make your head spin. If you have the next SpongeBob character, you'd better tell your printer to stay late to start cranking out the license contracts.

The problem, of course, is that either you can run with the big dogs or you have to stay on the porch. It's not by accident that these popular characters—Superman, Batman, Spider-Man—are all created and owned by the giant media companies like Sony, Warner Brothers, Disney, or Marvel. They're the ones that can invest millions in building up the characters' fame and consumer loyalty through movies or comic books or TV shows so that they can become desirable properties. A manufacturer might pay a small fortune to gain the rights to put Mickey Mouse on his products but wouldn't pay a dime for Melvin Mouse. Who ever heard of Melvin? Inventors send me their cute little figures all the time, and I tell them to come back when they've figured a way to get their character up in lights on Broadway.

Although we'd all like to be like Mr. Phillips and his wonder screw, most of us create products intended to be licensed to a single company, and that's the thrust of this chapter. Nevertheless, since the skills involved in successful negotiating are universal, and since most of the issues addressed in any good licensing agreement apply to either activity, I think you'll be interested, regardless of your intentions.

Professional Negotiating Techniques that Will Earn You the Respect and Goodwill of the Licensee plus All the Rewards You're Entitled To

Negotiating is not about grinding the other side into the dust; it's about coming to a meeting of minds where both sides can leave the table feeling that a harmonious partnership has been forged. The art of negotiation is time-honored, with successful negotiation techniques, strategies, and attitudes that have been honed and perfected over the ages. Here are some of them.

First, Know What You Want

When labor bosses come to the initial negotiating session with management, it's customary for them to plop a thick, bound document on to the table with a noisy thud, announcing it as the union's "nonnegotiable" demands. The other side yawns, expecting nothing less. Weeks later, when the settlement is announced in the newspapers, it's funny how few of those nonnegotiable demands are still intact. You, however, are a different story. You *do* have some truly nonnegotiable demands—and if the licensee digs in his heels about any one of them, in my view you are proceeding at your own peril. I will soon show you precisely what these demands are and why you're entitled to each and every one of them.

It's Your Game, You Bring the Ball and Bat

You are the seller, the licensor, so it's *your* job to provide the licensing agreement. Don't let anyone tell you differently. How else can each of your requirements be properly addressed? If you allow the licensee to have *his* attorney draw up the contract, you'll have a licensing agreement from hell to contend with and you'll wind up battling with the licensee word by word, comma by comma. The two of you might have started out as friends, but soon, in your eyes, the guy across the table will start to look like Attila the Hun and in his eyes you're starting to bear an uncanny resemblance to Ilsa Koch, the Beast of Buchenwald.

And when you do put your agreement on the desk, it's helpful if it looks like an official printed document rather than something specially prepared for the meeting. If the agreement has the appearance of being printed, it seems like something standard, not exceptional, and the licensee will be less likely to pick it apart. You are, after all, a product developer, accustomed to licensing products, and this is the agreement that every licensee signs (or at least that's the implication).

Bar the Door, Nellie, No Lawyers Allowed

There's an old saying that if there's only one lawyer living in town, he'll starve. If there are two, however, they'll both get rich. You and the licensee, both perfectly intelligent individuals, will have no difficulty in working out a mutually agreeable licensing agreement. It's not all that complicated; it's just business. Once all the points have been agreed on, of course you can have your attorney review the agreement and put it in proper legalese and point out anything that's glaringly amiss, as might the licensee, but, I beg you, don't put the two lawyers together, across from each other at the table. That is not a smart move. Those of you who have experienced that kind of situation know what I'm talking about, and those of you who haven't really don't want to know. It's too gruesome for tender ears. The upshot will be a legal bill as big as the national debt and an agreement (if there ever is one) that looks like a declaration of war. I'm not blaming the lawyers; that's what they're paid to do. But

When negotiating a licensing agreement, try to avoid putting two lawyers in the same room.

unless this is a very complicated deal, getting the lawyers together is rarely necessary, and is a move you will almost assuredly regret.

Understand the Nature of Your Relationship

Your intent, of course, is to achieve a licensing agreement that provides you with the rewards and protections that you're entitled to, but your intent should also be to conduct these negotiations in a calm and friendly manner, always keeping in mind that the licensee has rights as well. You are not dictating terms of surrender, you are striving to create a document that's fair and equitable and that serves as the benchmark for other new products that you intend to bring to this company as time goes on. The purpose of a negotiation is to resolve conflict, not to create it. Rudeness, shouting, insulting remarks, and threats have no place in a professional negotiation. "Take it or leave it" is not a negotiating technique, and the impossible anatomical act that you might like to see a person perform on himself is best left unsaid. Don't get personal. Remember, this is just business. Whatever the outcome, the world isn't coming to an end, you'll still have your health, and no one is holding your firstborn for ransom.

Remember that Reality Is Your Friend

As mentioned earlier, the principal cause of negotiation failure is the inventor's inflated view of the invention's value and the unrealistic demands the inventor might make because of it. That's not difficult to understand. You probably have invested a great deal of time, money, and passion in your creation, and so thinking more of it than someone else might is perfectly understandable. However, some honest research into the industry and the sales of similar products should give you a more realistic view—and that's the one that you should take with you into the negotiation. Otherwise, if you ask for the sky, you'll probably be given the gate.

Listen to the Other Side

Sometimes silence is more eloquent than speech, and so you should listen quietly, respectfully, and attentively to any objections or demands that might be raised by the other side. Jot the demands down to show that you take them seriously. If what the licensee is asking for seems out of reach by your standards, the correct stance is to put it aside and move on. That's what professionals do: They put to bed all that can be agreed on and put the sticky issues aside. The premise is that in the end, having come so far, it would be a shame for both sides not to make an extra effort to solve these one or two snags. "Let's put this aside for now and move on" is the phrase one side or another in a professional negation is apt to say when a particular clause gives them trouble.

If you truly understand what the other side hopes to achieve, you might be able to restate his demands in a manner that's mutually acceptable, or you can perhaps offer some "additional information" that might provide the other side with a face-saving way of shifting his position. Or, finally, you might be able to use your agreement to his demand as a bargaining chip for one of your own, as in: "If I agree to this proviso, will you agree to take another look at Article 4?" There are lots of ploys and tactics in your arsenal, but you can't employ any successfully without first listening carefully to what the other side has to say.

Assume the Right Attitude

President Kennedy once famously observed that we should never fear to negotiate, but we should never negotiate out of fear. I wish I had said that first because it makes my point precisely. Yes, certainly you should approach this negotiation with an open mind and be amiable and obliging, but you should also be prepared to end this negotiation and walk out the door if you have not not been able, despite your best efforts, to get the other side to agree to all the rights you're entitled to receive. Being able to create winning ideas, as you've proven yourself capable of doing, is an enormous asset, so don't forget it. There are few of you and many companies that can use your talents; if it's not this one, it'll be the one across town. If you have that attitude within your soul—that the other guy needs you more than you need him—it will in mysterious ways make itself known and you'll be the alpha one at the table.

Sample Licensing Agreement

Exhibit 10.1 is a licensing agreement I use for my own products and for those of inventors I represent. It was drawn up by me, not an attorney, but it has stood the test of time, having been executed more than 100 times without a hitch. The agreement contains just what I want it to include, and what is left out is not by carelessness; it's because those issues, no matter how settled, would not benefit me. The contract is deliberately couched in simple layperson's terms so that when the prospective licensee is ready to do the deal, the agreement is an abettor, not a stumbling block. Dozens of licensees' lawyers have critiqued this contract over the years with two guaranteed results: First, no opposing lawyer has ever looked at this agreement without making changes—a word here or a sentence there. It's the nature of the beast. And second, no opposing attorney has ever changed the spirit of the agreement.

As you'll see, this contract is for nonpatented products. If your product is patented, you would add a performance clause demanding that certain sales milestones be reached by specified dates, or else you have the right to end the deal and move your patent elsewhere. Other than that, and perhaps with some special clauses that might be unique to your own circumstances, I believe this agreement will serve your needs quite well, and you're welcome to use it. After you've looked it over, I'll explain the main provisions and review the 10 points contained therein that you have a right to insist on.

Date: _____

_____, located
at _____
(hereinafter referred to as LICENSOR), has given _____,
located at _____, (herein-
after referred to as LICENSEE), the exclusive production and marketing rights to [his/her] new product concept as herein described and as per drawings and/or prototype samples previously submitted). In exchange, LICENSEE agrees to pay LICENSOR a royalty in the amount and under the terms outlined in this Agreement.

PRODUCT DESCRIPTION:

_____

_____

_____

Exhibit 10.1   Licensing Agreement

1. <u>ROYALTY PAYMENTS</u>. A _____% (_____percent) royalty, based on net selling price, will be paid by LICENSEE to LICENSOR on all sales of subject product and all subsequent variations thereof by LICENSEE, its subsidiaries, and/or associate companies.

The term "net selling price" shall mean the price LICENSEE receives from its customers, less any discounts for volume, promotion, defects, or freight.

Royalty payments are to be made monthly on the 30th day of the month following shipment to LICENSEE's customers, and LICENSOR shall have the rights to examine LICENSEE's books and records as they pertain thereto. Further, LICENSEE shall reimburse LICENSOR for any costs [he/she] might incur in collecting overdue royalty payments.

2. <u>TERRITORY</u>. LICENSEE shall have the right to market this product [these products] throughout the United States, its possessions, Canada and Mexico, and may do so through any legal distribution channels it desires and in any manner it sees fit without prior approval from LICENSOR. However, LICENSEE agrees that it will not knowingly sell to parties who will resell the product(s) outside of the licensed territory.

3. <u>ADVANCE PAYMENT</u>. Upon execution of this Agreement, LICENSEE will make a non-refundable payment to LICENSOR of $_____, which shall be construed as an advance against future earned royalties.

4. <u>COPYRIGHT, PATENT AND TRADEMARK NOTICES</u>. LICENSEE agrees that on the product's [products'] packaging and collateral

Exhibit 10.1 *(Continued)*

material there will be printed notices of patents issued or pending and applicable trademark notices showing the LICENSOR as the owner of said patents, trademarks, or copyrights under exclusive license to LICENSEE.

In the event there has been no previous registration or patent application for the licensed product(s), LICENSEE may, at LICEN-SEE'S discretion and expense, make such application or registration in the name of the LICENSOR. However, LICENSEE agrees that at the termination or expiration of this Agreement, LICENSEE will be deemed to have assigned, transferred, and conveyed to LICENSOR all trade rights, equities, goodwill, titles, or other rights on and to licensed products which may have been attained by the LICENSEE. Any such transfer shall be without consideration other than as specified in this Agreement.

5. <u>TERMS AND WARRANTS</u>. This Agreement shall be considered to be in force for so long as LICENSEE continues to sell the original product(s) or subsequent extensions and/or variations thereof. However, it is herein acknowledged that LICENSEE makes no warrants to LICENSOR in regard to minimum sales and/or royalty payment guarantees. Further, LICENSOR agrees that, for the life of this Agreement, he [she] will not create and/or provide directly competitive products to another manufacturer or distributor without giving the right of first refusal to LICENSEE.

6. <u>PRODUCT DESIGNS</u>. LICENSOR agrees to furnish conceptual product designs, if requested, for the initial product(s) and all subsequent variations and extensions at no charge to LICENSEE. In addition, if requested, LICENSOR shall assist in the design of packaging, point-of-purchase material, displays, etc., at no charge to LICENSEE.

Exhibit 10.1 *(Continued)*

However, costs for finished art, photography, typography, mechanical preparation, etc., will be borne by LICENSEE.

7. QUALITY OF MERCHANDISE. LICENSEE agrees that the licensed product(s) will be produced and distributed in accordance with federal, state, and local laws. LICENSEE further agrees to submit a sample of said product(s), its cartons, containers, and packaging materials to LICENSOR for approval (which approval shall not be reasonably withheld). Any item not specifically disapproved within fifteen (15) working days after submission shall be deemed to be approved. The product(s) may not thereafter be materially changed without approval of LICENSOR.

8. DEFAULT, BANKRUPTCY, VIOLATION, ETC.

A. In the event LICENSEE does not commence to manufacture, distribute, and sell the product(s) within _____ months after the execution of this Agreement, LICENSOR, in addition to any other remedies that might be available to him [her], shall have the option of canceling this Agreement. Should this event occur, to be activated by registered letter, LICENSEE shall not continue with the product's development and is obligated to return all prototype samples and drawings to LICENSOR.

B. In the event LICENSEE files a petition in bankruptcy, or if the LICENSEE becomes insolvent, or makes an assignment for the benefit of creditors, the license granted hereunder shall terminate automatically without the requirement of written notice. No further sales of licensed product(s) may be made by LICENSEE, its receivers, agents, administrators, or assigns without the express written approval of the LICENSOR.

C. If LICENSEE shall violate any other obligations under the terms of this Agreement, and upon receiving written notice of this

Exhibit 10.1   *(Continued)*

violation by LICENSOR, LICENSEE shall have thirty (30) days to remedy such violation. If this has not been done, LICENSOR shall have the option of canceling this Agreement upon ten (10) days written notice. If this event occurs, all sales activity must cease and any royalties owing are immediately due.

9. <u>LICENSEE'S RIGHT TO TERMINATE</u>. Notwithstanding anything contained in this Agreement, LICENSEE shall have the absolute right to cancel this Agreement at any time by notifying LICENSOR of his [her] decision in writing to discontinue the sale of the product(s) covered by this Agreement. The cancellation shall be without recourse from LICENSOR other than for the collection of any royalty money that might be due him [her].

10. <u>INDEMNIFICATION</u>. LICENSEE agrees to obtain, at its own expense, product liability insurance for at least $2,000,000 combined single unit for LICENSEE and LICENSOR against claims, suits, loss, or damage arising out of any alleged defect in the licensed product(s). As proof of such insurance, LICENSEE shall submit to LICENSOR a fully paid certificate of insurance naming LICENSOR as an insured party. This submission is to be made before any licensed product is distributed or sold.

11. <u>NO PARTNERSHIP, ETC</u>. This Agreement shall be binding upon the successors and assigns of the parties hereto. Nothing contained in this Agreement shall be construed to place the parties in the relationship of legal representatives, partners, or joint venturers. Neither LICENSOR or LICENSEE shall have the power to bind or obligate in any manner whatsoever other than as per this Agreement.

Exhibit 10.1   *(Continued)*

12. <u>GOVERNING LAW.</u> This Agreement shall be construed in accordance with the laws of the state of _____.
IN WITNESS WHEREOF, THE PARTIES HERETO HAVE SIGNED THIS agreement as of the day and year written below.

_____   _____

LICENSEE   LICENSOR

DATE: _____   DATE: _____

Although I'm sure this agreement is quite clear, there are some matters that I'd particularly like to call to your attention.

Introduction

As is typical in any agreement, the first order of business is to identify the parties to it. Next follows the description of the product being licensed. Your goal is to offer enough information to clearly identify the licensed product, but to describe it broadly enough to encompass all of the derivatives and line expansions that you hope will follow. In other words, it's the *principle* of the product that's being licensed, not the fact that it's seven inches high and painted pink and purple.

Clause 1: Royalty Payments

Royalty percentages are negotiable. Usually, products that are associated with high profits and slow sales, like gift items, can carry a 6% or 7% royalty. High-volume, low-profit items, such as electronics or traffic appliances, might support a 2% royalty. For most other products, 5% is fairly average. You of course want a higher royalty percentage, and the licensee just as naturally wants a lower one. A compromise that often works is to accept the licensee's lower percentage up to a certain sales figure, when presumably the company has earned back its start-up costs. For sales beyond that figure, the royalty percentage is raised to the one that you requested.

Further, although this section calls for a monthly royalty payment, if you're dealing with a larger company, be prepared to be told that monthly payments are burdensome and that the company prefers to pay quarterly. Frankly, I seldom get monthly payments, and leave that provision in only to give the licensee a small victory.

Also note that payments are based on net sales, and the description of net sales in this agreement is the only one that you should settle for. There is one other very important point in this section. If you have to sue your licensee to collect royalties due you, the licensee pays your legal costs. You shouldn't have to pay a lawyer $20,000 to help you collect $19,000 that's due.

Clause 2: Territory

If your licensee has a strong export program, you might want to give the company world rights. If the licensee doesn't, you might decide to give the company rights to the United States, Canada and Mexico, the NAFTA partners, and to look for someone else to handle foreign sales. If you do give the licensee world rights (and assuming your product is patented), you should have two separate agreements: one for domestic sales, one for international. Domestic and international sales are usually separate departments within the company, and it might turn out that one is doing well with your product and the other isn't. By having separate agreements, you can fire one and keep the other.

Clause 3: Advance Payment

If your product is something that the licensee *really* wants badly, and if you're a skilled negotiator, you might be able to get the advance payment as a no-strings-attached signing bonus. Most often, however, it's an advance against future earned royalties. Authors get such advances from their publishers, and the size of the advance is a key arguing point that an agent might make for an author client. The idea is that the larger the advance, the more energetically the publisher will promote the book. However, regardless of the settled amount in your own case, or whether it's a bonus or an advance, *money should change hands at the time of the signing.* Otherwise, you don't have much of a contract, and if I were you, I wouldn't brag about it.

With the best of intentions, a manufacturer will enter into a licensing agreement with the inventor. As time passes, however, whatever can go wrong usually will. Company goals change or the competitive situation changes, or the company is sold, or the president resigns, or the company determines that it can't make the product as cheaply as it hoped to. Whatever can happen will. Months and months go by, until finally one day the inventor receives a call from the company saying that it decided not to proceed with the product. You'd be amazed at how often that happens. If the inventor did not receive an advance, what has he got for all this time that the company had him and his invention tied up? Zilch, nada, that's what he got. I've actually licensed one of my own products three times, and it still never reached the marketplace. At least I had the advances to keep me warm on cold winter nights.

An invention, being intellectual property, in this regard is no different from real estate property. If you think you might want to buy a vacant lot to erect a building, and if you want the owner to hold it off the market for you for a certain period of time so you can decide, you'll have to give the land owner option money. That's how it's done. If you do finally buy the lot, the option money applies to the price. If you don't, the owner keeps the money and hangs out the For Sale sign again. Why should you, the inventor, be treated any differently? By signing a licensing agreement, the company is, in effect, taking out an option on your property, and the company should have to pay for that option like anyone else. Don't let anyone tell you otherwise. Twice in a long career have I walked out of meetings because the company balked at paying the advance, and I've never regretted it for an instant.

Clause 4: Copyrights, Patents, and Trademark Notices

Putting proper legal notices on products and catalogs and packaging is to the licensee's benefit as well as yours, so the company will do it as a matter of course. Also, if your product isn't patented, but could be, you might be able to negotiate with the licensee to have the company pay to apply for the patent. Small companies will tell you its your job, but larger companies, with their own legal departments and patent attorneys on retainer, might do it without argument. Why not? It's to their benefit, and the cost for them to do so is minimal. On the patent, you would be named as the inventor, and you will have assigned merchandising rights to the licensee.

Clause 5: Terms and Warrants

If your product is patented, you'd indicate in Clause 5, Terms and Warrants, the performance standards that must be met, either in sales or royalties, for the licensee to keep the rights to produce and distribute it. If your product is not patented, then there's no basis for you to make these demands. If your licensee doesn't do a good job selling your nonpatented product, for all practical purposes there's not much you can do about it, since you have no intellectual property to move around.

Note also that this section expressly prohibits you from dreaming up a competitive product to your own and giving it to a competitor. I know it sounds great: two companies battling against each other, both with versions of your same product. But alas, I'm afraid your narrow-minded licensee won't stand for it.

I call your specific attention to this sentence: "This Agreement shall be considered to be in force for so long as LICENSEE continues to sell the original product(s) or subsequent extensions and/or variations thereof." My position is that as long as the licensee is earning money from my idea, whether it's 1 year or 20, it still must pay me my share. As years go by, the product that the company might be selling will have undergone so many changes that it bears little or no resemblance to the original. Nevertheless, if the original was the genesis, then royalties are due.

Clause 6: Product Designs

Clause 6, Product Designs, applies specifically to my own situation; a more general term might be something like "Services to

Be Rendered." Since I'm a product and graphic designer, this clause outlines what I'll do for free as part of the license and what I expect to be paid for. If, for instance, your invention is a new type of machinery or a new process, you might agree to provide shop-floor training to the licensee's employees. Will you do that for free? For how long? Whatever the nature of your invention dictates, this clause states what you'll do for free and what the licensee must pay for.

Clause 7: Quality of Merchandise

If you're a famous fashion designer like Ralph Lauren or Calvin Kline, your brand name is your principal licensing asset—and so all licensing contracts awarded contain a clause stating that no garment or accessory covered in the licensing agreement is to be produced by the licensee without your specific approval. If your name is on it, it has to meet a certain standard. Similarly, when an owner of characters, such as the Walt Disney Company, licenses the use of one of its characters, the licensee is provided with a thick style book that shows precisely how the character is to be drawn and precisely what colors are to be used. No product with a Disney character on it can be sold unless Disney approves the way the character has been rendered. In both instances, the licensor is protecting its brand.

However, since your licensees and mine aren't licensing our inventions because of our famous names or brands, we don't have the same latitude. Yes, you certainly are entitled to approve the product before it's produced—but only in terms of its legality and safety.

If you withhold approval because you don't like the shade of purple, the licensee's lawyers will be put on red alert, prepared to come down on you like the wrath of God.

Clause 8: Default, Bankruptcy, Violation, Etc.

There are three parts to clause 8, Default, Bankruptcy, Violation, Etc. First, a specific date is given by which time the licensee must be ready to produce and sell your product. This is an essential part of any licensing agreement since you can't allow the licensee to dawdle forever. The second part describes your rights if the licensee goes bankrupt. If that happens, the agreement is automatically canceled and the licensee cannot use the licensing agreement as an asset to be turned over to creditors as a part of a payment of debt. Otherwise, you might wind up as the licensor to the Broken Kneecap Collection Agency. And finally, the third part describes how infractions, such as late royalty payments or the lack of flaw correction in the product, are to be handled.

Clause 9: Licensee's Right To Terminate

If you're the owner of a famous character, such as Spiderman, or the owner of a famous brand, such as Martha Stewart, in order for you to award the license, the licensee guarantees to pay a minimum amount of money to you, the licensor; hopefully the money is earned by royalties, but it is due in any event. If the licensee decides to cease the sale of the licensed products, any shortfall below the guarantee must still be paid.

However, if you're a private inventor licensing a nonpatented product, you do not have the power to make that kind of demand because as soon as the first product appears on retailers' shelves, your idea's licensability to someone else is finished. You can, of course, demand to be paid for all royalties due, but other than that the licensee can walk away from the deal at any time.

If your product is patented, you can possibly demand minimum guarantees just as the famous licensors do. How successful you'll be depends on the value of your patent, but whatever you negotiate would be spelled out in this clause.

Clause 10: Indemnification

There are two things you can be sure of. First, if there's a way for your product to injure a person, no matter how remote, someone, somewhere, will figure out how to do it. And second, if the injury is severe enough, and if the potential financial awards are large enough, the plaintiff's attorney will name in the suit every person he can find that has some connection to the product. You would almost certainly be among those named, so clause 10, Indemnification, binds the licensee to protect you. Actually, for the licensee to do so is not such a big deal. No company selling products to the public would do so without substantial insurance, and it incurs only a minor cost to add your name to the policy.

In the enthusiasm of getting the signed agreement, often both sides overlook this clause. However, if you allow that to happen, your nights of restful sleep will be at an end.

Clause 11: No Partnership, Etc.

Clause 11, No Partnership, Etc., is routine boilerplate that, by defining the nature of the relationship, protects both parties to the agreement. This clause states that the only connection between you and the licensee has to do with the production and marketing of a mentioned product. Period. If it turns out that your licensee is part of an international drug ring, that has nothing to do with you; or if you turn out to be the Scarlet Pimpernel, that has nothing to do with your licensee.

Clause 12: Governing Law

Since this is your agreement, it would be smart to show that it has been drawn up in accordance with the laws of your own home state. Any lawsuits that might thereafter be initiated would have to take place in the governing state, meaning the licensee has to send lawyers to your state, rather than you sending them to the licensee's. Lawyers charge even while snoozing on the train. Also, although it hasn't been proven, there is the implied home field advantage on the part of jurors. You're just a decent, innocent local citizen, and these city slicker thugs from out of town are trying to take advantage.

The Phantom Clauses That Never Appear

Most often, this contract is executed directly between the licensor and the licensee without benefit of lawyers. It's a simple agreement between two businesspeople, and the matters are quickly agreed on and settled. The fact that the agreement is already printed with my letterhead at the top makes it appear to be a standard, routine document, requiring only the blanks to be filled in. However, the contract deliberately does not address several matters because no decision on them would be to our advantage. Fortunately, the licensee seldom thinks of these issues, and so we just let them pass.

1. Who Defends Whom?

If you licensed a nonpatented product, and if, despite your own investigations and those of the licensee, it turns out that you have inadvertently violated someone else's patent, and if that person sues, who defends the lawsuit? The licensee is going to say "Hey, you sold us a bill of goods! It's your product, you're the one who has to defend it." But you say "Wow! What a shock! You investigated and so did I, but we both missed it. But wait a minute—since you get 95% of the proceeds and I only get 5%, why should I have to pay for everything? Let's split the costs just like the income: 95% and 5%." Back and forth you go, while the unsigned agreement sits there on the table gathering dust.

You have the same problem if your product is patented, except this time the licensee might demand that you bring suit against companies that have copied your patent. "You got us into this," they'll say, "and now you've got to protect us from those lousy knockoff bastards!"

Who's right? Beats me. All I know is that I would *never* sign an agreement that obligated me to sue or defend against a lawsuit. I could easily spend $250,000 to protect a paltry $25,000 in royalties. The best conclusion is to leave this matter out of the licensing agreement and to address it on an individual basis if and when it shows up. Fortunately, in my case it never has, which I suppose is a tribute to the amount of research I do before presenting a product to a potential licensee.

2. Getting Rid of the Goods

There's an old saying that merchants should never count profits until all of the goods are out of the warehouse. Fad items, novelties, toys, and other products of that sort have an unpredictable life span, and when they die, it's not a long, lingering death; it's more like a heart attack. Overnight, hot products turns cold. A company might one day be shipping the product out of the door as fast as the trucks can be loaded, and the next day, all of a sudden, no more orders! Meanwhile the warehouse is bursting with merchandise that must be disposed of at fire-sale prices to the bargain barns and closeout vultures. So now what?

"Hey," says the licensee, "I'm losing my shirt on each sale just to get rid of this stuff, so why should I pay you a royalty?" And you say, "But look, it says in our agreement that I'm to get 5% of the proceeds on each sale; it doesn't say anything about whether you're making a profit or not." This matter would be a sticking point in any agreement, as is the matter of who pays for lawsuits, so the agreement I provide licensees does not address either one. As a practical matter, regarding closeouts, since you want to maintain the licensee's goodwill for future dealings, you should make some accommodation. If you cut your royalties in half for closeout sales, that might show your willingness to be a good partner.

3. Defective Merchandise

Suppose there's a manufacturing defect in the product, necessitating a recall and a reimbursement of many thousands of dollars to customers. The licensee might say, "Hey, since we had to give all this money back, we're taking back the royalties we paid you for the sales." And you might answer, "Not so fast, big guy, I'm not your partner; I didn't manufacture the products. Quality control is your responsibility, and I shouldn't be penalized for your sloppiness. Once you ship it, I'm supposed to get paid." Who wins?

These are pesky problems with enough right on both sides to make any arguments legitimate and long lasting. In real life they rarely become issues, and if they do, the actual circumstances usually dictate an intelligent response. The "what if?" game is the one that lawyers like to play, and it's what earns them their thousand-dollar suits. Mere mortals like us should avoid them when we can.

Ten Nonnegotiable Demands

You might be the salt of the earth, the most amiable and understanding, easiest-going person anyone has the pleasure of knowing. For that I salute you. However, when it comes to signing a licensing agreement, a little iron in the spine will serve you well. You are entitled to all 10 of these points, and if your licensee won't agree to any of them, you might want to take a closer look at what you're letting yourself in for.

Demand No. 1. Royalty Percentages Should Always Be Based on Sales, Never on Profits

"Hey, we'll be partners!" the licensee might say. "I'll cut you in on a share of the profits." That sounds great, but don't buy it. Profits are the licensee's business, sales are yours. A clever person can interpret profits in many ways: one way for the tax collector, another for the investors, and another for you. Sales, however, are absolute and provable, and that's what your royalties should be based on. Accept nothing else.

Demand No. 2. Sales Are Sales, Period

A duplicitous licensee might want to deduct all sorts of items from the sales figures before figuring out your cut: commissions, trade show expenses, brochures, travel, and whatever else he can think of. "Forget it, pal," you might say. "That's why you get the 95% of every dollar and I only get 5." The expenses are the licensee's and have nothing to do with royalties. Sales are sales, period. You can't tell the licensee how to price your product and you can't dictate what terms he can offer his customers. However, whatever he collects, you get your share.

Demand No. 3. You Have the Right to Examine the Books

During the cold war, when we were trying to have détente with the Soviets, President Reagan is known for his repeated warning "Trust, but verify." That works here as well. Certainly you trust your esteemed licensee, but it doesn't hurt to have a peek at the books once in a while. If any licensee balks at this provision, I suggest you pack your bag and leave. The only books you're entitled to see, however, are the ones pertaining to sales. Whatever profits the licensee is earning is between him, his conscience, and the tax collectors.

Demand No. 4. The Licensee Picks Up the Legal Bill

If the licensee keeps stalling when it comes to paying your royalties, or if your examination of the books finds some glaring omissions, and if you have to sue the crook in order to get paid, the beautiful part is that he has to pay your legal fees. Sometimes an attorney will modify that right by saying the licensee has to pay your legal fees if you prevail in court, but not if your claim proves frivolous.

That's fair and it does not in any way alter the intent to this clause. If your licensee's a crook, he has to pay what's due and he has to pay for your legal action to collect it.

Don't settle for anything less. Some wise guys like to say "You don't like it? So sue me!" knowing full well that the cost to do so is more than it's worth. But nobody ever said "So sue me! The treat's on me!"

Demand No. 5. No End to Royalty Payments

"Hey, I'll pay you royalties for five years, and that should be enough." That was said to me one time. I ended the negotiations because I couldn't get the company president to change her mind. Fortunately, however, this is rarely a problem. Licensees are ordinarily not opposed to paying royalties for so long as the licensed product and its variations continue to earn money for them. Fair's fair. They might ask that the percentage be lowered as competition enters the picture, and that remains to be negotiated, but at least paying something is usually not the issue.

However, if your product is patented, what the licensee is actually licensing is the patent, not the product and so asking for a termination of royalty payments when the patent expires is a legitimate demand. But, hey, that's 20 years down the road, so I don't think it's worth fighting about. By then we might be living on Mars and flying around like the Jetsons.

Demand No. 6. Defining Your Product Properly

You're the licensor, so you have the right to describe what you're licensing under your own terms, and you have the right to expect royalty payments for any other products that spring from your basic concept. If the licensee tries to limit the description, that shouts a warning that he's planning to work around it to avoid paying royalties. Even though you're able to shoot down that attempt, the mere fact that it was made should give you a clue about the person you're dealing with. Lucky for us, most licensees are honest people, so an event like this is extremely rare. My only suggestion is that you be alert for it.

Demand No. 7. Getting a Nonrefundable Advance

From time to time I've encountered companies (always small ones) that, because of the owner's personal pique, refuse to pay an advance to license an inventor's product. The company owner feels that since he's spending the money to produce the product, and assuming all of the risks, he shouldn't have to pay an advance on top of it. When I've encountered this attitude (fortunately rarely), I've never been able to change the owner's mind (and on occasion I've tried mightily). By now, however, I've learned that a person like this is impossible to budge, and so I will just thank him for his time and leave. I figure it's his loss, not mine.

Because I do this work for a living and have no personal attachment to the products I create, and particularly since I know that if I have a good product I can almost always find a licensee for it, I don't hesitate to end a meeting if the licensee won't meet what I consider reasonable demands. However, if this is a new venture for you, I do understand your own personal passion for your idea and can see how you might be persuaded to enter into the deal even if no advance money is to be paid. I can only urge you not to do so. You have every reason to receive an advance (no matter what size), and the licensee has no reason to withhold it. Don't sell yourself short.

One other thing: Inventors are always asking me how much of an advance they should get. I might suggest that they estimate the first year's royalty earnings and get an advance for 25% of it. However, that's totally arbitrary. The advance should be large enough to establish the licensee's sincerity, but not that large that it stands in the way of making the deal. I'm sorry I can't give you a more definitive answer, but business is still an art, not a science.

Demand No. 8. Establishing a Performance Date-Certain

Any real licensing agreement demands that the licensee have the licensed product on the market by a certain date or be subjected to penalties outlined in this clause. That's usually expressed as a date certain instead of certain date because that seems to emphasize its seriousness, with no exceptions allowed. No licensee will argue with you about the need for this provision; the argument might be about when that date should be. The licensee, of course, wants it far in the future, and you want it as soon as possible. This is one example of why understanding the industry in which your product is intended to compete is important. Most consumer product industries have product introduction cycles tied in to when retail customers place orders. These orders are usually connected to industry trade shows, where buyers come to see what's new and place orders for the forthcoming season. Companies that make swimming pool accessories are looking for new products at a different time of the year from companies making skiing accessories. It's not hard to gather that information.

Manufacturers of holiday products, for instance, usually need to have their product lines set, at least on paper, at least a year before the date of the holiday itself. The larger chains start looking at toys and decorations in October for the following year's Christmas, and the smaller retailers make their Christmas buying decisions in January and February. That means if you don't have your new Christmas product idea in the hands of the manufacturer by September for the following year's Christmas season, you probably will have missed the cycle and will have to wait another year. By then, who knows what might happen?

Professionals know these cycles and show products to management when companies are starting to plan their forthcoming lines. By showing a new product idea at the precise time that the company is looking for them, deals are made more quickly and lead times are reduced.

Demand No. 9. Requiring Product Liability Insurance Protection

Don't let any licensee tell you that it's difficult for him to add you to his coverage, because it isn't. And don't let him tell you that for a product like yours, the insurance isn't necessary, because it is. In our litigious society, and with product liability lawyers all over America waiting by their phones, any licensee who doesn't have insurance up to his eyeballs is not someone who should be allowed to play with scissors or use other sharp objects. I guarantee you, any company that you're dealing with has this insurance, and it only takes a phone call to their insurance agent to get you included by name. Don't do the deal without a receipt showing that you're covered. If you do proceed without it, don't write to me from debtor's prison to say that I didn't warn you.

Demand No. 10. Make No Promise to Sue

Although, for reasons already discussed, my standard agreement makes no mention about me protecting the licensee from infringers, every once in a while the licensee's attorney tries to add a paragraph to address the issue. "Look, Jerry," you have to say, "you know I can't sign a blanket agreement to sue everybody who wants to be a competitor, and neither can you. That would be crazy. The situation probably will never arise, but if it does, you and I will take a look at it together as partners and decide between us what the appropriate action should be."

What's that? you say. You say that sounds like double-talk? Well, I guess it is, and if you can come up with a better line, I hope you'll send it to me. All I know is that I would *never* sign an agreement forcing me to sue someone, and in the strongest way possible, I urge you not to either. Instead, I suggest you heed the words of Voltaire, the famous French philosopher. He said he was driven to ruin twice in his life: once when he lost a lawsuit and once when he won one.

Now that we've reviewed a typical licensing agreement, I hope you agree that there's nothing complicated or mysterious about it; it's something you can easily handle on your own. It's nothing more than a simple, plain language business deal; the kind that business-people make every day.

When I make a presentation, the prospective licensee will frequently ask, "OK, so what's the deal?" As I take a printed agreement out of my briefcase I can answer the question in one sentence. "It's easy, Jack, the royalty is 5%, the advance against royalties is $10,000 with no minimum guarantee requirements, and you can quit at any time." Know what you want, know what you're entitled to, be open to the licensee's legitimate requests, and you will almost certainly have a done-deal.

ELEVEN

Meet Our Panel
of Successful Inventors

> *1. It's impossible!*
> *2. It's possible, but not worth doing.*
> *3. I knew it was a good idea as soon as I heard it.*
> —Arthur C. Clark, author, inventor

"**G**ood morning, ladies and gen-
tlemen! On behalf of the Institute, I would like to welcome you all to
our first annual Inventors' Success Conference. I'm pleased so many
of you were able to come, and I'm amazed that you all got here on
time—what with the terrible weather we've been having and all the
flight delays. Anyhow, I thank you all for being here and I applaud
you for the seriousness with which you are taking the whole idea of
inventing for profit. You're among the few who are going about this
business in the right way, and I'm sure such diligence will pay off for
you. Those of us here at the Institute are ready to do our part, and I'm
sure our carefully selected panel of successful inventors will make
this morning a memorable one for you all.

"Can you all hear me in the back? Raise your hands. Good. Most
of you, I see, have already found our hospitality table with compli-
mentary coffee and coffee cakes located in the main entrance area
by the elevators. Those who haven't, please help yourselves. Also,
I must say, I'm glad to see that so many of you have brought along

the Institute's latest book, *The 12 Amazing Secrets of Millionaire Inventors*. We'll be referring to it during the conference.

"One little piece of business before we start; I'm told that some of you have not made your final registration payments. If that applies to you, please see Mrs. Green at the registration desk during the intermission. Those of you who don't comply, I'm sorry to say, will be forcefully evicted by our security staff, and your *12 Amazing Secrets* book will be taken from you.

"And now, if you'll please turn off your cell phones or put them on vibrate, let's not waste any more time in getting this seminar started. Let's meet our panel!

"First, sitting here to my immediate left is John Higgins, inventor of the famous Re-Pillable Card. Stand up, John, and let the folks see you."

John stands and waves; the audience applauds.

John Higgins

"I love products like John's because they're so simple and so practical—the kind of product that any one of us could have invented it. No offense, John, but the beauty of the Re-Pillable Card is its sheer simplicity. Of course, even though it's the kind of product that any of us could have come up with, the credit all goes to John, because he's the one who did something about it. John got the idea of the Re-Pillable Card by reading of the life-saving benefits of immediately taking ordinary aspirin if one experiences a heart attack. No one would argue the fact that we should all have aspirin with us, if only just to address a headache, but few of us go to the trouble. That's where John's brainstorm comes in.

"John's card, which can hold four aspirin (or other pills), slips into the wallet just like a credit card. Because of the way most current wallets are designed, with cascading slots for cards, by putting the Re-Pillable Card into the top slot, the wallet is virtually no thicker that it was before. More details can be found on John's website, www.Re-Pillable.com.

"At first John tried to license the idea, but had no success. He then decided to market it himself and, with the help of a local plastics injection molder, developed the tools and dies to get into business. However, now with a product to sell and a website up and running, still no one was buying. That's when John got the marketing idea that put him and the Re-Pillable Card on the map. He saw an article in *Men's Health* magazine about the importance of aspirin, called the editor and told him about his patented new product. The rest, as they say, is history. *Men's Health* ran a story on the Re-Pillable Card; orders by the thousands flew into John's website, and the fame of the card quickly spread. Only recently John shipped an order to Bayer Levitra Mexico for *a half million* specially engraved Re-Pillables, which Bayer is using as a giveaway promotion. Orders from other pharmaceutical companies around the world may be coming in even as we speak.

"Bucking the odds against having success in marketing one product, John has obviously figured out the formula for making it happen, and he has graciously agreed to give us his own tips and suggestions. Thank you, John.

"Sitting directly next to John is Rodney Long, a guy who could probably write the book on successful inventing. You might not recognize his name, but if you've ever gone fishing, you've probably used one of his many licensed inventions. Rodney has been interviewed by *Modern Marvels* on the History Channel and has appeared on many TV fishing shows. He has been the subject of numerous newspaper and magazine articles, everything from the *New York Times* to *Bassmaster* magazine, and whenever I personally need help with a fishing product, Rodney is the guy I go to.

"Stand up, Rodney, and let the folks see you."

Rodney stands and waves; the audience, some with knowing nods, applauds.

Rodney Long

"Rodney, you're like the Leonardo da Vinci of the fishing industry. I hardly know where to start. I suppose the best place would be to list some of your inventions. Let's see: I know you've invented and licensed the the EZKnot, the Stand Out Hook, the Wiggle Rig with the SpecTastic Thread, the Rock Hopper, the Rig Saver, and, along with a partner, the Nutri Shield insect repellent. Whew! I may have missed some, folks, so I urge you to visit Rodney's website, www.EZKnot.com, for a full description of what these products are and where to buy them.

"I especially wanted Rodney on the panel, not just because he has many wise tips to give us, but because he exemplifies what *The 12 Amazing Secrets* book is all about—doing things right and enjoying the rewards his creativity entitles him to. Rodney dropped out of high school, joined the army at 17, and was married by the time he was 19. One might think that would be the end of the story; that he'd get out of the army, maybe go into construction, and that would be it. However, fortunately for our story, Rodney, a natural engineer with almost no formal education, managed to have his talents recognized. While still in his 20s, he became an expert in water pollution control and was placed in charge of the world's first functioning flue gas desulfurization system ever built. Rodney stayed in the field until 1999, having had a hand in over 300 inventions still used today in heavy industry, before deciding to try his luck as a full-time inventor.

"After a few false starts and lots of mistakes, Rodney did what most successful inventors do: He finally focused in on an industry that he was familiar with, fishing, and made himself the source that companies in that business go to when they're looking for new products. When he tried inventing for industries where he had no familiarity, he found little acceptance; the products had been done before, or had been succeeded by newer, improved models, or had little financial potential. But by sticking to what he knew and what he loved, Rodney has made himself a renowned expert in the field— someone who companies are happy to see when he calls to say that he has a new product to show them. With all the successful products that Rodney has invented and licensed, any company making fishing products would be crazy not to invite him in.

"By being an expert in this one industry, instead of gadding about here and there as so many others do, Rodney has the insider knowledge of what the companies are looking for, what niches have been overlooked, and what issues have not been satisfactorily resolved. And only then, when he has the target product and the target company in mind, does he do the actual inventing. There are lots of talented people who can invent products, but the key is in uncovering what needs to be invented; and that's where Rodney excels.

"Rodney will later join with the other panelists in offering tips and advice, but he sums up his own success in what he calls 'the three rights': finding the right problem, creating the right solution, and presenting it effectively to the right company. We'll hear more on that later. Thank you, Rodney.

"Our next panelist, Dr. Larry Loo, probably has the most interesting, varied, and rich background of all, and I can't wait to tell you about it. Stand up Larry, and say hello."

Larry Loo stands, and the audience applauds.

Larry Loo, M.D.

"Larry was born in Hawaii, got a BS degree in chemical engineering from Stanford University, and worked as a plant manager for Allied Chemical Company. That would be a big enough career for almost anyone, but after eight years as a plant manager, Larry decided to go back to school to become a medical doctor. After completing a three-year residency in family practice, Larry, along with his wife and children, moved to Africa to serve as a medical missionary; eventually working in Kenya, Tanzania, and Ghana. Later Larry again moved his family, this time back to America, to open a private practice.

"But wait, that's only the half of it! After eight years of a private family medicine practice in California, Larry closed his offices to become a physician with the California Department of Correction, eventually becoming the chief medical officer for several prisons in the system.

"What does all of this have to do with inventing? And when would he find the time?

"Well, it turns out that all through this interesting and multilayered career, Larry maintained a lifelong interest in woodworking. As Larry knew, most woodworking hobbyists have a table saw, and the most dangerous function one can do on a table saw is rip narrow lengths of wood, particularly the last few inches when the fingers can accidentally come in contact with the whirling blade. At one point in Larry's career he worked as an emergency room physician, and more than once he saw what can happen to careless table saw operators.

"Since he had loved woodworking from when he was a child, and since he personally always had a fear about safely using the table saw, Larry was sure that others shared this trepidation. The result is Larry's WondeRip Fence, a wonderful product that eliminates the old push stick, enables the operator to rip boards safely, and rips wood with almost machinelike accuracy. You can get full details of how this amazing tool works, along with glowing testimonials from professional woodworkers, by visiting Larry's website at www. wonderip.com. You'll see why this interesting and useful product earned a full half-page article in the *New York Times,* plus articles in media like *Fine Woodworking Magazine, This Old House* magazine, *Wood Magazine,* along with others.

"I am particularly happy to have Larry here, not only because of his unique invention, but because he made a careful analysis and determined that marketing the product himself was the right course of action. He tried licensing but didn't like it; didn't like the profit potential, and determined that he'd be happier calling all the shots in running his own business. Rodney Long, on the other hand, did an equally intelligent analysis and determined that he didn't have the skills to run a business. He decided to become a full-time professional product developer. So we have two successful, intelligent inventors deciding on different career paths by honestly examining their own skills, resources, goals, and talents. Both of these men, I'm happy to say, are glad they made the decisions they did. Many of you in the audience, I believe, are at similar crossroads, and I can only hope that the book in your hands and this seminar can be useful in helping you make your decision.

"Our next panelist is Brian Conant who, along with his wife, Myra, has invented and patented what is certainly the oddest invention of any mentioned by our panelists, and one of the most odd, and yet perfectly sensible, inventions you'll ever hear about. Before I tell you about the invention itself, please give a big hand to the co-inventor, Brian Conant."

Brian rises in his seat and the audience responds with warm applause.

Brian Conant

"Brian and his wife live in Hawaii, where he spent more than 20 years in the U.S. National Guard. While on an active duty stint that required him to wear chemical protective clothing, Brian released gas. Unlike other times, when he was not wearing the garb, he couldn't smell anything, and neither could anyone else. Interesting, he thought, but just filed it away. One morning, some time later, his wife had a gas episode, and Brian mentioned his experience with the chemical protective clothing. "Too bad," she said, "that there's not underwear that can be worn and you don't have to worry about the odor." That set the wheels in motion. After five years of experimentation, Brian invented and patented the Flat-D, the flatulence control underwear for men and women.

"I see some of you are smiling, as did I when I first learned about it, but I assure you, it's the real deal! Brian's underwear is recommended by doctors, it's FDA registered, and it really works in neutralizing the odors associated with human flatulence. All of us have gas episodes from time to time, but for some folks—sufferers of colitis, Crohn's disease, diabetes, and so on—it's a real problem. If you visit Brian's website at www.flat-d.com, you'll see how this product works and you'll read some of the appreciative letters that Brian has received. He even was considered for a slot on *American Inventor,* the hit TV show.

"The reason I particularly wanted to have Brian with us, aside from the fact that I thought you'd like knowing about his invention, is that he represents the determination and adaptability that's typical of successful entrepreneurs. Brian's entire work career was with the post office, and so, with no business experience, he was bound to make mistakes. His first, a big one, was to throw $15,000 down the drain with an invention submission company. Next, he tried to interest other manufacturers in licensing the product, but none had the slightest interest. When trying to license a product, the product itself of course is everything, and unfortunately, Brian's flatulence underwear interested no one. However, in self-marketing, many other factors are at least equally important in contributing to the idea's success. In this instance, Brian, of necessity, was forced to learn about marketing fast—and in the end that's what turned the product into a success.

"Brian knew he'd have to create the demand for the product on his own, without money, relying on bootstrapping—and the way to do that was by capitalizing on the product's uniqueness. With a website up and running and with merchandise in the warehouse ready to be shipped, Brian and his partner started a media blitz. Through phone calls and press releases they were able to get Brian and his product featured in a number of magazine and newspaper stories, and orders by the thousands started pouring in. Now that single product has grown into a line, the company is advertising on radio, doctors are recommending the products to their patients, and, as Brian envisioned all along, the product concept is helping thousands and thousands of folks all across the country. Great job, Brian!

"And now we turn to these two attractive women sitting directly to my right, Mary Sarao and Barbara Pitts, sisters in life and partners in inventing a marvelous, popular, and useful product that you'll find in many of the major retail chain stores in the country. Barbara, Mary, please take a rightfully deserved bow."

Mary and Barbara stand and the audience applauds heartily.

Barbara Pitts and Mary Sarao

"Every once in a while we see a new product on the market, or an improvement on an old one, that's so sensible that we say to ourselves, 'Now that's such a great idea, how come nobody thought of that before?' What Barbara and Mary invented and patented fits that description perfectly: It's the Ghostline poster board. Probably by now all of you know what that is, but for the few who don't, it's regular poster board or foam board with a very faint grid printed on it that is virtually invisible from a few feet away. Anyone who has ever turned a poster board or foam board into a sign has probably wished for boards like this, as has probably every schoolchild (and parent!) who ever had to measure and cut poster board for homework projects. The need for a product like this was so obvious to companies in the business that the several largest ones were actually bidding against each other to get the licensing contract. How often does that happen?

"Mary, a former school teacher and mother of two daughters, has dealt with a good share of poster board projects over the years, and the idea for Ghostline came to her in a dream. Naturally she called her sister, Barbara, and the two of them invented and patented the product we see in stores today. This is an inventing family, with the sisters' father and brother both being patent holders as well. Sales for the Ghostline poster boards are in the tens of millions of dollars, and the product is now so basic and entrenched that who knows how far into the future sales will continue? For many years, I'm sure.

"Mary and Barbara now spend much of their time helping other inventors by giving free talks, lectures, and seminars and through their website, www.AskTheInventors.com and through their two books, *The Everything Inventions and Patents Book* and *Inventing on a Shoestring Budget*. Both books can be bought through their website or through electronic booksellers like Amazon.com and Barnes&Noble.com

"I knew Barbara and Mary before their success, and I am proud to have played a very small, minor role in helping them achieve it. We've stayed in touch over the years, and I know you'll find a great deal to learn from their experiences in first attempting to self-market and later successfully licensing this wonderful product.

"To Barbara and Mary's right is seated another highly successful inventor. You might not recognize his name when I mention it, but if you're a golfer, I'll bet you've heard of the amazing product that this gentleman and his father invented. Ladies and gentlemen, meet John Breaker, the co-inventor of the popular BirdieBall!"

John rises and is greeted with enthusiastic applause.

John Breaker

"The BirdieBall, for you nongolfers, is a uniquely designed and patented golf training ball with the mass and heft of a real golf ball, but since it's designed for limited flight, it provides excellent training regardless of the club being used. The BirdieBall, according to John, will do everything a regular golf ball does, but does it in short enough space to be used in a typical backyard. You can get the full details at John's website, www.birdieball.com.

"What typically happens is an inventor will try to license his product and, finding no success, will then decide to market it himself. Or, conversely, the inventor starts out with the intention of marketing his invention himself but, having no success, decides to look for a licensee. Either way can work; the trick is to remain flexible and amenable to change. When one door closes, another one opens. John and his co-inventor father, in this instance, started by hoping to make a deal with one of the conventional golf ball companies, but then decided to become their own licensee. John and his friend Paul Olson formed a company to market the BirdieBall, licensing the invention from John and his father. A double play! John the inventor receives royalties for his creativity and John the entrepreneur achieves profits for his abilities. What a great idea.

"That's how it is now, but that's not how it started out. The first few years were grim. The BirdieBall is oddly shaped, sort of like a rectangular napkin ring, and John and Paul had a difficult time breaking into the retail market with a product that didn't offer immediate visual understanding. Yes, the BirdieBall worked better than any other practice ball, but it didn't *look* as if it would—and perception trumps reality every time. Retailers aren't in the business of educating consumers, they're in the business of selling what consumers want to buy, and the BirdieBall was on few shopping lists. However, John and his partner were not to be denied, and so with some creative marketing moves they began to reposition their BirdieBall into markets more receptive to innovative new products.

"First, because the ball has four flat plain, printable surfaces, the product was a natural for the advertising specialty business, which is all about imprinting. And second, the BirdieBall was picked up by high schools for their phys ed and golf team use. Through these avenues, news of the BirdieBall's value as a training aid spread to the golfing public, and now regular retail selling is growing and prospering. *Reader's Digest* named the BirdieBall one of the best under-$50 Christmas gifts, as did *Good Morning America.* The BirdieBall has been featured in almost too many magazines to mention: *US News & World Reports, Business Week, USA Today, Golf Magazine,* and so on.

"John, who majored in marketing in college, understands full well the difficulties in getting distribution if you're a one-product company. And so, if you visit John's Web site, you'll see that the BirdieBall has become the cornerstone for a full offering of interesting golf products to help make the company an established source in the industry. More important, John is now enjoying the kind of satisfactions that every inventor hopes to achieve: satisfaction in seeing his product being used and enjoyed across the land and satisfaction in earning financial rewards for his creativity.

"And finally, but certainly not least, I'd like to introduce you to the gentleman sitting to John's left. Please give a warm welcome to the inventor of the game Going-Going Crazy, Mr. Kurt Kirckof!"

Kurt rises and waves as the audience applauds.

Kurt Kirckof

"I'm particularly pleased that Kurt accepted our invitation because this panel wouldn't be complete without a game inventor, and Kurt's story is one from which we can all benefit. Of all the categories of products I see from inventors, probably the largest is new ideas for board games. That's not difficult to understand. Lots of bright, imaginative folks like to think up board games. It's a fun, challenging, and creative thing to do. The problem is that nobody needs and few people want all of these new games, so getting the creativity to pay off is extremely difficult. Licensing is virtually impossible, and getting a retailer to stock an unknown board game from an unknown source is just about as hard.

"Because of the explosion in electronic games, fewer families are sitting around in the evening playing the kind of regular board games that you and I might remember from our own childhoods. And for those families that are still playing board games, the established companies like Parker and Pressman have talented and skilled in-house designers able to easily fill the demand. Few of these companies will even look at games from outside inventors. A shrinking market and with more than enough games already floating around to fill the demand several times over does not bode well for a new entrant.

"Doug Larson, a writer, once said, 'Some of the world's greatest feats were accomplished by people not smart enough to know that they were impossible.' I don't mean to suggest that Kurt isn't smart enough, but even knowing how hard it is to launch an unknown game from an unknown sources, Kurt, undaunted, showed that he has the grit, determination, and unbounded zeal needed to make it happen. Few among you, I believe, would have taken the chances or done the things that that Kurt has done (and continues to do) to get his game, Going-Going Crazy, out there before the public. For instance, how many of you would take a second (and third and fourth!) mortgage on your home, and how many of you would order 13,700 pieces of your own product from China and have them delivered to your own house? And do it with virtually no orders on hand?

"Kurt did what few inventors are willing to do: He hit the road, going from shop to shop, convincing local retailers to take in his game. 'If it doesn't sell, I'll take it back,' he told them. Then, with his game in stores all over western Minnesota, Kurt went to the local radio station and bought some commercials. And sure enough, his games did sell! The following year Wal-Mart put the game in a few local stores, and the year after that, it added another 40. Oh, I forgot to mention, as sales and expenses grew, Kurt remortgaged his house three more times!

"Thanks to Kurt's fierce determination and passion, Going-Going Crazy (which, he says, came to him in a dream) is now also available in Spanish, French, and Japanese versions as more and more kids enjoy and learn from the game and more retail outlets are selling the game. Kurt is managing to ground out success in an arena scattered with the bodies of failures, so what he has to tell us is certainly worth hearing. Also, I hope you'll find a few moments to visit Kurt's website at www.going-goingcrazy to see what this great game is all about.

"And that's our panel, ladies and gentlemen. Lots of other successful inventors wanted to be included, but for one reason or another we were forced to turn them away. We wanted a group that would be as representative as possible of inventors all over, and I think we achieved that goal. As you see, we have men and women, young and old, from coast to coast, border to border. Some panel members are licensing their inventions, some are self-marketing them, and some have switched from one to the other. What all these folks have in common is that through their individual creativity, intelligence, and drive, they have accomplished what inventors everywhere hope for themselves: success with their inventions and financial reward for their creativity."

Twelve Tips, Suggestions, and Pieces of Advice Offered by Our Panelists to Help You Achieve Your Own Personal Triumphs

"Time does not permit us to have each of these men and women address you individually, although you can reach them through their own websites. However, in preparation for this seminar, we had each panelist complete a questionnaire, and so we know the kind of tips and suggestions that they'd like to pass on. I am proud to present a general amalgamation of their collective thinking on matters that can impact on your individual success. Here are the 12 most important ones.

Tip No. 1. The Money; It's Always the Money

"Although not every panelist has precisely the same 12 most important pieces of advice to pass on, no topic has wider agreement than the need to have enough money to accomplish your goals. One of our panelists, Kurt Kirckof, as you saw, mortgaged and remortgaged his home, others borrowed from whomever they could, others took in partners, and others spent years scrambling to pay their bills. Virtually all of the panelists caution that self-marketing takes more money than they ever imagined it would, and if they didn't have the resources to pay the bills, or the willingness to go into debt, they would have surely folded. What I hear the panelists strongly caution is to not quit your day job. And if you do have to quit it, don't do so until the last possible minute.

"Some highly successful entrepreneurs started out on a shoestring – for instance, Bill Gates with his partner, Paul Allen, and Bill Hewlitt and his partner, David Packard. However, these were young men with the support of their families behind them. They didn't have to scramble to put food on the table, and they knew where to reach out for money when they needed it. That's not to take anything away from their enormous accomplishments, but for every Gates, Allen, Hewlitt, and Packard there are literally thousands of unknown, unsung entrepreneurs, done in by the lack of financial resources.

"I know I'm repeating myself, but it can't be said too often. More than anything else—more than the poor value of the idea, more than a lack of business skills—the principal reason for business failure is lack of money to sustain the company during the first rocky years. If you don't have it, if you can't get it—don't do it.

Tip No. 2. Forget This "Inventor" Stuff

"When Mary Sarao and Barbara Pitts first tried to make contact with companies to show their Ghostline poster board, they announced themselves as "sister inventors." Nobody wanted to see them; nobody wanted to do business with them. What these executives imagined, I'm sure, is two crazy ladies coming into their office with some weird, stupid invention and not being able to get rid of them. This quickly became obvious to Barbara and Mary, and so they turned themselves into "product developers" with official-looking business cards and letterheads. What these two sisters easily understood is that companies like to deal with other companies, and so that's what they made themselves into. Certainly there's nothing wrong with being an inventor, but the title comes with certain baggage and to ignore that reality is not a smart move. I know of no one who licenses products for a living who doesn't call himself a product developer. Surely there must be a reason.

"Similarly, if you intend to self-market your invention, looking for investors or lenders, don't identify yourself as an inventor in your business plan unless you have folks on your management team with impressive business backgrounds. Being a genius inventor is great, but not when you're asking people for money.

Tip No. 3. Loose Lips Sink Ships

"During World War II, German submarines were sinking American ships one after another in the North Atlantic, and with the U-boats apparently knowing just where to strike, it seemed that spies were all around. In an effort to help stem these tragic losses, the government put up posters with pictures of sinking ships, urging citizens not to say anything about ship sailings if they were privy to that information. "Loose Lips Sink Ships!" the posters warned, or "Shhh, the enemy may be listening."

"Of course, an idea for a new product is not as important as ship sailings during war, but it's an important secret for you and it deserves protection. If your idea is still just that, an idea in your head, it's particularly important that you tell *no one* about it who doesn't need to know. You might think to tell your favorite uncle George, whom you trust with your life, but don't do it. Certainly, good old Uncle George is not going to steal your idea, but he might brag about his smart nephew to the guys at work. Who knows who might learn of your idea second or third hand? And if the idea's as good as you think it is, and if it's not legally protected, who knows what they might do with it?

"That doesn't mean you should be secretive to the point of not telling anyone; what good it that? It just means that you should keep your wits about you. When you show your idea to a potential licensee or potential investor, leave a paper trail. Also, spend the money for a provisional patent application. If you apply yourself, the cost is $100. If you have an attorney do it for you, the cost is probably $1,000. Yes, I realize that's not cheap, but if only for your peace of mind I urge you to do so. But even if you don't, the most basic protection is to simply not talk about your idea to anyone who doesn't have to know about it. And for those service folks who do have to know, like model makers or graphic designers, have them sign a non-disclosure agreement. Just don't blab about it. The enemy might be listening.

"Also, as an aside, Dr. Loo strongly suggests that you first check the credentials of anyone you plan to hire. The doctor wasted thousands of dollars with so-called specialists who proved unable to do the assigned prototype work, and he wouldn't like to see you repeat his mistake.

Tip No. 4. The Product Is the McGuffin

"Earlier, as you'll recall, I mentioned how Alfred Hitchcock, the famous director of suspense movies, said the crime itself was not important; it was simple a "McGuffin": the dramatic device to move

Tip No. 3.
Do not tell others of your idea except when necessary.

the story along. Similarly, for successful inventor/entrepreneurs, that's how the invention itself is viewed: It's simply as a means to an end, not something to fall in love with. Your McGuffin only has one purpose—to earn royalties for you or profits for your company. If it can't do that, put it aside and move on. Your next idea will be better.

"If you look at the business skills, talents, zeal, and ambitions that the self-marketing inventors on our panel have displayed, it's easy to see that it's not only the brilliance of their particular product that gave them success; it's equally their skills and dermination that made it happen. Any of these folks would have been just as success-ful regardless of what product they were selling.

"Even if you're clever enough to build a better mousetrap, the world will not beat a path to your door unless you're also clever enough to figure out how to make them do it (and with cash in their hands).

"Similarly, if your desire is to build a career by dreaming up and licensing products, you're urged to stop thinking of yourself as an inventor and to consider yourself a product developer for two rea-sons. First, as already mentioned, it makes you a professional, which is more palatable to the companies that you'll be dealing with. And second, describing yourself as a product developer helps you view yourself as someone who does this work professionally. Inventors have love affairs with their inventions; product developers never do. Product developers understand that if they can come up with one product, they can just as easily come up with another one, and another one after that. They're one-person McGuffin factories.

Tip No. 5. "Ya Gotta Know the Territory"

"Do you remember that great musical, *The Music Man*? In the open-ing scene the traveling salesmen on the train sing about 'Ya gotta know the territory.' And if you don't know the territory, so the song goes, you'll never become a star salesman (like Professor Harold Hill). Well, in the business of licensing for profit, we're all Music Men, and if we don't know the territory, our chances for success are doubtful.

"Every professional product developer I know, like our own panelist Rodney Long, specializes in an industry in which he's an expert (or is prepared to make himself one). They will all agree that inventing the product is usually the easier part of the business; success comes from knowing *what* to invent. But if you're not in the business, how can you know what the business is looking for?

"Some professionals even specialize down to specific companies. In the toy business, for instance, I know of some independent product developers who just specialize in creating toys for Mattel. They've made themselves specialists in knowing what products each division is looking for, when they want them, and who makes the decisions. With that kind of knowledge, and being creative in the first place, these folks are able to come up with one winner after another.

"Some amateur inventors, boasting of their creativity in being able to continually dream up new product ideas, will send me a string of them. However, after seeing a few samples, it becomes obvious that these folks are just dabblers—inventing something here and something there—without any real understanding of the assorted industries in which their products are intended to compete. That's not how this business works; that's like tailoring a custom-made suit and then looking around for someone it fits. What tailor would do that? What inventor would invent a new surgical tool if she wasn't already a surgeon or surgical nurse?

"It's a small miracle if you can pop into any industry in which you have no prior experience with a new product idea that will cause those who have spent their entire careers in that business to say 'WOW!' as they rub their hands together in greedy anticipation. Most often they'll just yawn. Usually your proposed product either has already been done or doesn't deserve to be done. Sometimes that small miracle does occur: a lone inventor with a lone invention can have that success. However, that happens so infrequently that we hear about it when it does. What we don't hear about are the hundreds or thousands of others for whom it doesn't. So, whether you're selling 76 trombones or anything else, ya gotta know the territory.

Tip No. 6. The Curse of the One-Trick Pony

"If you intend to self-market your product in the conventional manner, through retail stores, you have to understand that no retailer will greet you like a new savior if you only have one product to sell. Yes, you can perhaps sell one product to folks who run specialty catalogs or have commercial websites, but the real business comes when your product is in thousands of Wal-Marts or Kmarts across the land. However, the hard truth is that these chains have little interest in doing business with you. Either have a plan to deal with it, or don't get started in the first place.

"First, large chains are hesitant to deal with small companies because they're afraid they don't have the wherewithal to supply their needs. And second, adding a new vendor is expensive for retailers, and the continuing trend for them is to reduce the numbers, rather than increase them. All retailers, especially large ones, prefer to deal with companies that can supply them with entire product categories rather than buying one product from one source and one from another. Yes, sometimes that policy will prevent consumers from having absolutely the best product for the money, but seldom does that really matter. If you can demonstrate to retailers that consumers want your product and will go elsewhere if his store doesn't sell it, then they'll be interested. Otherwise, they probably won't. Retailers view their role as providing access to products that customers want, not to convince the customers of what products they should have. You might have a perfect product idea for licensing to a company with a full line of allied products, but one product alone might not support self-marketing. Vanity and ego should play no role; understanding the nature of the business world should be the determining factor. That's why John Breaker quickly used his BirdieBall as the Cornerstone for a full line of similar products. He understood the need and had the ability to make it happen.

"Also, as our panel well knows, all products have a life cycle. One common reason for new-start failures is that the entrepreneur doesn't have powerful new product ideas in the pipeline to take the place of the fast-fading old one. It often happens that when the product that started the company dies, sadly, so does the company. Know the business, know the competition, and know what you're getting into before investing your own money or the money of others.

Tip No. 7. Reach for the Top; Accept No Substitutes

"When our panelist Rodney Long decided on what industry to specialize in, he picked fishing because he likes it and understands it, but also, he told me, because the fishing industry is made up mainly of small companies and so he knew he could deal directly with the presidents. Also, when panelists Barbara Pitts and Mary Sarao were being wooed by the leading companies in the office supply business, it was the company presidents themselves or principal corporate officers who did the wooing, not someone in the engineering department or some marketing assistant.

"I know I harp on this almost to the point of being a pest, but I feel it's impossible to overstate. If you want to license your product, you have to do it face to face, and you have to deal with the person who can make the decision. Accept no substitutes. First of all, these folks are called decision makers because that's what they do—make decisions. If you're in front of the company president or divisional vice president and if he likes what he sees, you'll get the deal. Period, end of story. If, instead, you spend your time with some engineer who views you as his enemy to begin with, you'll just get one stall after another. He couldn't say yes to the deal even if you held his mother-in-law as hostage.

"Also, with any new product, you need a champion in the company to push it through, someone who's enthusiastic enough about it to stick his neck out to make it happen. Who can you depend on to be your champion: Wilbur Q. Feeble, second marketing assistant, or Lance J. Morgan, the guy who runs the company?

Tip No. 8. Develop Mentors

"Woodrow Wilson once said that in order to do his job as President he needed all the brains he had, plus all he could borrow. For those about to enter the business world, there are lots of brains to borrow and plenty of others to rent. None of us knows everything, and so it's the wise person who understands this and seeks help as needed. Running a start-up company is lonely enough as it is, so certainly you should reach out to mentors to help lighten the load. Heaven knows, there are plenty of them around. Why guess, make false starts, and proceed down wrong paths when so many experienced folks are there to help you? Even Bill Gates talks about the valuable advice from mentors he received when just starting out.

"You might find mentors among your friends or relatives or simply by networking. It's been my experience that folks are usually quite generous with their time and advice if you ask them nicely. You would, of course, have to pay for the advice of the lawyers, accountants, and other specialists you might hire, but they might have friends in other areas who'd be happy to offer pro bono advice. One person leads to another. Either in your hometown or within easy driving distance is probably an inventors' club for you to join for a modest membership fee. Many of the members have already done what you're aspiring to do, and the whole point of these clubs is for members to help each other.

"Beyond your own circle of mentor contacts, a good place to start is with SCORE (www.score.org). This is a nonprofit organization of retired executives whose pleasure is to help inventors and new entrepreneurs. It would be difficult for me to think of any facet of business that can't be intelligently discussed by one or another of the SCORE volunteers. They're just sitting there, hoping you'll call. Also, you might pose a question to one of the Internet inventor chat rooms; they're easy to track down. Further, our own panelists, Barbara and Mary, host a website dedicated to helping other inventors (www.ask-theinventors.com), and I myself am happy to answer inventor questions (www.Money4ideas.com). I suppose many of you already know of the famous 50-50-90 rule. It states that anytime you have a 50-50 chance of doing something right, there's a 90% chance that you'll get it wrong. With mentors by your side, that won't happen.

Tip No. 9. Step One: Insert Tab A into Slot B

"As my C.R.A.S.H. course explains, there's a precise order in the way successful inventors proceed, as all of our panelists would happily point out, and the first two steps are (1) make sure your product idea is original and (2) make sure there's really a market for it. Just because you can't find the product idea at your local retailer doesn't mean that it's original; and just because your aunt Minnie said she'd buy one doesn't mean that a true market for it exists. No matter how you intend to proceed after that, first do steps 1 and 2, and do them *exhaustively*. Do *not* rush off to see a patent attorney. Do *not* rush to hire an invention submission company. Do *not* rush off to hire a model maker to build you a prototype. Do *not* rush out to look for investors. Do *not* make appointments with prospective licensees. And do *not* blab about your idea to anyone who doesn't need to know. Read my lips: Research your idea to make sure it's original. Research your idea to see if it's really of value.

"First, go to Google, Yahoo, or one of the other search engines and search to see if your product exists. Try a couple of different definitions. Next, search the patent files on your own. If you don't find anything, let a professional search again. Visit stores, chat with clerks. You can ask about your idea without giving away precisely what you have in mind. Don't ask friends and relatives, and don't just hear what you want to hear. Talk with folks in the business. Search, and search, and search some more because the results of steps 1 and 2 will determine everything that follows. Finally, if you are utterly convinced that your idea is unique and original, and if you're utterly convinced that a sizable market for it exits, then, *and only then,* proceed to the next steps on the way to fame and glory.

Tip No. 10. Remember, It's the How, Not the What, that Might Pique Someone's Interest

"That's a paraphrase of a comment by Rodney Long and mentioned by some of our other panelists as well. Rodney, being a professional licensor, was of course thinking about licensing when he made the observation, but it's just as true for any inventor looking for investors or lenders. Lots of folks will come up with the "what" and think they've done something; but until they can figure out the "how," all they have is an idea, which, by itself, has little or no commercial value. The "what" is simply an observation ("What this country needs is . . .") that might earn you a thank-you-for-your-suggestion note from the company, but a fully designed product that shows the "how," as evidenced by a working prototype, might command their attention.

"After steps 1 and 2, researching your idea for originality and commercial value, the next step is to actually invent it. That is, after all, what makes someone an inventor; the act of inventing the product. As obvious as that might be, not everyone who calls herself an inventor seems able to grasp its meaning. Once you've invented the product and made a working prototype to demonstrate that your invention works, then (and only then) you can think about patenting it or licensing it or looking for investors. Not before; after.

Tip No. 11. Have Clear Goals

"You're in charge. Remember that. If you're negotiating a licensing deal with a manufacturer, you're in charge if you have clearly defined goals and clear justifications for everything you're demanding. If you're negotiating with an investor, you're in charge if you have clearly defined investment requirements and if you can clearly justify the funds being requested in return for the shares being offered. And if you're embarking on a new business, you're in charge if you have clearly defined goals as to what you intend for this business to achieve and if you have a clearly defined strategy for how to achieve them. A plan to build quick profits and sell out is different from a plan to build a company to be left to your children.

"With a clear vision of where you're going and how you expect to get there, you can proceed with enthusiasm and confidence. Whether you're looking for a licensee, a lender, or an investor, this business requires all of your focus, all of your strength, and all of your commitment. Nothing good can come from giving less. When Alice met the Cheshire Cat, she asked him for directions. The Cat asked Alice where she wanted to go. "I don't much care where," she replied. "Then it doesn't matter where you go," replied the Cat. Unlike Alice, we here at the institute realize that you *do* care where you're going. We're here to help you make the right choice and to help you do it in the most successful way possible. That's the whole purpose of this seminar, and it neatly brings us to the final point that our panel would like to express.

Tip No. 12. Don't Dawdle!

"Why are you folks still just sitting there? Don't you realize that whatever your idea is, someone else has probably also thought of it? Don't you know that even as we speak, someone else might be searching to see if the product's original and may in fact already be building a prototype? Why wait? Why do nothing? If you just continue to do what you've always done, won't you still be what you've always been? I believe I speak for the entire panel when I say it's obvious that you're all bright, ambitious, and enterprising; and I have no doubt that your product ideas are brilliant, original, and useful. I assume it only remains for you to decide how you wish to proceed—through licensing your idea, selling your idea, building a company around it, or using it as a vehicle for franchising. I hope we here at the Institute have been able to provide you some guidance in this matter and that you will all now go out with confidence to find the rewards that your creativity entitles you to. And so, as this conference draws to a close, on behalf of the panel, the Institute, and myself, we wish you all luck, and we wish you great fortune. As Dr. Seuss aptly said,

> Will you succeed?
> Yes indeed, yes indeed.
> Ninety eight and three quarters
> percent guaranteed.

Thank you all for coming!"

The meeting hall erupts in a cacophony of noise as books are slammed shut, laptops quickly closed, bags snapped and locked, chairs pushed back, and the inventors of every stripe rush off to confidently face the wonderful adventures awaiting them.

CONTRACTS AND LICENSING AGREEMENTS FOR INVENTORS

Inventor's Confidential Disclosure Agreement*

INFORMATION the parties (the party disclosing the CONFIDEN-TIAL INFORMATION and the party receiving same are hereinafter called "DISCLOSER" and "RECIPIENT," respectively) agree as follows:

1. To be protected hereunder, CONFIDENTIAL INFORMATION must be disclosed in written or graphic form conspicuously labeled with the name of the DISCLOSER as CONFIDENTIAL INFOR-MATION, or disclosed orally and documented in detail, labeled as above, and submitted by DISCLOSER in written or graphic form to RECIPIENT within twenty (20) business days thereafter.

2. RECIPIENT agrees to receive and hold all such CONFIDENTIAL INFORMATION acquired from DISCLOSER in strict confidence and to disclose same within its own organization only, and only to those of its employees who have agreed in writing (under RECIPIENT's own blanket or specified agreement form) to pro-tect and preserve the confidentiality of such disclosures and who are designated by RECIPIENT to evaluate the CONFIDENTIAL INFORMATION for the aforementioned purposes. Without affect-ing the generality of the foregoing, RECIPIENT will exercise no less care to safeguard the CONFIDENTIAL INFORMATION acquired from DISCLOSER than RECIPIENT exercises in safeguarding its own confidential or proprietary information.

3. RECIPIENT agrees that it will not disclose or use CONFIDEN-TIAL INFORMATION acquired from DISCLOSER, in whole or

Exhibit A.1 Inventor's Confidential Disclosure Agreement
1997-2001 PatentCafe.com, Inc.

*To download and customize this form for your own personal use, please visit www.wiley.com/go/amazingsecrets.

in part, for any purposes other than those expressly permitted herein. Without affecting the generality of the foregoing, RECIPI-ENT agrees that it will not disclose any such CONFIDENTIAL INFORMATION to any third party, or use same for its own benefit or for the benefit of any third party.

4. The foregoing restrictions on RECIPIENT's disclosure and use of CONFIDENTIAL INFORMATION acquired from DISCLOSER shall not apply to the extent of information (i) known to RECIPI-ENT prior to receipt from DISCLOSER (ii) of public knowledge without breach of RECIPIENT's obligation hereunder, (iii) rightfully acquired by RECIPIENT from a third party without restriction on disclosure or use, (iv) disclosed by DISCLOSER to a third party without restriction on disclosure or use, or (v) independently developed by RECIPIENT relies as relieving it of the restrictions hereunder on disclosure or use of such CONFIDENTIAL INFOR-MATION, and provided further that in the case of any of events (ii), (iii), (iv), and (v), the removal of restrictions shall be effective only from and after the date of occurrence of the applicable event.

5. The furnishing of CONFIDENTIAL INFORMATION hereunder shall not constitute or be construed as a grant of any express or implied license or other right, or a covenant not to sue or forbearance from any other right of action (except as to permitted activities hereunder), by DISCLOSER to RECIPIENT under any of DISCLOSER's patents or other intellectual property rights.

6. This Agreement shall commence as of the day and year first written above and shall continue with respect to any dislosures of CONFIDENTIAL INFORMATION by DISCLOSER to RECIPIENT within twelve (12) months thereafter, at the end of which time the Agreement shall expire, unless terminated earlier by either party at any time on ten (10) days prior written notice to the other party.

Exhibit A.1   *(Continued)*

Upon expiration or termination of this Agreement, RECIPIENT shall immediately cease any and all disclosures or uses of CONFIDENTIAL INFORMATION acquired from DISCLOSER (except to the extent relieved from restrictions pursuant to paragraph 4 above) and at DISCLOSER's request RECIPIENT shall promptly return all written, graphic, and other tangible forms of the CONFIDENTIAL INFORMATION (including notes or other write-ups thereof made by RECIPIENT in connection with the disclosures by DISCLOSER) and all copies thereof made by RECIPIENT except one copy for record retention only.

7. The obligations of RECIPIENT respecting disclosure and use of CONFIDENTIAL INFORMATION acquired from DISCLOSER shall survive expiration or termination of this Agreement and shall continue for a period of three (3) years thereafter or, with respect to any applicable portion of the CONFIDENTIAL INFORMATION, until the effective date of any of the events recited in paragraph 4, whichever occurs first. After such time RECIPIENT shall be relieved of all such obligations.

8. In the event that the parties enter into a written contract concerning a business relationship of the type contemplated herein, the provisions of such contract concerning confidentiality of information shall supersede and prevail over any conflicting provisions of this Agreement. Each party acknowledges its acceptance of this Agreement by the signature below of its authorized officer on duplicate counterparts of the Agreement, one of which fully executed counterparts is to be retained by each party.

Date: _____   Signature: _____
                                                    (yours)

Date: _____   Signature: _____
                                                    (theirs)

Exhibit A.1   *(Continued)*

Supplier Nondisclosure Agreement*

Date: _____

This agreement between _____ hereinafter referred to as INVENTOR and _____ hereinafter referred to as SUPPLIER is entered into under the following terms and conditions.

INVENTOR invites supplier to provide cost information for the following work: To perform engineering work on product concept as per sketches and specifications to be submitted. To enable SUPPLIER to perform this service, it is necessary for the INVENTOR to provide certain secret or confidential information (herein referred to as "Subject Matter") relating to his invention or product concept concerning a _____.

1. SUPPLIER agrees not to reveal, publish, or communicate the Subject Matter to any other party for any purpose without the written consent of the INVENTOR.

2. SUPPLIER agrees to use this information strictly for the purpose of performing his service to the INVENTOR and agrees to hold it in the strictest confidence at all times.

3. All of the work done by the SUPPLIER in connection with the Subject Matter, whether or not patentable, is and shall remain the sole property of the INVENTOR.

4. Upon completion of the assignment, if awarded, SUPPLIER agrees to return all material and objects that may have been provided by the INVENTOR, plus any copies he might have made.

Exhibit A.2   Supplier Nondisclosure Agreement
*To download and customize this form for your own personal use, please visit www. wiley.com/go/amazingsecrets.

5. If portions of the Subject Matter are already in the public domain, or if SUPPLIER can document that he has prior knowledge of the material from another source, he is not obligated to hold that specific material in confidence.

6. Except for possible exclusions indicated in Point 5, this Agreement shall be in force for five (5) years, commencing with the above date. After this time, the obligations of confidentiality are canceled.

This Agreement shall be construed in accordance with the laws of the State of _____ and contains the entire understanding of the parties hereto.

IN WITNESS WHEREOF, the parties have indicated their agreement to all of the above terms by signing and dating where below indicated.

INVENTOR: _____ Date: _____

SUPPLIER: _____ Date: _____

Exhibit A.2   *(Continued)*

Company Confidentiality Agreement*

Date: _____   Inventor Name: _____
Harvey Reese Associates   Inventor Address: _____
614 South 8ᵗʰ Street
Philadelphia, PA 109147   _____
TheReeseCo@aol.com   Name of Invention: _____

INVENTOR confirms that to the best of his or her knowledge, he or she is the originator of the subject product idea and has the full power to submit it for REESE's evaluation.

REESE confirms his policy not to show the invention outside of his organization without express INVENTOR permission. REESE also confirms his agreement not to use this information for his own advantage without INVENTOR's express permission.

All information about the INVENTOR's idea shall remain confidential except in the following circumstances:

1. If information about the idea becomes public knowledge through no fault of REESE.

2. If inventor on his/her own discloses product information to the public, or if such product information comes to REESE in good faith from outside sources.

3. If REESE is already working on a similar or identical product concept as evidenced by REESE's internal records or files.

Exhibit A.3 Company Confidentiality Agreement
*To download and customize this form for your own personal use, please visit www.wiley.com/go/amazingsecrets.

REESE confirms that any design changes he might make in the product idea will automatically be assigned to the INVENTOR without cost or obligation.

UNDERSTOOD AND AGREED: _____
Inventor's Signature

CONFIRMED: _____
Harvey Reese Associates

Exhibit A.3 *(Continued)*

Licensing Agreement*

Date: _____

_____, located

at _____

(hereinafter referred to as LICENSOR), has given _____,
located at _____ (hereinafter
referred to as LICENSEE), the exclusive production and marketing
rights to [his/her] new product concept as herein described and
as per drawings and/or prototype samples previously submitted).
In exchange, LICENSEE agrees to pay LICENSOR a royalty in the
amount and under the terms outlined in this Agreement.

PRODUCT DESCRIPTION:

_____

_____

_____

1. ROYALTY PAYMENTS. A _____ % (_____ percent) royalty,
based on net selling price, will be paid by LICENSEE to LICENSOR
on all sales of subject product and all subsequent variations thereof
by LICENSEE, its subsidiaries, and/or associate companies.

The term "net selling price" shall mean the price LICENSEE
receives from its customers, less any discounts for volume, promotion, defects, or freight.

Royalty payments are to be made monthly on the 30th day of the
month following shipment to LICENSEE's customers, and LICENSOR

Exhibit A.4 Licensing Agreement

*To download and customize this form for your own personal use, please visit
www.wiley.com/go/amazingsecrets.

shall have the rights to examine LICENSEE's books and records as they pertain thereto. Further, LICENSEE shall reimburse LICENSOR for any costs [he/she] might incur in collecting overdue royalty payments.

2. TERRITORY. LICENSEE shall have the right to market this product [these products] throughout the United States, its possessions, Canada and Mexico, and may do so through any legal distribution channels it desires and in any manner it sees fit without prior approval from LICENSOR. However, LICENSEE agrees that it will not knowingly sell to parties who will resell the product(s) outside of the licensed territory.

3. ADVANCE PAYMENT. Upon execution of this Agreement, LICENSEE will make a non-refundable payment to LICENSOR of $_____, which shall be construed as an advance against future earned royalties.

4. COPYRIGHT, PATENT AND TRADEMARK NOTICES. LICENSEE agrees that on the product's [products'] packaging and collateral material there will be printed notices of patents issued or pending and applicable trademark notices showing the LICENSOR as the owner of said patents, trademarks, or copyrights under exclusive license to LICENSEE.

In the event there has been no previous registration or patent application for the licensed product(s), LICENSEE may, at LICENSEE'S discretion and expense, make such application or registration in the name of the LICENSOR. However, LICENSEE agrees that at the termination or expiration of this Agreement, LICENSEE will be deemed to have assigned, transferred, and conveyed to LICENSOR all trade rights, equities, goodwill, titles, or other rights on and to licensed products which may have been attained by the LICENSEE. Any such transfer shall be without consideration other than as specified in this Agreement.

Exhibit A.4 *(Continued)*

5. TERMS AND WARRANTS. This Agreement shall be considered to be in force for so long as LICENSEE continues to sell the original product(s) or subsequent extensions and/or variations thereof. However, it is herein acknowledged that LICENSEE makes no warrants to LICENSOR in regard to minimum sales and/or royalty payment guarantees. Further, LICENSOR agrees that, for the life of this Agreement, he [she] will not create and/or provide directly competitive products to another manufacturer or distributor without giving the right of first refusal to LICENSEE.

6. PRODUCT DESIGNS. LICENSOR agrees to furnish conceptual product designs, if requested, for the initial product(s) and all subsequent variations and extensions at no charge to LICENSEE. In addition, if requested, LICENSOR shall assist in the design of packaging, point-of-purchase material, displays, etc., at no charge to LICENSEE.

However, costs for finished art, photography, typography, mechanical preparation, etc., will be borne by LICENSEE.

7. QUALITY OF MERCHANDISE. LICENSEE agrees that the licensed product(s) will be produced and distributed in accordance with federal, state, and local laws. LICENSEE further agrees to submit a sample of said product(s), its cartons, containers, and packaging materials to LICENSOR for approval (which approval shall not be reasonably withheld). Any item not specifically disapproved within fifteen (15) working days after submission shall be deemed to be approved. The product(s) may not thereafter be materially changed without approval of LICENSOR.

8. DEFAULT, BANKRUPTCY, VIOLATION, ETC.

A. In the event LICENSEE does not commence to manufacture, distribute, and sell the product(s) within _____ months

Exhibit A.4 *(Continued)*

after the execution of this Agreement, LICENSOR, in addition to any other remedies that might be available to him [her], shall have the option of canceling this Agreement. Should this event occur, to be activated by registered letter, LICENSEE shall not continue with the product's development and is obligated to return all prototype samples and drawings to LICENSOR.

B. In the event LICENSEE files a petition in bankruptcy, or if the LICENSEE becomes insolvent, or makes an assignment for the benefit of creditors, the license granted hereunder shall terminate automatically without the requirement of written notice. No further sales of licensed product(s) may be made by LICENSEE, its receivers, agents, administrators, or assigns without the express written approval of the LICENSOR.

C. If LICENSEE shall violate any other obligations under the terms of this Agreement, and upon receiving written notice of this violation by LICENSOR, LICENSEE shall have thirty (30) days to remedy such violation. If this has not been done, LICENSOR shall have the option of canceling this Agreement upon ten (10) days written notice. If this event occurs, all sales activity must cease and any royalties owing are immediately due.

9. LICENSEE'S RIGHT TO TERMINATE. Notwithstanding anything contained in this Agreement, LICENSEE shall have the absolute right to cancel this Agreement at any time by notifying LICEN-SOR of his [her] decision in writing to discontinue the sale of the product(s) covered by this Agreement. The cancellation shall be without recourse from LICENSOR other than for the collection of any royalty money that might be due him [her].

10. INDEMNIFICATION. LICENSEE agrees to obtain, at its own expense, product liability insurance for at least $2,000,000

Exhibit A.4 *(Continued)*

combined single unit for LICENSEE and LICENSOR against claims, suits, loss, or damage arising out of any alleged defect in the licensed product(s). As proof of such insurance, LICENSEE shall submit to LICENSOR a fully paid certificate of insurance naming LICENSOR as an insured party. This submission is to be made before any licensed product is distributed or sold.

11. NO PARTNERSHIP, ETC. This Agreement shall be binding upon the successors and assigns of the parties hereto. Nothing contained in this Agreement shall be construed to place the parties in the relationship of legal representatives, partners, or joint venturers. Neither LICENSOR or LICENSEE shall have the power to bind or obligate in any manner whatsoever other than as per this Agreement.

12. GOVERNING LAW. This Agreement shall be construed in accordance with the laws of the state of _____. IN WITNESS WHEREOF, THE PARTIES HERETO HAVE SIGNED THIS agreement as of the day and year written below.

_____   _____
LICENSEE   LICENSOR

Date: _____   Date: _____

Exhibit A.4   *(Continued)*

U.S. Patent and Trademark Office Application Forms

PTO/SB/95 (07-05)
Approved for use through 07/31/2008. OMB 0651-0030
U.S. Patent and Trademark Office; U.S. DEPARTMENT OF COMMERCE
Under the Paperwork Reduction Act of 1995, no persons are required to respond to a collection of information unless it displays a valid OMB control number.

Disclosure Document Deposit Request

Mail to:

Mail Stop DD
Commissioner for Patents
P.O. Box 1450
Alexandria, VA 22313-1450

Inventor(s): _____

Title of Invention: _____

Enclosed is a disclosure of the above-titled invention consisting of _____ sheets of description and _____ sheets of drawings. A check or money order in the amount of _____ is enclosed to cover the fee (37 CFR 1.21(c)).

The undersigned, being a named inventor of the disclosed invention, requests that the enclosed papers be accepted under the Disclosure Document Program, and that they be preserved for a period of two years.

_____	_____
Signature of Inventor	Address
_____	_____
Typed or printed name	Address
_____	_____
Date	City, State, Zip

NOTICE OF INVENTORS

It should be clearly understood that a Disclosure Document is not a patent application, nor will its receipt date in any way become the effective filing date of a later filed patent application. A Disclosure Document may be relied upon only as evidence of conception of an invention and a patent application should be diligently filed if patent protection is desired.

Your Disclosure Document will be retained for two years after the date it was received by the United States Patent and Trademark Office (USPTO) and will be destroyed thereafter unless it is referred to in a related patent application filed within the two-year period. The Disclosure Document may be referred to by way of a letter of transmittal in a new patent application or by a separate letter filed in a pending application. Unless it is desired to have the USPTO retain the Disclosure Document beyond the two-year period, it is not required that it be referred to in the patent application.

The two-year retention period should not be considered to be a "grace period" during which the inventor can wait to file his/her patent application without possible loss of benefits. It must be recognized that in establishing priority of invention an affidavit or testimony referring to a Disclosure Document must usually also establish diligence in completing the invention or in filing the patent application since the filing of the Disclosure Document.

If you are not familiar with what is considered to be "diligence in completing the invention" or "reduction to practice" under the patent law or if you have other questions about patent matters, you are advised to consult with an attorney or agent registered to practice before the USPTO. The publication, *Attorneys and Agents Registered to Practice Before the United States Patent and Trademark Office*, is available from the **Superintendent of Documents, Washington, DC 20402.** Patent attorneys and agents are also listed in the telephone directory of most major cities. Also, many large cities have associations of patent attorneys which may be consulted.

You are also reminded that any public use or sale in the United States or publication of your invention anywhere in the world more than one year prior to the filing of a patent application on that invention will prohibit the granting of a patent on it.

Disclosures of inventions which have been understood and witnessed by persons and/or notarized are other examples of evidence which may also be used to establish priority.

There is a nationwide network of Patent and Trademark Depository Libraries (PTDLs), which have collections of patents and patent-related reference materials available to the public, including automated access to USPTO databases. Publications such as *General Information Concerning Patents* are available at the PTDLs, as well as the USPTO's Web site at www.uspto.gov. To find out the location of the PTDL closest to you, please consult the complete listing of all PTDLs that appears on the USPTO's Web site or in every issue of the Official Gazette, or call the USPTO's General Information Services at 800-PTO-9199 (800-786-9199) or 703 308-HELP (703-308-4357). To ensure assistance from a PTDL staff member, you may wish to contact a PTDL prior to visiting to learn about its collections, services, and hours.

Burden Hour Statement: This collection of information is used to file (and by the USPTO to process) Disclosure Document Deposit Requests. Confidentiality is governed by 35 U.S.C. 122 and 37 CFR 1.14. This collection is estimated to take 12 minutes to complete, including gathering, preparing, and submitting the completed application form to the USPTO. Time will vary depending upon the individual case. Any comments on the amount of time you require to complete this form and/or suggestions for reducing this burden, should be sent to the Chief Information Officer, U.S. Patent and Trademark Office, U.S. Department of Commerce, P.O. Box 1450, Alexandria, VA 22313-1450. DO NOT SEND FEES OR COMPLETED FORMS TO THIS ADDRESS. **SEND TO: Mail Stop DD, Commissioner for Patents, P.O. Box 1450, Alexandria, VA 22313-1450.**

If you need assistance in completing the form, call 1-800-PTO-9199 and select option 2.

Exhibit B.1   Disclosure Document Deposit Request

To download and customize this form for your own personal use, please visit www.wiley.com/go/amazingsecrets.

PTO/SB/16 (05-07)
Approved for use through 05/31/2007. OMB 0651-0032
U.S. Patent and Trademark Office; U.S. DEPARTMENT OF COMMERCE
Under the Paperwork Reduction Act of 1995, no persons are required to respond to a collection of information unless it displays a valid OMB control number.

PROVISIONAL APPLICATION FOR PATENT COVER SHEET – Page 1 of 2

This is a request for filing a PROVISIONAL APPLICATION FOR PATENT under 37 CFR 1.53(c).

Express Mail Label No. _____

INVENTOR(S)		
Given Name (first and middle [if any])	Family Name or Surname	Residence (City and either State or Foreign Country)

Additional inventors are being named on the _____ *separately numbered sheets attached hereto*

TITLE OF THE INVENTION (500 characters max):

Direct all correspondence to: **CORRESPONDENCE ADDRESS**

☐ The address corresponding to Customer Number: [   ]

OR

☐ Firm or Individual Name

Address

City	State	Zip
Country	Telephone	Email

ENCLOSED APPLICATION PARTS *(check all that apply)*

☐ Application Data Sheet. See 37 CFR 1.76   ☐ CD(s), Number of CDs _____

☐ Drawing(s) *Number of Sheets* _____   ☐ Other (specify) _____

☐ Specification (e.g. description of the invention) *Number of Pages* _____

Fees Due: Filing Fee of $200 ($100 for small entity). If the specification and drawings exceed 100 sheets of paper, an application size fee is also due, which is $250 ($125 for small entity) for each additional 50 sheets or fraction thereof. See 35 U.S.C. 41(a)(1)(G) and 37 CFR 1.16(s).

METHOD OF PAYMENT OF THE FILING FEE AND APPLICATION SIZE FEE FOR THIS PROVISIONAL APPLICATION FOR PATENT

☐ Applicant claims small entity status. See 37 CFR 1.27.

☐ A check or money order is enclosed to cover the filing fee and application size fee (if applicable).

☐ Payment by credit card. Form PTO-2038 is attached   **TOTAL FEE AMOUNT ($)**

☐ The Director is hereby authorized to charge the filing fee and application size fee (if applicable) or credit any overpayment to Deposit

Account Number: _____.   A duplicative copy of this form is enclosed for fee processing.

USE ONLY FOR FILING A PROVISIONAL APPLICATION FOR PATENT

This collection of information is required by 37 CFR 1.51. The information is required to obtain or retain a benefit by the public which is to file (and by the USPTO to process) an application. Confidentiality is governed by 35 U.S.C. 122 and 37 CFR 1.11 and 1.14. This collection is estimated to take 8 hours to complete, including gathering, preparing, and submitting the completed application form to the USPTO. Time will vary depending upon the individual case. Any comments on the amount of time you require to complete this form and/or suggestions for reducing this burden, should be sent to the Chief Information Officer, U.S. Patent and Trademark Office, U.S. Department of Commerce, P.O. Box 1450, Alexandria, VA 22313-1450. DO NOT SEND FEES OR COMPLETED FORMS TO THIS ADDRESS. **SEND TO: Commissioner for Patents, P.O. Box 1450, Alexandria, VA 22313-1450.**
If you need assistance in completing the form, call 1-800-PTO-9199 and select option 2.

Exhibit B.2   Provisional Application for Patent

To download and customize this form for your own personal use, please visit www.wiley.com/go/amazingsecrets.

PTO/SB/16 (05-07)
Approved for use through 05/31/2007. OMB 0651-0032
U.S. Patent and Trademark Office; U.S. DEPARTMENT OF COMMERCE
Under the Paperwork Reduction Act of 1995, no persons are required to respond to a collection of information unless it displays a valid OMB control number.

The invention was made by an agency of the United States Government or under a contract with an agency of the United States Government.

☐ No.

☐ Yes, the name of the U.S. Government agency and the Government contract number are: _____

WARNING:

Petitioner/applicant is cautioned to avoid submitting personal information in documents filed in a patent application that may contribute to identity theft. Personal information such as social security numbers, bank account numbers, or credit card numbers (other than a check or credit card authorization form PTO-2038 submitted for payment purposes) is never required by the USPTO to support a petition or an application. If this type of personal information is included in documents submitted to the USPTO, petitioners/applicants should consider redacting such personal information from the documents before submitting them to the USPTO. Petitioner/applicant is advised that the record of a patent application is available to the public after publication of the application (unless a non-publication request in compliance with 37 CFR 1.213(a) is made in the application) or issuance of a patent. Furthermore, the record from an abandoned application may also be available to the public if the application is referenced in a published application or an issued patent (see 37 CFR 1.14). Checks and credit card authorization forms PTO-2038 submitted for payment purposes are not retained in the application file and therefore are not publicly available.

SIGNATURE _____   Date_____

TYPED or PRINTED NAME _____   REGISTRATION NO. _____
(if appropriate)

TELEPHONE _____   Docket Number: _____

Exhibit B.2   *(Continued)*

PTO/SB/18 (05-07)
Approved for use through 05/31/2007. OMB 0651-0032
U.S. Patent and Trademark Office; U.S. DEPARTMENT OF COMMERCE
Under the Paperwork Reduction Act of 1995, no persons are required to respond to a collection of information unless it displays a valid OMB control number.

DESIGN
PATENT APPLICATION
TRANSMITTAL

(Only for new nonprovisional applications under 37 CFR 1.53(b))

Attorney Docket No.	
First Named Inventor	
Title	
Express Mail Label No.	

ADDRESS TO:
Commissioner for Patents
P.O. Box 1450
Alexandria, VA 22313-1450

DESIGN V. UTILITY: A "design patent" protects an article's ornamental appearance (e.g., the way an article looks) (35 U.S.C. 171), while a "utility patent" protects the way an article is used and works (35 U.S.C. 101). The ornamental appearance of an article includes its shape/configuration or surface ornamentation upon the article, or both. Both a design and a utility patent may be obtained on an article if invention resides both in its ornamental appearance and its utility. For more information, see MPEP 1502.01.

APPLICATION ELEMENTS
See MPEP 1500 concerning design patent application contents.

1. ☐ Fee Transmittal Form *(e.g., PTO/SB/17)*
   (Submit an original, and a duplicate for fee processing)

2. ☐ Applicant claims small entity status.
   See 37 CFR 1.27.

3. ☐ Specification   [Total Pages _____]
   (preferred arrangement set forth below, MPEP 1503.01)
   - Preamble
   - Cross References to Related Applications
   - Statement Regarding Fed sponsored R & D
   - Description of the figure(s) of the drawings
   - Feature description
   - Claim (only one (1) claim permitted, MPEP 1503.03)

4. ☐ Drawing(s) *(37 CFR 1.152)* [Total Sheets _____]

5. Oath or Declaration   [Total Pages _____]

   a. ☐ Newly executed (original or copy)

   b. ☐ A copy from a prior application (37 CFR 1.63(d))
      (for continuation/divisional with Box 16 completed)
      DELETION OF INVENTOR(S)
      i. ☐ Signed statement attached deleting
         inventor(s) named in the prior application,
         see 37 CFR 1.63(d)(2) and 1.33(b)

6. ☐ Application Data Sheet. See 37 CFR 1.76

ACCOMPANYING APPLICATION PARTS

7. ☐ Assignment Papers (cover sheet & document(s))

8. ☐ 37 CFR 3.73(b) Statement   ☐ Power of
   (when there is an assignee)   Attorney

9. ☐ English Translation Document *(if applicable)*

10. ☐ Information Disclosure Statement (IDS)
    PTO/SB/08 or PTO-1449
    ☐ Copies of foreign patent documents,
       publications, & other information

11. ☐ Preliminary Amendment

12. ☐ Return Receipt Postcard (MPEP 503)
    (Should be specifically itemized)

13. ☐ Certified Copy of Priority Document(s)
    (if foreign priority is claimed)

14. ☐ Request for Expedited Examination of a Design Application
    (37 CFR 1.155) (NOTE: Use "Mail Stop Expedited Design")

15. ☐ Other:

16. **If a CONTINUING APPLICATION,** check appropriate box, and supply the requisite information below and in the first sentence of the specification following the title, or in an Application Data Sheet under 37 CFR 1.76:

☐ Continuation   ☐ Divisional   ☐ Continuation-in-part (CIP) of prior application No.: _____

Prior application information: Examiner _____ Art Unit: _____

17. CORRESPONDENCE ADDRESS

☐ The address associated with Customer Number:		**OR**	☐ Correspondence address below

Name	
Address	

City		State		Zip Code	

Country		Telephone		Email	

Signature		Date	
Name (Print/Type)		Registration No. (Attorney/Agent)	

Exhibit B.3   Design Patent Application

To download and customize this form for your own personal use, please visit www.wiley.com/go/amazingsecrets.

PTO/SB/05 (05-07)
Approved for use through 05/31/2007. OMB 0651-0032
U.S. Patent and Trademark Office. U.S. DEPARTMENT OF COMMERCE
Under the Paperwork Reduction Act of 1995, no persons are required to respond to a collection of information unless it displays a valid OMB control number.

UTILITY PATENT APPLICATION TRANSMITTAL

(Only for new nonprovisional applications under 37 CFR 1.53(b))

Attorney Docket No.	
First Inventor	
Title	
Express Mail Label No.	

APPLICATION ELEMENTS
See MPEP chapter 600 concerning utility patent application contents.

ADDRESS TO: Commissioner for Patents
P.O. Box 1450
Alexandria VA 22313-1450

1. ☐ **Fee Transmittal Form** (e.g., PTO/SB/17)
   (Submit an original and a duplicate for fee processing)
2. ☐ **Applicant claims small entity status.**
   See 37 CFR 1.27.
3. ☐ **Specification** [*Total Pages_____*]
   Both the claims and abstract must start on a new page
   (For information on the preferred arrangement, see MPEP 608.01(a))
4. ☐ **Drawing(s)** (35 U.S.C. 113) [*Total Sheets _____*]

5. **Oath or Declaration** [*Total Sheets _____*]
   a. ☐ Newly executed (original or copy)
   b. ☐ A copy from a prior application (37 CFR 1.63(d))
      (for continuation/divisional with Box 18 completed)
      i. ☐ **DELETION OF INVENTOR(S)**
         Signed statement attached deleting inventor(s)
         name in the prior application, see 37 CFR
         1.63(d)(2) and 1.33(b).

6. ☐ **Application Data Sheet.** See 37 CFR 1.76

7. ☐ **CD-ROM or CD-R** in duplicate, large table or
   Computer Program *(Appendix)*
   ☐ Landscape Table on CD

8. **Nucleotide and/or Amino Acid Sequence Submission**
   (if applicable, items a. – c. are required)
   a. ☐ Computer Readable Form (CRF)
   b. ☐ Specification Sequence Listing on:

      i. ☐ CD-ROM or CD-R (2 copies); or
      ii. ☐ Paper

   c. ☐ Statements verifying identity of above copies

ACCOMPANYING APPLICATION PARTS

9. ☐ **Assignment Papers** (cover sheet (PTO-1595) & document(s))

   Name of Assignee_____

   _____

10. ☐ **37 CFR 3.73(b) Statement**   ☐ Power of
    (when there is an assignee)   Attorney

11. ☐ **English Translation Document** *(if applicable)*

12. ☐ **Information Disclosure Statement** (PTO/SB/08 or PTO-1449)
    ☐ Copies of foreign patent documents,
       publications, & other information

13. ☐ **Preliminary Amendment**

14. ☐ **Return Receipt Postcard** (MPEP 503)
    (Should be specifically itemized)

15. ☐ **Certified Copy of Priority Document(s)**
    (if foreign priority is claimed)

16. ☐ **Nonpublication Request** under 35 U.S.C. 122(b)(2)(B)(i).
    Applicant must attach form PTO/SB/35 or equivalent.

17. ☐ **Other:**_____

18. If a CONTINUING APPLICATION, check appropriate box, and supply the requisite information below and in the first sentence of the specification following the title, or in an Application Data Sheet under 37 CFR 1.76:

☐ Continuation   ☐ Divisional   ☐ Continuation-in-part (CIP)   of prior application No.: ....

Prior application information: Examiner _____   Art Unit: _____

19. CORRESPONDENCE ADDRESS

☐ The address associated with Customer Number: [_____]   **OR**   ☐ Correspondence address below

Name	
Address	

City		State		Zip Code	
Country		Telephone		Email	

Signature		Date	
Name (Print/Type)		Registration No. (Attorney/Agent)	

This collection of information is required by 37 CFR 1.53(b). The information is required to obtain or retain a benefit by the public which is to file (and by the USPTO to process) an application. Confidentiality is governed by 35 U.S.C. 122 and 37 CFR 1.11 and 1.14. This collection is estimated to take 12 minutes to complete, including gathering, preparing, and submitting the completed application form to the USPTO. Time will vary depending upon the individual case. Any comments on the amount of time you require to complete this form and/or suggestions for reducing this burden, should be sent to the Chief Information Officer, U.S. Patent and Trademark Office, U.S. Department of Commerce, P.O. Box 1450, Alexandria, VA 22313-1450. DO NOT SEND FEES OR COMPLETED FORMS TO THIS ADDRESS. **SEND TO: Commissioner for Patents, P.O. Box 1450, Alexandria, VA 22313-1450.**
If you need assistance in completing the form, call 1-800-PTO-9199 and select option 2.

Exhibit B.4   Utility Patent Application

To download and customize this form for your own personal use, please visit www.wiley.com/go/amazingsecrets.

PTO/SB/01 (05-07)
Approved for use through 05/31/2007. OMB 0651-0032
U.S. Patent and Trademark Office; U.S. DEPARTMENT OF COMMERCE
Under the Paperwork Reduction Act of 1995, no persons are required to respond to a collection of information unless it contains a valid OMB control number.

DECLARATION FOR UTILITY OR DESIGN PATENT APPLICATION (37 CFR 1.63)

Attorney Docket Number	
First Named Inventor	
	COMPLETE IF KNOWN
Application Number	
Filing Date	
Art Unit	
Examiner Name	

☐ Declaration Submitted With Initial Filing   **OR**   ☐ Declaration Submitted after Initial Filing (surcharge (37 CFR 1.16 (e)) required)

I hereby declare that:

Each inventor's residence, mailing address, and citizenship are as stated below next to their name.

I believe the inventor(s) named below to be the original and first inventor(s) of the subject matter which is claimed and for which a patent is sought on the invention entitled:

(Title of the Invention)

the specification of which

☐ is attached hereto

OR

☐ was filed on (MM/DD/YYYY) [＿＿＿＿] as United States Application Number or PCT International

Application Number [＿＿＿＿] and was amended on (MM/DD/YYYY) [＿＿＿＿] (if applicable).

I hereby state that I have reviewed and understand the contents of the above identified specification, including the claims, as amended by any amendment specifically referred to above.

I acknowledge the duty to disclose information which is material to patentability as defined in 37 CFR 1.56, including for continuation-in-part applications, material information which became available between the filing date of the prior application and the national or PCT international filing date of the continuation-in-part application.

I hereby claim foreign priority benefits under 35 U.S.C. 119(a)-(d) or (f), or 365(b) of any foreign application(s) for patent, inventor's or plant breeder's rights certificate(s), or 365(a) of any PCT international application which designated at least one country other than the United States of America, listed below and have also identified below, by checking the box, any foreign application for patent, inventor's or plant breeder's rights certificate(s), or any PCT international application having a filing date before that of the application on which priority is claimed.

Prior Foreign Application Number(s)	Country	Foreign Filing Date (MM/DD/YYYY)	Priority Not Claimed	Certified Copy Attached?	
				YES	NO
			☐	☐	☐
			☐	☐	☐
			☐	☐	☐
			☐	☐	☐

☐   Additional foreign application numbers are listed on a supplemental priority data sheet PTO/SB/02B attached hereto.

[Page 1 of 2]

This collection of information is required by 35 U.S.C. 115 and 37 CFR 1.63. The information is required to obtain or retain a benefit by the public which is to file (and by the USPTO to process) an application. Confidentiality is governed by 35 U.S.C. 122 and 37 CFR 1.11 and 1.14. This collection is estimated to take 21 minutes to complete, including gathering, preparing, and submitting the completed application form to the USPTO. Time will vary depending upon the individual case. Any comments on the amount of time you require to complete this form and/or suggestions for reducing this burden, should be sent to the Chief Information Officer, U.S. Patent and Trademark Office, U.S. Department of Commerce, P.O. Box 1450, Alexandria, VA 22313-1450. DO NOT SEND FEES OR COMPLETED FORMS TO THIS ADDRESS. **SEND TO: Commissioner for Patents, P.O. Box 1450, Alexandria, VA 22313-1450.**
If you need assistance completing the form, call 1-800-PTO-9199 and select option 2.

Exhibit B.5   Declaration for Utility or Design Patent Application

To download and customize this form for your own personal use, please visit www.wiley.com/go/amazingsecrets.

PTO/SB/01 (05-07)
Approved for use through 05/31/2007. OMB 0651-0032
U.S. Patent and Trademark Office; U.S. DEPARTMENT OF COMMERCE
Under the Paperwork Reduction Act of 1995, no persons are required to respond to a collection of information unless it contains a valid OMB control number.

DECLARATION — Utility or Design Patent Application

Direct all correspondence to:	☐	The address associated with Customer Number:		OR ☐	Correspondence address below

Name

Address

City	State	ZIP

Country	Telephone	Email

WARNING:

Petitioner/applicant is cautioned to avoid submitting personal information in documents filed in a patent application that may contribute to identity theft. Personal information such as social security numbers, bank account numbers, or credit card numbers (other than a check or credit card authorization form PTO-2038 submitted for payment purposes) is never required by the USPTO to support a petition or an application. If this type of personal information is included in documents submitted to the USPTO, petitioners/applicants should consider redacting such personal information from the documents before submitting them to the USPTO. Petitioner/applicant is advised that the record of a patent application is available to the public after publication of the application (unless a non-publication request in compliance with 37 CFR 1.213(a) is made in the application) or issuance of a patent. Furthermore, the record from an abandoned application may also be available to the public if the application is referenced in a published application or an issued patent (see 37 CFR 1.14). Checks and credit card authorization forms PTO-2038 submitted for payment purposes are not retained in the application file and therefore are not publicly available.

I hereby declare that all statements made herein of my own knowledge are true and that all statements made on information and belief are believed to be true; and further that these statements were made with the knowledge that willful false statements and the like so made are punishable by fine or imprisonment, or both, under 18 U.S.C. 1001 and that such willful false statements may jeopardize the validity of the application or any patent issued thereon.

NAME OF SOLE OR FIRST INVENTOR:	☐ A petition has been filed for this unsigned inventor	
Given Name (first and middle [if any])		Family Name or Surname

Inventor's Signature	Date

Residence: City	State	Country	Citizenship

Mailing Address

City	State	Zip	Country

☐ Additional inventors or a legal representative are being named on the _____ supplemental sheet(s) PTO/SB/02A or 02LR attached hereto.

[Page 2 of 2]

Exhibit B.5 *(Continued)*

235

RESOURCES FOR INVENTORS

Local Inventor Clubs and Organizations

Alabama

Invent Alabama
Montevallo, AL 35115
Phone: 205-663-9982

Alaska

Alaska Inventors and
  Entrepreneurs
Anchorage, AK 99525
Phone: 907-563-4337

Inventors Institute of Alaska
Wasilla, AK 99687
Phone: 907-376-5114

Arkansas

Inventors Congress, Inc.
Dandanell, AR 72834
Phone: 501-229-4515

Arizona

Inventors Association of
  Arizona
Tucson, AZ 85732
Phone: 520-721-8540

California

American Inventor Network
Sabastopol, CA 95472
Phone: 707-823-3865

Central Valley Inventors
  Association
Manteca, CA 95336
Phone: 209-239-5414

Idea to Market Network
Santa Rosa, CA 95406
Phone: 1-800-ATM 3210

Inventors Alliance
Mountain View, CA 94039
Phone: 650-964-1576

Inventors Alliance of
  Northern California
Redding, CA 96001
Phone: 530-225-2770

Inventors Forum
Huntington Beach, CA 92648
Phone: 714-540-2491

Inventors Forum of
  San Diego
San Diego, CA 92127
Phone: 858-673-4733

Innovators Forum/Whittier
Whittier, CA 90605
Phone: 562-464-0069

Exhibit C.1   Local Inventor Clubs and Organizations

Colorado
Rocky Mountain Inventors
   Congress
Denver, CO 80236
Phone: 303-670-3760

Connecticut
Inventors Association of
   Connecticut
Bridgeport, CT 06606
Phone: 203-866-0720

Innovators Guild
Danbury, CT 06811
Phone: 203-790-8235

Delaware
Delaware Entrepreneurs
   Forum
Yorklyn, DE 19736
Phone: 302-234-4440

District Of Columbia
Inventors Network of the
   Capital Area
Arlington, VA 22215
Phone: 703-971-9216

Florida
Inventors Society of South
   Florida
Boynton Beach, FL 33424
Phone: 954-486-2426

Edison Inventors Association
Fort Myers, FL 33919
Phone: 239-275-4332

Inventors Council of Central
   Florida
Orlando, FL 32806
Phone: 407-859-4855

Space Coast Inventors Guild
Indian Harbour Beach,
FL 32937
Phone: 407-773-4031

Tampa Bay Inventors Council
St. Petersburg, FL 33705
Phone: 727-866-0669

Georgia
Inventors Association of
   Georgia
Macon, GA 31220
Phone: 912-474-6948

Iowa
Drake University Inventure
   Program
Des Moines, IA 50311
Phone: 515-271-2655

Idaho
East Iowa Inventors Forum
Shelly, ID 83274
Phone: 208-346-6763

Illinois
Illinois Innovators and
   Inventors Club
Edwardsville, IL 62035
Phone: 618-656-7445

Inventors Council
Chicago, IL 60605
Phone: 312-939-3329

Exhibit C.1   *(Continued)*

Indiana

Indiana Inventors Association
Marion, IN 46953
Phone: 765-674-2845

Kansas

Inventors Association of
South Central Kansas
Wichita, KS 67205
Phone: 316-721-1866

Kentucky

Central Kentucky Inventors
& Entrepreneurs
Nicholasville, KY 40356
Phone: 606-885-9593

Louisiana

Louisiana Inventors
Association
Baton Rouge, LA 70816
Phone: 225-752-3783

Maine

Portland Inventors Forum
Orono, ME 04469
Phone: 207-581-1488

Maryland

Inventors Network of the
Capital Area
Arlington, VA 22215
Phone: 707-971-9216

Massachusetts

Cape Cod Inventors
Association
Wellfleet, MA 02667
Phone: 508-349-1629

Inventors Association of
New England
Lexington, MA 02420
Phone: 781-229-6614

Innovators Resource
Network
Shutesbury, MA 01072
Phone: 413-259-2006

Worcester Area Inventors
West Boylston, MA 01583
Phone: 508-835-6435

Michigan

Inventors Club of Michigan
Farmington Hills, MI 48335
Phone: 810-870-9139

Inventors Clubs of America
E. Lansing, MI 48823
Phone: 517-332-3561

Inventors Council of
Mid-Michigan
Flint, MI 48502
Phone: 810-232-7909

Minnesota

Inventors Network
St. Paul. MN 55103
Phone: 651-602-3175

Minnesota Inventors Congress
Redwood Falls, MN 55070
Phone: 507-637-2344

Society of Minnesota
Inventors
St. Francis, MN 55070
Phone: 763-753-2766

Exhibit C.1 *(Continued)*

Missouri

Inventors Association of
  St. Louis
St. Louis, MO 63141
Phone: 314-432-1291

Mid-America Inventors
  Association
Kansas City, MO 64129
Phone: 816-254-9542

Mississippi

Society of Mississippi
  Inventors
University, MS 38677
Phone: 601-232-5650

Montana

Montana Inventors
  Association
Bozeman, MT 59178
Phone: 406-586-1541

Yellowstone Inventors
Billings, MT 59102
Phone: 406-259-9110

North Dakota

North Dakota Inventors
  Congress
Jamestown, ND 58401
Phone: 701-252-4959

Nebraska

Lincoln Inventors Association
Brainard, NE 68626
Phone: 402-545-2179

Nevada

Inventors Society of South
  Dakota
Las Vegas, NV 89121
Phone: 702-435-7741

Nevada Inventors Association
Reno, NV 89506
Phone: 775-677-4824

New Hampshire

New Hampshire Inventors
  Association
Concord, NH 03202
Phone: 603-228-3854

New Jersey

Jersey Shore Inventors Club
Bradley Beach, NJ 07720
Phone: 732-776-8467

National Society of Inventors
Livingston, NJ 07039
Phone: 973-994-9282

New Jersey Entrepreneurs
  Forum
Westfield, NJ 07090
Phone: 908-789-3424

New Mexico

New Mexico Inventors Club
Albuquerque, NM 87190
Phone: 908-266-2541

New York

Inventors Alliance—
  Rochester Chapter
Rochester, NY 14616
Phone: 716-225-3750

Exhibit C.1 *(Continued)*

Long Island Forum of
Technology
Farmingdale, NY 11735
Phone: 613-755-3321

New York Society of
Professional Inventors
Farmingdale, NY 11735
Phone: 516-798-1490

Ohio

Inventors Connection
Greater Cleveland
Cleveland, OH 44136
Phone: 440-543-3594

Inventors Council of
Cincinnati
Milford, OH 45150
Phone: 513-831-0664

Inventors Council of Canton
North Canton, OH 44720
Phone: 330-499-1262

Inventors Council of Dayton
Dayton, OH 45409
Phone: 937-293-2770

Inventors Network, Inc.
Columbus, OH 43212
Phone: 614-470-0144

Inventors Network of
Greater Akron
Twinsburg, OH 44087
Phone: 330-425-1749

Youngstown-Warren
Inventors Association
Youngstown, OH 44503
Phone: 330-744-4481

Oklahoma

Oklahoma Inventors
Congress
Oklahoma City, OK 73157
Phone: 405-348-7794

Oregon

South Oregon Inventors
Council
Medford, OR 97501
Phone: 541-772-3478

Pennsylvania

American Society of
Inventors
Philadelphia, PA 19102
Phone: 215-546-6601

Pennsylvania Inventors
Association
Erie, PA 16510
Phone: 814-825-5820

South Carolina

Carolina Inventors Council
Easley, SC 29640
Phone: 864-859-0066

Inventors and Entrepreneurs
Association
of South Carolina
Greenville, SC 29608

Exhibit C.1   *(Continued)*

South Dakota

South Dakota Inventors
  Congress
Brookings, SD 57007
Phone: 605-688-4184

Tennessee

Inventors Association of
  Middle Tennessee
Nashville, TN 37215
Phone: 615-269-4346

Tennessee Inventors
  Association
Knoxville, TN 37939
Phone: 423-869-8136

Texas

Amarillo Inventors
  Association
Amarillo, TX 79109
Phone: 806-351-0702

Houston Inventors
  Association
Houston, TX 77018
Phone: 713-686-7676

Laredo Inventors Association
Laredo, TX 78041
Phone: 956-725-5863

Network of American
  Inventors
Houston, TX 77006
Phone: 713-523-3923

Vermont

Inventors Network of
  Vermont
Springfield, VT 05156

Virginia

Association for Science,
  Technology & Innovation
Arlington, VA 22210
Phone: 703-241-2850

Blue Ridge Inventors Club
Charlottesville, VA 22906
Phone: 804-973-3708

Inventors Network Capital
  Area
Arlington, VA 22215
Phone: 703-971-9216

Washington

Inventors Network
Vancouver, WA 98668
Phone: 503-239-8299

Northwest Inventors Guild
PO Box 226
Port Hadlock, WA 98339

Tri-Cities Enterprise
  Association
Richland, WA 99352
Phone: 509-375-3268

Wisconsin

Central Wisconsin Inventors
  Association
Manawa, WI 54949
Phone: 920-596-3092

Exhibit C.1   *(Continued)*

242

U.S. Small Business Administration Local Development Centers

Alabama SBDC
University of Alabama
2800 Milan Court, Suite 124
Birmingham, AL 35211-6908
Phone: 205-943-6750

Alaska SBDC
University of Alaska—
    Anchorage
430 West Seventh Avenue,
Suite 110
Anchorage, AK 99501
Phone: 907-274-7232

American Samoa SBDC
American Samoa Community
    College
P.O. Box 2609
Pago Pago, American Samoa
96799
Phone: 011-684-699-4830

Arizona SBDC
Maricopa County
    Community College
2411 West 14th Street,
Suite 132
Tempe, AZ 85281
Phone: 480-731-8720

Arkansas SBDC
University of Arkansas
2801 South University
Avenue
Little Rock, AR 72204
Phone: 501-324-9043

California
Santa Ana SBDC
California State
    University—Fullerton
800 North State College
Boulevard, LH640
Fullerton, CA 92834
Phone: 714-278-2719

San Diego SBDC
Southwestern Community
    College District
900 Otey Lakes Road
Chula Vista, CA 91910
Phone: 619-482-6388

Fresno SBDC
University of California—
    Merced
550 East Shaw, Suite 105A
Fresno, CA 93710
Phone: 559-241-6590

Exhibit C.2   U.S. Small Business Administration Local Development Centers

Sacramento SBDC
California State
  University —Chico
Chico, CA 95929-0765
Phone: 530-898-4598

San Francisco SBDC
Humboldt State University
Office of Economic
  Development
1 Harpst Street 2006A,
Siemens Hall
Arcata, CA, 95521
Phone: 707-445-9720 x317

Los Angeles SBDC
Long Beach Community
  College District
3950 Paramount Boulevard,
Suite 101
Lakewood, CA 90712
Phone: 562-938-5004

Colorado SBDC
Office of Economic
  Development
1625 Broadway, Suite 170
Denver, CO 80202
Phone: 303-892-3864

Connecticut SBDC
University of Connecticut
1376 Storrs Road, Unit 4094
Storrs, CT 06269-1094
Phone: 860-870-6370

Delaware SBDC
Delaware Technology Park
1 Innovation Way, Suite 301
Newark, DE 19711
Phone: 302-831-2747

**District of Columbia
SBDC**
Howard University
2600 6th Street,
NW Room 128
Washington, DC 20059
Phone: 202-806-1550

Florida SBDC
University of West Florida
401 East Chase Street,
Suite 100
Pensacola, FL 32502
Phone: 850-473-7800

Georgia SBDC
University of Georgia
1180 East Broad Street
Athens, GA 30602
Phone: 706-542-6762

Hawaii SBDC
University of Hawaii—Hilo
308 Kamehameha Avenue,
Suite 201
Hilo, HI 96720
Phone: 808-974-7515

Idaho SBDC
Boise State University
1910 University Drive
Boise, ID 83725
Phone: 208-426-3799

Exhibit C.2 *(Continued)*

Illinois SBDC
Department of Commerce
and Economic
Opportunity
620 E. Adams, S-4
Springfield, IL 62701
Phone: 217-524-5700

Indiana SBDC
Indiana Economic
Development Corporation
One North Capitol, Suite 900
Indianapolis, IN 46204
Phone: 317-232-2464

Iowa SBDC
Iowa State University
340 Gerdin Business
Building
Ames, IA 50011-1350
Phone: 515-294-2037

Kansas SBDC
Fort Hays State University
214 SW Sixth Street,
Suite 301
Topeka, KS 66603
Phone: 785-296-6514

Kentucky SBDC
University of Kentucky
225 Gatton College of
Business Economics
Building
Lexington, KY 40506-0034
Phone: 859-257-7668

Louisiana SBDC
University of Louisiana—
Monroe
College of Business
Administration
700 University Avenue
Monroe, LA 71209
Phone: 318-342-5506

Maine SBDC
Mr. John Massaua, State
Director
University of Southern Maine
96 Falmouth Street
P.O. Box 9300
Portland, ME 04103
Phone: 207-780-4420

Maryland SBDC
University of Maryland
7100 Baltimore Avenue,
Suite 401
College Park, MD 20742
Phone: 301-403-8300

Massachusetts SBDC
University of Massachusetts
School of Management,
Room 205
Amherst, MA 01003-4935
Phone: 413-545-6301

Michigan SBTDC
Grand Valley State University
510 West Fulton Avenue
Grand Rapids, MI 49504
Phone: 616-331-7485

Exhibit C.2 *(Continued)*

Minnesota SBDC
Minnesota Small Business
   Development Center
1st National Bank Building
332 Minnesota Street,
Suite E200
St. Paul, MN 55101-1351
Phone: 651-297-5773

Mississippi SBDC
University of Mississippi
B-19 Jeanette Phillips Drive
P.O. Box 1848
University, MS 38677
Phone: 662-915-5001

Missouri SBDC
University of Missouri
410 S. Sixth Street
200 Engineering North
Columbia, MO 65211
Phone: 573-882-1348

Montana SBDC
Department of Commerce
301 South Park Avenue,
Room 114 P.O. Box 200505
Helena, MT 59620
Phone: 406-841-2746

Nebraska SBDC
University of Nebraska—
   Omaha
60th & Dodge Street, CBA
Room 407
Omaha, NE 68182
Phone: 402-554-2521

Nevada SBDC
University of Nevada—Reno
Reno College of Business
Administration, Room 411
Reno, NV 89557-0100
Phone: 775-784-1717

New Hampshire SBDC
University of New
   Hampshire
108 McConnell Hall
Durham, NH 03824-3593
Phone: 603-862-4879

New Jersey SBDC
Rutgers University
49 Bleeker Street
Newark, NJ 07102-1993
Phone: 973-353-5950

New Mexico SBDC
Santa Fe Community College
6401 Richards Avenue
Santa Fe, NM 87505
Phone: 505-428-1362

New York SBDC
State University of New York
SUNY Plaza, S-523
Albany, NY 12246
Phone: 518-443-5398

North Carolina SBDTC
University of North Carolina
5 West Hargett Street,
Suite 600
Raleigh, NC 27601
Phone: 919-715-7272

Exhibit C.2   *(Continued)*

North Dakota SBDC
University of North Dakota
1600 E. Century Avenue,
Suite 2
Bismarck, ND 58503
Phone: 701-328-5375

Ohio SBDC
Ohio Department of
  Development
77 South High Street
Columbus, OH 43216
Phone: 614-466-5102

Oklahoma SBDC
Southeast Oklahoma State
  University
517 University, Box 2584,
Station A
Durant, OK 74701
Phone: 580-745-7577

Oregon SBDC
Lane Community College
99 West Tenth Avenue,
Suite 390
Eugene, OR 97401-3021
Phone: 541-463-5250

Pennsylvania SBDC
University of Pennsylvania
The Wharton School
3733 Spruce Street
Philadelphia, PA 19104-6374
Phone: 215-898-1219

Puerto Rico SBDC
Inter-American University of
  Puerto Rico
416 Ponce de Leon Avenue,
Union Plaza, 4th Floor
Hato Rey, PR 00918
Phone: 787-763-6811

Rhode Island SBDC
Johnson & Wales University
270 Weybosset Street,
4th Floor
Providence, RI 02903
Phone: 401-598-2704

South Carolina SBDC
University of South Carolina
College of Business
Administration
1710 College Street
Columbia, SC 29208
Phone: 803-777-4907

South Dakota SBDC
University of South Dakota
414 East Clark Street,
Patterson Hall
Vermillion, SD 57069
Phone: 605-677-6256

Tennessee SBDC
Middle Tennessee State
  University
PO Box 98
Murfreesboro, TN 37123
Phone: 615-849-9999

Exhibit C.2 *(Continued)*

Texas

Houston SBDC
University of Houston
2302 Fannin, Suite 200
Houston, TX 77002
Phone: 713-752-8425

North SBDC
Dallas County Community
  College
1402 Corinth Street
Dallas, TX 75215
Phone: 214-860-5835

NW SBDC
Texas Tech University
2579 South Loop 289,
Suite 114
Lubbock, TX 79423
Phone: 806-745-3973

**South-West Texas Border
Region SBDC**
University of Texas—
  San Antonio
501 West Durango Boulevard
San Antonio, TX 78207-4415
Phone: 210-458-2742

Utah SBDC
Salt Lake Community
  College
9750 South 300 West
Sandy, UT 84070
Phone: 801-957-3493

Vermont SBDC
Vermont Technical College
PO Box 188, 1 Main Street

Randolph Center,
VT 05061-0188
Phone: 802-728-9101

Virginia SBDC
George Mason University
4031 University Drive,
Suite 200
Fairfax, VA 22030-3409
Phone: 703-277-7727

Washington SBDC
Washington State University
534 E. Trent Avenue
P.O. Box 1495
Spokane, WA 99210-1495
Phone: 509-358-7765

West Virginia SBDC
West Virginia Development
  Office
Capital Complex, Building 6,
Room 652
Charleston, WV 25301
Phone: 304-558-2960

Wisconsin SBDC
University of Wisconsin
Room 423
432 North Lake Street,
Madison, WI 53706
Phone: 608-263-7794

Wyoming SBDC
University of Wyoming
P.O. Box 3922
Laramie, WY 82071-3922
Phone: 307-766-3505

Exhibit C.2   *(Continued)*

U.S. Patent and Trademark Office Local Patent Depositories

Alabama

Auburn	Ralph Brown Draughon Library, Auburn	334-844-1737
Birmingham	Birmingham Public Library	205-226-3620

Alaska

Anchorage	Loussac Public Library, Municipal Libraries	907-562-7323

Arkansas

Little Rock	Arkansas State Library	

California

Los Angeles	Los Angeles Public Library	213-228-7220
Sacramento	California State Library, Courts Bldg.	916-654-0069
San Diego	San Diego Public Library	619-236-5813
San Francisco	San Francisco Public Library	415-557-4500
Sunnyvale	Sunnyvale Public Library	408-730-7300

Colorado

Denver	Denver Public Library	720-865-1711

Delaware

Newark	University of Delaware Library	302-831-2965

District of Columbia

Washington	Founders Library, Howard University	202-806-7252

Florida

Fort Lauderdale	Broward County Main Library	954-357-7444
Miami	Miami-Dade Public Library	305-375-2665
Orlando	University of Central Florida Libraries	407-823-2562

Exhibit C.3 U.S. Patent and Trademark Office Local Patent Depositories

Georgia

Atlanta	Georgia Institute of Technology	404-894-1395

Hawaii

Honolulu	Hawaii State Library	808-586-3477

Idaho

Moscow	University of Idaho Library	208-885-6584

Illinois

Chicago	Chicago Public Library	312-747-4450
Springfield	Illinois State Library	217-782-5659

Indiana

Indianapolis	Indianapolis Marion County Public Library	317-269-1741
West Lafayette	Siegesmund Engineering Library, Purdue	765-494-2872

Iowa

Des Moines	State Library of Iowa	515-242-6541

Kansas

Wichita	Ablah Library, Wichita State University	800-572-8368

Kentucky

Louisville	Louisville Free Public Library	502-574-1611

Louisiana

Baton Rouge	Troy H. Middleton Library, LSU	225-578-8875

Maine

Orono	Raymond H. Fogler Library, University of Maine	207-581-1678

Maryland

College Park	Engineering & Physical Sciences Library, University of Maryland	301-405-9157

Exhibit C.3 *(Continued)*

Massachusetts

Amherst	W.E.B. DuBois Library, UMass	413-545-2765
Boston	Boston Public Library	617-536-5400 Ext. 2226

Michigan

Ann Arbor	Art, Architecture & Engineering Library, University of Michigan	734-647-5735
Big Rapids	Ferris Library for Information, Technology & Education (FLITE), Ferris State University	231-591-3602
Detroit	Detroit Public Library	313-833-1450

Minnesota

Minneapolis	Minneapolis Public Library	612-630-6000

Mississippi

Jackson	Mississippi Library Commission	601-432-4111

Missouri

Kansas City	Linda Hall Library	816-363-4600 Ext. 724
St. Louis	St. Louis Public Library	314-241-2288 Ext. 390

Montana

Butte	Montana Tech Library, University of Montana	406-496-4281

Nebraska

Lincoln	Engineering Library, Nebraska Hall, 2nd Floor West, University of Nebraska-Lincoln	402-472-3411

Nevada

Las Vegas	Clark County District Library	702-507-3421
Reno	University Library, University of Nevada	775-784-6500 Ext. 257

Exhibit C.3 *(Continued)*

New Jersey

Newark	Newark Public Library	973-733-7779
Piscataway	Library of Science & Medicine, Rutgers University	732-445-2895

New Mexico

Albuquerque	Centennial Science & Engineering Library, University of New Mexico	505-277-4412

New York

Albany	New York State Library	518-474-5355
Buffalo	Buffalo and Erie County Public Library	716-858-8900
New York	Science, Industry & Business Library, New York Public Library	212-592-7000
Rochester	Central Library of Rochester and Monroe County	585-428-8110
Stony Brook	Science & Engineering Library, SUNY at Stony Brook	631-632-7148

North Carolina

Charlotte	University of North Carolina-Charlotte	704-687-2241
Raleigh	D.H. Hill Library, North Carolina State University	919-515-2935

North Dakota

Grand Forks	Chester Fritz Library, University of North Dakota	701-777-4888

Ohio

Akron	Akron Summit County Public Library	330-643-9075
Cincinnati	Public Library of Cincinnati & Hamilton	513-369-6932
Cleveland	Cleveland Public Library	216-623-2870
Columbus	Ohio State University	614-292-3022
Dayton	Wright State University	937-775-3521
Toledo	Toledo/Lucas County Public Library	419-259-5209

Exhibit C.3 *(Continued)*

Pennsylvania

Philadelphia	The Free Library of Philadelphia	215-686-5331
Pittsburgh	Carnegie Library of Pittsburgh	412-622-3138
University Park	PAMS Library, Penn State University	814-865-7617

Puerto Rico

Bayamón	Learning Resource Center, Bayamón Campus, University of Puerto Rico	787-993-0000 Ext. 3244
Mayagüez	General Library, Mayagüez Campus, University of Puerto Rico	787-832-4040 Ext. 2307

Rhode Island

Providence	Providence Public Library	401-455-8027

South Carolina

Clemson	R.M. Cooper Library, Clemson University	864-656-3024

South Dakota

Rapid City	Devereaux Library, South Dakota School of Mining & Technology	605-394-1275

Tennessee

Nashville	Stevenson Science & Engineering Library, Vanderbilt University	615-322-2717

Texas

Austin	McKinney Engineering Library, ECJ 1.300, University of Texas in Austin	512-495-4500
College Station	Texas A&M University Libraries	979-745-2111
Dallas	Dallas Public Library	214-670-1468
Houston	Fondren Library – MS 225, Rice University	713-348-5483
Lubbock	Texas Tech University Library	806-742-2282
San Antonio	San Antonio Public Library	210-207-2500

Exhibit C.3   *(Continued)*

Utah		
Salt Lake City	Marriott Library, University of Utah	801-581-8394
Vermont		
Burlington	Bailey/Howe Library, University of Vermont	802-656-2542
Virginia		
Richmond	James Branch Cabell Library, Virginia Commonwealth University	804-828-1101
Washington		
Seattle	Engineering Library, University of Washington	206-543-0740
West Virginia		
Morgantown	Evansdale Library, West Virginia University	304-293-4695 Ext. 5113
Wisconsin		
Madison	Kurt F. Wendt Library, University of Wisconsin-Madison	608-262-6845
Milwaukee	Milwaukee Public Library	414-286-3051
Wyoming		
Cheyenne	Wyoming	State	Li-

Exhibit C.3 *(Continued)*